Immigrant From Paradise Valley

Immigrant From Paradise Valley

Larry D. McIntosh

Disclaimer

This book is a work of creative nonfiction. It is based on the author's imperfect memory of actual events in his life. To protect the privacy of individuals, the names of some persons and organizations have been changed, as well as the sequence and other details of some events.

Table of Contents

Part 1: Colonialism and Independence 11

School for Subjects 1

Roots 8

Family 14

Licks 20

The Valley 24

Homework 31

Independence 41

Coming to America 51

Deployment 57

Part 2: The Surprising Limits of Superpower 1

Tet 66

Jungle Operation: Tay Ninh 78

Doreen 94

Dragons and Monster Cows 115

Black and White 124

Bill Conway 130

Eagle Trap: Bad Day at Ben Tre 142

Thien Ngon *(Tin Neon)* 156

Leaving 178

Home 184

The Army and the Klan 195

Bearcat Library 205

Op Tempo 216
Night Tactical Emergency (Tac-E) 228
Stevens 238
Cambodia 245
Goodbye Vietnam 266
The Big RIF 280
Part 3: American Awakening 1
ERAU 301
The Old Country 311
Office Politics 327
A Second Chance 347
Ballade 349
New Year's Day 354
You Can Stop Fighting 366
Postscript 380
About the Author 382

To Sarah

Part 1: Colonialism and Independence

School for Subjects

At Miss Carrington's preschool, we made our letters and numbers on slates. We didn't yet know how to write, but with encouragement from Miss, we made shapes on our slates with our slate pencils. Miss was always pleased with our markings, even if they didn't look like her letters or numbers. Some children had rectangular slates set in wooden frames. These were sold in the store where our parents bought our schoolbooks. My slate was a broken tile with an irregular shape and no wooden borders. This made me envious of the kids with neat slates. I told my parents I wanted a real slate. They got me a book bag for my slate and showed me how to carry it over my shoulder and across my chest like a big boy. Then I didn't feel so bad about my slate.

Miss Carrington lived on Bengal Street, three doors down from our house at the corner of Bengal and Delhi streets in St James. (No, we are not in India.) The area was once agricultural but, by the late 1940s, had been gradually converted into a suburb of the Capital, Port of Spain. (No, we are not in Europe.) Miss Carrington rearranged her home to accommodate the little school. There were six to eight toddlers and a few babies. Miss taught us rhythmic rhymes to help us learn our letters and numbers. Each day we sang and clapped our way through the alphabet. She read us stories and gave us biscuits, milk, and sometimes sweet candies if we behaved well. If one of us was being naughty, she was firm but never yelled or hit anyone. If someone started crying, she was attentive and consoling and would offer water or some juice or a few governor plums from her tree. When I could not make my letters look like hers, she would gently take my hand as I held the slate pencil, and make a perfect D or T, or L, just like those in the picture book.

This was my first experience of taking my place in the world beyond home and family, beyond the comfort of parents, siblings, and grandparents, and measuring myself against children I didn't know. I felt like a big boy and looked forward to going to Miss Carrington's school every day, except for the angry dog snarling at us from behind our neighbor's gate when I walked to and from school.

Eventually, it was time for me to attend preschool at big school. My older brother attended St John's Catholic Boys school in the heart of Port of Spain, the capital of Trinidad at the southern end of the Caribbean island chain. I was filled with excitement but also apprehension based on some of the stories my brother told about big school. He was alarmingly brave and would readily do things I would never do, like climbing over someone's fence to snatch a few mangoes off their tree or throwing stones onto metal roofs, alarming the occupants, and running away just for the fun of being daring. I could hardly wait to wear my new school uniform and be driven to school in Daddy's Ford Prefect. But I was a little nervous too. My brother said some of the bigger boys were mean and got into fights. And if you were caught running in the schoolyard or talking in class, you could get licks! He said he didn't care about licks.

NO TALKING! They were the first words I heard from a teacher in big school and the first rule I learned. She was fearsome, and she had a blaring raspy voice that sounded like when Daddy grated a coconut but much louder, like the coconut vendor's donkey across the street from the school. Those words were shouted at us many times each day. We were the 1951 preschool class of three and four-year-olds at St. John's. Talking was one of the few things we knew how to do on our own while sitting still.

"Little boys must sit still and not speak unless spoken to", the teacher said. "No talking!"

We sat on toddler-sized benches, four to a bench, on opposite sides of low wooden tables. The preschool occupied a corner of the ground floor of the two-story school building on one of the busiest intersections in the capital. It was separated from kindergarten and first-grade classes by tall partitions with a gap at the top to allow air to circulate. I could hear children on the other side of the partitions getting licks and crying.

Mrs. Walsh had one group of pre-schoolers. She was light-skinned like my mother but much older and with white hair. She wore glasses that made her look fierce, like our cat when we pulled its tail too hard. She reigned over us from her lectern-style desk in the corner of the room from where she could see everything that happened. Her stern glare was enough to frighten most of the class into silence, but she would often add an angry yell and a firm thump or slap. "What is this? No, no, no!" She always said no. I think her voice had become raspy from so much yelling. As far away as the boys' bathroom, she could be heard yelling "no!" at someone. Mrs. Walsh said sternly that school was not a place for having fun. Children were sent to school to learn to behave and do as they were told. If she came near me when I was trying to make my letters, my hands shook, and my letters became scrawls that looked like cracks on the sidewalk.

We learned about King George the Sixth. His head was on our coins, and a large picture of him was over the school entrance. We didn't have our own king. This is what a real King looked like. He didn't look like us. He looked a bit like our policemen on parade. But he was white. We were his Subjects, and we were to behave like proper British Subjects, not like little savages. I didn't know why we were called "Subjects" or how a Subject was supposed to behave. I didn't know what savages were either, except that they lived far away, were frightful, and had no manners.

Miss Miller had very dark, nearly black skin. She looked soft and warm and always smelled nice. She was younger than Mrs. Walsh. She smiled a lot and made perfect letters on the blackboard that seemed like a magic trick because they were too perfect for someone to make by hand. My letters were misshapen and ugly, producing a sharp rebuke and a smack on the knuckles daily from Miss Miller's wooden ruler. No matter how hard I tried, I couldn't make my pencil go where I wanted it to go.

Not talking was not a challenge for me; I was too afraid. But for some of my classmates, sitting still and not talking was not going to happen for more than ten seconds.

Mikey and Cyril were buddies even before coming to St John's. They chattered away with each other constantly, sometimes in fun, sometimes in rivalry, paying little attention to the two teachers. I shrunk down into my little bench in fear as the punishment for repeated violations of the no-talking rule was about to be administered. Mikey was to have his lips sewn together. The older teacher, Mrs. Walsh, lifted the struggling child and held him firmly while Miss Miller approached with a shiny needle. A length of white sewing thread hung from the end of the needle. Mikey struggled and screamed in terror as Miss Miller brought the needle close to his face. I could feel the piercing of the needle. I put my hand over my mouth and pursed my lips tightly together. The torture and screaming continued until the teachers decided to release the child with a stern warning that they would not be so lenient next time. He returned to his bench, screaming, "Mommy! I want my mommy!" The teachers yelled at him to be quiet, or he would get licks. He cried softly for his mother.

Cyril was already sobbing when Mrs Walsh picked him up. He was to have his tongue cut out. He struggled and screamed, but Mrs Walsh held him firmly. Miss Miller brought a pair of scissors close to his face. He made a loud gurgling sound as he tried to keep his tongue from being exposed while screaming uncontrollably. Mrs Walsh suddenly held him out at arm's length because he had lost control of his bladder. Miss Miller laughed as Cyril ran screaming to the boys' bathroom. In a release of the tension, some of the boys laughed too. Mrs Walsh stared at us fiercely as if she were about to pounce on another victim. Then, when we were all quiet, she and Miss Miller smiled and chatted with each other. They seemed pleased with their dramatic demonstration.

I dared not draw attention to myself and risk a similar punishment. I tried to hide my terror and act normal. I sat still and looked down at our low wooden table. I did not want to be noticed. I tried but couldn't make my letters and numbers come out right. They looked much worse than normal. The harder I tried, the worse they looked. WHACK WHACK! I pulled my hand away. My knuckles ached from the wooden ruler. "Stop making these scrawls in your exercise book! Make your letters and numbers the way I showed you, or you'll get licks!"

As I grew older and progressed through the primary grades, all this punishing and shaming continued and seemed more wicked and pointless with each passing year. But it was not pointless. This colonial system for producing compliant Subjects, so casually cruel and destructive, was where and when, and how it started, the journey that would take me, sixteen years later, to the middle of the most casually cruel and destructive human activity of all.

Roots

During WWII, the US had two important military bases in the British Colony of Trinidad in the Caribbean. In September 1940, America had agreed to provide warships to Britain, and in return, the British had leased the two bases in Trinidad to the US for ninety-nine years; Chaguaramas, a naval base with an excellent natural harbour in the Northwest corner of the island, and Fort Read/Waller Field, an Army Air Force base on the wide central plain of the island. Trinidad had oilfields and a refinery that could produce fuel for military ships, planes, and ground vehicles. Many US Army Air Force planes, including bombers and their fighter escorts, stopped at Wallerfield to refuel and continue their journey to war. The naval base helped protect the vital petroleum facilities from naval attack and possible capture by the Germans.

Many Trinidadian locals were employed at these bases, including one young man who found the American way of doing things a welcome contrast to the aloofness and superior attitude of the British colonizers. In 1942, at the height of the war, he married his sweetheart, and they went on to have a family of seven children, of which I was the middle child, arriving in April 1947. My father's positive view of America never faded throughout his long life, and this had a significant influence on the lives of several of his children, including me.

My Father, Cecil E. McIntosh, was born to Edgar James and Floretta McIntosh in September 1912. Shortly thereafter, Edgar James moved to Martinique, married his sweetheart, and raised a family of four children. My mother, Germaine, was born in Martinique in 1913 to Inez Angel, an attractive light-skinned woman from the village of St Francois in Martinique. Inez's maternal grandfather had endured slavery, and from what little Inez said of her past, it appears she had grown up in poverty. All Germaine knew of her father was that he was European. Imbert Boulon, a soldier in the French Army, fell in love with Inez and sought to marry her and adopt her daughter, Germaine. Inez allowed him to adopt Germaine but refused his offer of marriage. (Many Vietnamese women would similarly decline to marry American soldiers, fearing the loss of their family and friends and the inability to fit into a world where everything would be unfamiliar.) Imbert Boulon eventually returned to France with a broken heart, leaving Inez and his adopted daughter behind. For a while, he wrote letters to Germaine which became among her most treasured possessions.

When my mother was eight, Inez moved with her to Trinidad.

Families often have their closely guarded secrets, things that remain too painful or too deeply embarrassing to be revealed, things that might change who you are perceived to be. The existence of such things is betrayed not so much by what is said in an unguarded moment but by what is evaded, or never mentioned, or never answered: what was it like growing up in Martinique? Why did you and Mama move to Trinidad? How many siblings do you have?

Mama Inez was immensely proud of her seven grandchildren. They were the joy of her life. But there seemed to be nothing about her life in Martinique that Mama was proud of or eager to share with her grandchildren. Mom, too, seemed to remember nothing of Martinique that she might want to share with her children. But with Mama, she often spoke the French Creole of that island. Maybe she remembered her early childhood in that language.

After learning in school about the Mt Pelée eruption in Martinique, I asked Mama if she had been there when it happened. When I said the words Mt Pelée, she shouted, "Oh God!", turned her face up to heaven, and then covered her face with her hands. She rocked forward in her rocking chair and lowered her covered face toward her lap. When she came up, she wiped away tears. She said, "When de volcano bust . . .!" When she said bust, she threw her arms outward as if she were exploding. She covered her face and bent forward again for a moment. "We run, run, run. The air was getting hot." She grasped at the air with her hands. "I see people run into the sea, but the sea started to boil! Jesus, Mary, and Joseph." She got up and went to her bedroom, muttering softly in her French Creole. A little while later, she returned with her bible, rosary, and reading glasses.

Mama was a teenager when Mt. Pele erupted in 1902. The volcano destroyed the town of St Pierre in just a few minutes, killing thirty thousand people. Mama must have seen the disaster unfolding from across the bay. She lived not far away and must have lost friends in the disaster.

Inez and Germaine started their new life in a poor section of Port of Spain, an area with a bad reputation. They both had light complexions and light eyes, evidence of their mixed European and African heritage. Grandmother Inez (Mama) had to find a school for little Germaine. The staff at Holy Trinity Girls School in Port of Spain included nuns from Ireland. Inez took Germaine to these nuns and begged them to look out for her. They took the poor little "white" girl who spoke no English under their wing.

Mama made a living making and selling jams, jellies, and other sweets directly to a small clientele of well-off customers. In return, they helped to supply her with the guavas, shaddock, and other fruits, which she made into the sweet and savoury treats they then bought from her. Making ends meet was a daily struggle for her and her daughter. They never identified to us the location where they lived in those early days, a testament to how embarrassed they were about having lived there. Little Germaine would often take a long, circuitous deviation on her walk home from school to ensure that her friends would not discover where she lived or the dire poverty of her circumstances. The most Mom revealed to her children was that it was a one-room unit and that she did her studies by candlelight.

With the attention and support of the nuns, who would certainly have deduced her home circumstances, Germaine was eventually able to become a primary school teacher, beginning a successful career at Holy Trinity Girls School, the school of her childhood. She grew into an attractive young woman and was courted by several eligible bachelors, including privileged "white" young men, to the delight of my grandmother Inez. But she and my father, Cecil, fell in love, initially alarming my grandmother.

Cecil was raised by his single mother. Floretta McIntosh was a primary school teacher as well as a music teacher. She was from a respectable family in Woodbrook, a middle-class suburb of Port of Spain. Cecil became an apprentice auto mechanic and a rising local musician, leading one of the more successful and enduring dance bands of the late forties and 1950s, the Ces McIntosh Orchestra.

Cecil was black like his mother, closer in skin tone to ebony than to his father's light cedar complexion. This was not what Inez had in mind for her precious daughter. She initially objected firmly to the courtship, steering Germaine towards one of the nice (white) young men who were very keen to have her and whose families owned businesses. Inez relented, however, when she discovered that Monsieur Edgar James, a highly regarded designer, and producer of bespoke clothing for upper-class (white) gentlemen in Fort-de-France, the capital of Martinique, was Cecil's father. As a young man, Cecil had been sent to live with his father in Martinique for two years and could speak fluently to Mama in her French Creole dialect. Mama grew increasingly fond of him but had one stipulation; he had to become a Catholic, which he did. Cecil and Germaine married and raised a happy family of seven children.

Family

Most of my formative boyhood experiences unfolded during the transformation of the Diego Martin Valley in Trinidad from a rural agricultural district about ten miles West of the capital to the bustling, overcrowded suburb of Port of Spain that it became from the late 1960s onwards. In the 1950s, parents could still allow their young children to explore the surrounding environment for hours at a time without adult supervision. On weekends and during school holidays, my brothers and I would spend all morning – sometimes all day – exploring the forested hills of Petit Valley, a subdivision on the eastern side of the Diego Martin Valley, discovering on our own the sights and sounds of life in the natural world; the birds, manicou, snakes; being stung by wasps as we climbed secret fruit trees known only to us and a few of our friends. Afternoons were often spent swimming and fishing in the crystal-clear pools of the Diego Martin River. We tried various fishing techniques and, most days, caught nothing. On the rare days when we caught three or four fish – *Guabine* or *Coscarob* four to eight inches from nose to tail – we celebrated with a grand fish fry, retelling the adventure like triumphant seafarers as we struggled with the tiny fish bones and tried to ignore the lingering aftertaste in the little fish of insecticide sprays that everyone used at home to control mosquitoes: DDT.

"Hurry up, hurry up! You're holding everyone up!" Mom was yelling from the front seat of the light blue Ford Consul as my younger brother, and I raced down the stairs. My sister opened the back door of the car to let us in, but there was nowhere to fit. The car was packed from floor to ceiling with pots, pans, foodstuffs, supplies for a three-week stay at a beach house, and of course, people. The trunk was overstuffed with the lid tied down. The back of the car sagged alarmingly. "Get in, get in!" Pop shouted impatiently. There were three adults and one child in the front seat and six people of varying sizes in the back. We scrambled over everything and everyone, hoping to find a space to survive the nearly three-hour trip to the beach house.

We started out with the little engine straining to pull the load. My brother and I were bursting with excitement in anticipation of three weeks at the beach. Each time we went over a slight bump or dip in the road, there was an ominous grinding noise from beneath the car, and each time the grinding was longer and louder. People were gawking and pointing as we went by. We waved back cheerfully. Finally, the grinding of metal on asphalt wouldn't stop and could no longer be ignored. Pop decided that some of us would have to get the bus to Sangre Grande, a town about half the way to our destination. He would go ahead with the rest of the group, unload the car at the beach house in Mayaro, and return to Sangre Grande to get us.

A variation of this scene played out almost every year in August. Vacations at Mayaro Beach were idyllic and magical. Mayaro was still a rural and largely undeveloped village. Seven miles of undeveloped and unspoiled tropical beach fringed by groves of mile-high coconut trees begged to be explored by adventurous kids with weeks of nothing else to do and long hours without adult supervision. This forced us to supervise ourselves and respect boundaries not far beyond those our parents would set. My siblings and I agree; nothing you might find at Disneyworld could generate the magic and wonder of those precious weeks at Mayaro Beach. There were no man-made fantasies, no bright lights or whirling rides. Mayaro was closer in ambiance to a natural wilderness than an amusement park. We always invited friends along, often doubling the number of kids from seven to fourteen or more, with Mom and Pop adding two or three of their adult friends. Whether it was the old Austin Devon, the English Vanguard, or the fading but willing British-built Ford Consul, our Mayaro vacations were enchanting adventures.

With sleeping space at a premium in the small house, some of the kids opted to sleep on the beach, taking care to avoid the tall coconut trees. These giants could suddenly unleash a deadly missile in the form of a heavy coconut, known to cause serious injury or death to someone beneath their flight path. At sunrise, we headed up the beach to help the fishermen pull in their Seine nets. As the nets came close to shore, with its catch of struggling fish, the older fishermen, weathered like black slate, warned us to watch out for dangers like stinging jellyfish and stingrays. "Look out! Look out! *La Ray, La Ray*!" the old guy shouted, using the French *Creole* name for the sting ray. Recognizing something more sinister among the fish struggling in the shallows to escape the net, the old man suddenly let go of his section of the net and sprinted like a young athlete for the safety of the beach.

By the third or fourth day, we became friendly with several of the fishermen. We were usually rewarded with a fish big enough to provide lunch for the family. After breakfast, we spent endless hours playing and bodysurfing in the heavy breakers. At low tide, we dug in the soft sand for *Chip-chip*, tiny molluscs (think miniature mussels) that, when boiled and shelled, produced a tasty side dish if one could tolerate the occasional grinding of sand against teeth.

In the cool of the late afternoon, as the sun dipped behind the tall coconut trees, we headed up the beach playing our *quatros* and singing the latest calypso hits, accompanied by a percussion section made up of whatever noise makers could be found. Our impromptu beach band gradually grew as other holidaymakers joined the carnival jump-up along the beach at sunset. Time seemed to stand still on these Mayaro vacations; they remain some of my happiest memories.

But they were more than just happy interludes in the course of family life. These expeditions to the rural countryside helped to knit our family more tightly together. Away from the daily routines of chores and homework, of minor irritations and petty bickering, we enjoyed a warm fondness for each other. There was more laughter and spontaneity, less focus on rules and rivalries. The unique qualities of individual family members became more evident and thus more deeply appreciated and valued.

At Christmas time, our parents turned our house into a dream world of lights and decorations, and Christmas music. My siblings and I helped with the cleaning, painting, and hanging of new curtains – but especially with the cooking as the house filled with rich, warm aromas of slowly roasted meats, plus sauces, breads, pastries, and cakes all freshly prepared using recipes reserved for Christmas only. I still marvel at how our parents were able to give their seven children such a rich and varied childhood, ensuring there would be three meals for all each day while constantly struggling to make ends meet. We never heard them speak of that struggle, and they showed little signs of the stresses they must have endured. They seemed to live by a simple rule: stay happy and stick together no matter what.

Licks

I attended St John's Roman Catholic Elementary from Kindergarten to 6th Standard (7th Grade). School was punishment; for running in the schoolyard; for not walking properly; for talking in class; for not speaking up; for not knowing your twelve times tables; for making your "o" like an "a"; for not knowing when Francis Drake sailed around the world; for not knowing when Spain fought the British when the British fought the French when the French fought the Russians; for laughing in church; for not knowing all five mysteries of the Rosary; for asking why Mary was called The Virgin; for having dirty shoes and fingernails; for losing your pencil or your pen. School was punishment for being a child. And the punishment was licks.

Extreme corporal punishments and shaming were the norm. The state-of-the-art in corporal punishment - and hated instrument of terror - was The Strap! From 2nd to 4th Standard, the administration of licks was done using an ordinary leather belt intended to hold a man's trousers in place. But for the purposes of the 5th and 6th Standard teachers and the Headmaster, these belts were too light. These men, obsessed with the aim of eradicating all manifestations of indiscipline from their most hardened students, went to the tanners and cobblers at the leather shop not far from the school to choose the perfect length of heavy leather, about an inch and a half wide, and have it worked and finished to just the right combination of flexibility and stiffness. These weapons would leave raised and sometimes bloody welts along the arms and backs of 11 and 12-year-old children. Two or three times each year, there was high drama as a teacher would be punched out by a parent enraged by the bloody streaks down his child's back. Among my classmates, the highest admiration went to the rare student brave enough to steal and dispose of Sir's Strap, even though several of us would be beaten for not disclosing the perpetrator. But for at least a week or two, Sir was reduced to using a lighter belt on us.

Even after you left the school at the end of the day, there was no escape from the fear of the strap. There was a psychological barbed wire fence that served to keep you mentally in school and under surveillance, reserving your punishment for when you physically returned to school; it was called Homework. When I left that school compound at the end of the day, I left behind everything related to school and the fear that always hovered over me within the school walls. This meant I never even thought about homework until I was on my way to school the next day, even though this all but guaranteed regular beatings from the teacher. It was such a silly ritual, painful but tiresome all the same; the small group of boys who hadn't done their homework stepping up to be beaten with the leather strap even though, in my case, at least, the beatings never achieved the desired effect. If I made it to school early, I would sneak into the church next door and scribble as much as I could, my shaking hand making my homework all but illegible. Sometimes this worked, most times not. Eventually, I abandoned this feeble and embarrassing attempt at appeasement and accepted my fate.

Witnessing the violent beatings received by friends who were more rebellious or adventurous than me may have been even more emotionally disturbing than the "licks" I endured. Sometimes the beatings were just inexplicably depraved. In 4th Standard, the teacher took perverse delight in putting a boy whom I'll call James (not his real name) in front of the class and hitting him with the leather strap until Sir achieved his cruel and shameful result. Sir would swing the leather strap high above his head and crash it down over James' shoulder so that it would flex and deliver searing pain down James' back until, after about five or six blows, James lost control of his bladder. We all wore short trousers to school at that age. Some of the boys giggled when this happened. I sat riveted by the expression in James' eyes, at once a question, a plea, a challenge, and a defiant refusal to submit. He stood tall and erect and looked directly into the teacher's eyes, trying to deflect the blows with his forearms. He never said a word, never cried, or sought forgiveness or mercy. He never lost his dignity, and his demeanor never wavered, even as his dripping urine made darkening splotches on the chalk-dusted wooden floor.

The Valley

The community of Petit Valley in the Diego Martin Valley in northwest Trinidad was still an undeveloped rural area when my family moved there from Port of Spain in 1953. I was then a rambunctious 6-year-old. Housing was sparse along the road that snaked around the base of the densely wooded hills on the eastern side of the valley. My parents somehow managed to get a mortgage on an aging three-bedroom house clinging to the steep hillside just above the road and the valley floor below. It had the potential for expansion into a comfortable home for two parents and, eventually, seven kids. There were a few farms scattered around the fertile valley, producing citrus, cocoa, and coconut. Still, others had been abandoned and had reverted to swampy forests interspersed with large patches of bamboo. From the vantage point of our front porch sixty feet above the valley floor, all I could see were forest treetops and large stands of towering bamboo swaying back and forth in the breeze like happy drunks who couldn't stop laughing. Flocks of Yellowtails stopped by the bamboo briefly to cackle at us and move on, wary of hunters and young boys throwing stones or using homemade slingshots crafted from the discarded inner tubes of bicycle tyres.

As the years passed, farmers and other landowners in the valley began converting their holdings to housing developments to take advantage of the burgeoning demand fuelled by a growing petroleum economy. Groceries and other shops sprang up. The center of the capital city, Port of Spain, was less than ten miles away, and the country was in transition from a British colony to an independent parliamentary democracy and from an agricultural economy to one based on oil and, later, natural gas.

At the end of the 1950s, a small minority of ethnic white Europeans still controlled the economy and had the final say in governance and law enforcement. But that was changing fast. More than eighty percent of the population were people of colour - mostly descendants of Africans and Indians - plus smaller numbers of Chinese, Venezuelans, Syrians, and Lebanese, plus every ethnic mixture imaginable. The local political leaders, some of whom had earned degrees from some of the best universities in the UK, Canada, and the US, were vigorously championing the people's insistence on ending British rule and the privileged life of the tiny European white minority. Although non-whites did not have to endure the extreme racial oppression and degradation being cruelly enforced by the white majority in the southern US States, the subtle but widespread exclusion from better jobs, especially management and executive positions, was becoming intolerable.

On 31st August 1962, at age 15, my classmates and I were taken out of school to the Oval, the cricket stadium in the Capital, Port of Spain, along with children from many other schools around the island. We waved our new Trinidad and Tobago national flags and sang the new National Anthem we had learned at school. My classmates and I pretended not to notice how the girls' ankle-length skirts sometimes flared in the breeze, showing their pretty legs as they went through their much-rehearsed dance routines in celebration of our Independence. In his first Independence Day speech, the new Prime Minister exhorted us to work hard in school because we carried the nation's future in our bookbags.

By the middle of the nineteen-sixties, the trickle of development that began in our valley in 1960 became a flood. Tiny rural communities mushroomed into a sprawling suburb of Port of Spain. Middle and working-class families of all ethnic groups and mixtures, plus a few truly wealthy families, lived peacefully side by side. As I went from childhood to adolescence, this was internalized as normal. I assumed this was just how people lived, not just here but everywhere. War and ethnic strife were stories we read about and saw in cinemas because they were abnormal events in faraway places. Life in this peaceful valley was the way all people were meant to live.

In a departure from what was the norm - around our island and around the world - no single ethnic group rose to dominance or claimed ancestral rights to our beloved Valley. I was not yet aware that this was in stark contrast to other regions, such as the central plains where descendants of indentured Indians had worked the sugarcane fields for generations and built communities infused with their ancestral traditions, or the low hills to the East of the Capital where the descendants of African slaves developed close-knit communities that celebrated their African ancestry. The families moving into the Valley were mostly people who, whether through hard work, entrepreneurship, or family connections, had acquired the means to raise their kids in a home and community much nicer than the ones in which they grew up. They tended to identify more strongly with the new rainbow nation of Trinidad and Tobago than with the lands and traditions of their ancient ancestors.

In our Valley (it became known simply as The Valley), neighbours still gossiped and quarreled and even sometimes used racial slurs behind each other's backs. But these lacked the power to inflict lasting pain and were generally laughed at or ignored because, except for the colonial rulers, no racial group had any enduring power to deprive the others of opportunity or to frustrate their aspirations. Petty bickering and name-calling happen among all people, even those of the same race and class. These same neighbours partied together, worshipped together, and sent their children to the same schools. My friends and I grew up without either the self-delusions of a privileged class or the fear, anger, and resentment of an exploited underclass. But I would eventually discover that this Valley, this beautiful, diverse micro-society in which I grew up, was a rare accident, unlikely to be found in many places around the world, and virtually non-existent in developed countries.

It's often been said children learn what they live. What I internalized as a child growing up in this environment was that it was normal for people of all ethnicities, races, colours, religions, and incomes to be living together harmoniously in the same community. This does not mean that we grew up without prejudices. Children automatically absorb the biases, both positive and negative, of their parents and authority figures. But as I grew up, I found that these biases were not supported by my everyday experiences. Still, prejudices can be frustratingly stubborn and intractable; they never seem to completely fade away. I find I still must be on my guard against instant thoughtless reactions influenced by biases learned at an early age.

As a teenager, I learned from books, radio, and newspapers that prejudice, suspicion, exploitation, and strife between different groups were the norm in many places around the world. But it was something outside of our lived experience. On the radio, I heard the words of Martin Luther King and other African American leaders and tried to reconcile those with the wonderful America portrayed on movie screens. I tried to imagine what it might be like to grow up under slavery or Jim Crow deprivation. Would I hate white people? Would I be ashamed of my skin colour and hair? I found it impossible to imagine what kind of person I would be had I grown up under those horrific conditions. I also tried to imagine growing up with the presumption of superiority over people of colour; to have such a cruel prejudice be the reality you were born into; to believe that any person of colour who was doing better than you must have been given an unfair advantage, some form of "reverse racism", because every person of colour was inherently deficient compared to whites. I couldn't imagine living with such a distorted reality. Two of my siblings were dark-skinned, two of us were brown, and three had very light complexions. It was a wonderful family to be born into. The idea that skin colour had anything to do with a person's inherent value or potential was simply inconceivable. But I knew that racial prejudice was deeply ingrained in many cultures and, because of the advantages it conferred, would not be easily or quickly eradicated.

Homework

At seven-thirty on Saturday morning, my mother came into the bedroom I shared with my younger brother to collect our dirty laundry. Mom always did laundry on Saturday morning, but she was earlier than usual, which meant she had errands later that morning. I was still in my pyjamas. As she gathered up our dirty school uniforms, she said briskly, "Take those off and take the sheets off the bed." As I stepped out of my pyjama bottoms and underwear, I reached for a towel and quickly wrapped it around myself. At age twelve I was no longer fully comfortable being nude in my mother's presence. I heard my mother say, "Wait, wait! What's that?" I turned around and stared at her in confusion and some apprehension: "What's what?". She came over, turned me around, lifted the towel from behind, bent down, and ran her hand over a slightly raised spot on my backside. It was still a little sensitive, and I squirmed away. "Ouch, I told you, I got licks in school for not doing my homework." She turned me around to face her. "But that was two or three weeks ago; did you get licks again?"

"No, I already told you about this." She looked at me for a few moments, then stood up with a look of deep concern on her face. Before I was born, she had been a young teacher at that school. She probably never imagined that her children might be subject to the kind of beatings that she must have seen there. I hurried into the bathroom and twisted around to see the bruise in the mirror. I didn't know that the raised black and blue mark left by the beating was still visible on my mahogany-coloured backside.

Successful people often speak of that one special teacher in elementary or high school who made them believe in themselves for the first time and inspired them to pursue their dreams regardless of the obstacles facing them. I had the opposite experience in 6th Standard (7th Grade?); a highly respected teacher who became frustrated at my stubborn refusal to produce satisfactory homework assignments despite regular beatings, or floggings, as he called them.

Mr. Bradshaw (not his real name) was almost a legend at St John's Boys Primary School for two reasons. Parents connived and pleaded to get their children into St John's because of the school's reputation for getting kids into the best high schools based on their performance on the island-wide secondary entrance exams. These exams were taken on the same day each year by nearly twenty thousand children across the two islands. The top five or six students were celebrated in the leading newspapers with front-page headlines and photos. Their schools were also highlighted, which fuelled the pressure on parents to get their children into those schools. Those students scoring among the top one hundred or so would have their pick of the best high schools. At St John's Boys, Standard 6A was the class where children were prepared for taking the secondary entrance exams. Standard 6A was Mr. Bradshaw's class.

As early as the second grade, we learned the reason for Mr. Bradshaw's other reputation. It was almost whispered by the bigger boys when Mr. Bradshaw's name was mentioned: "HE DOH MAKE JOKE! He does beat BAD!" The fear of Mr. B grew slowly over the years as we got closer to the dreaded Standard 6A. Mr. B was always serious and always focused. He never joked or laughed with us as some of the other teachers did. He seemed to believe that academic excellence could only be achieved through the liberal application of licks. Of all the teachers at St John's Boys, he delivered the fiercest and most frequent beatings. He was feared by every boy in that school. When he walked through the school at recess or lunch, there was a hush among the students as he passed by. Despite his lofty reputation for producing high academic scorers, a few parents pulled their sons out of the school each year because of the beatings, which earned him his second reputation.

Mr. Bradshaw was probably in his mid-forties, about five feet seven or eight inches in height, with a complexion the shade of weathered teak. He was always well groomed, white shirt, grey jacket, and tie. His voice was a bit thin and slightly higher than normal in pitch. He began his classes an hour before the rest of the school. Punctual attendance was compulsory. Sometimes he got to school an hour or two later than normal, looking subdued, even dazed, as if he'd just woken up, yet even more menacing than normal. This made us tense and quiet; somebody was going to get some bad licks today. When he briefly stepped away from the class, some of the boys giggled and said he had been drunk the night before. Their parents were friends of Mr. B.

He taught us all our subjects: Math, Science, History, Geography, Civics, English. He taught us about T. A. Marryshow and William Wilberforce, Francis Drake, and Kublai Khan; the capitals and geography of all the Caribbean islands, that Dominica produced limes, Grenada spices, and Barbados sugar. He showed us where the great rivers of the world ran, the Yangtze Kiang, the Ganges, the Congo River, the Murray-Darling, the Nile, the Amazon, and the Orinoco. He taught us about Chimborazo and Cotopaxi, the Atacama and the Andes, the Aztecs and Incas, the Prairies of North America, the Great Lakes, and the St Lawrence Seaway. He taught us about Argon and Ozone and why they were important, about Latitude and Longitude, the Tropic of Cancer and Tropic of Capricorn, the tilt of the Earth's axis, and the seasons. I learned more things from Mr. Bradshaw than from any other single teacher. He had opened a wide window through which I began to see the world as an exciting and wondrous place begging to be explored. I was in awe of this man. But I was also terrified of him.

Long before I got to Standard 6A, I had largely given up on homework and resigned myself to regular licks as a consequence, usually three of four strokes with a leather strap, sometimes on my outstretched palm and forearm, sometimes on my back, in which case I twisted my arm up against my back to dissipate the force of the blows. Mr. B must eventually have become frustrated that, in my case, his standard floggings were not producing the desired effect. He decided to deliver a beating so fierce, I would never again dare to neglect one of his homework assignments.

He put me into a kneeling position in front of and facing the class and stood next to me to my left. In the standing position, we had learned how to deflect some of the force of the blows by shifting or twisting slightly just before the belt landed. This could not be done in the kneeling position. He rose up on his toes and brought the strap down on my buttock with his full force. The pain was like a red-hot iron against my right buttock. The crack of the strap went out across the open plan upper floor of the school, momentarily distracting the other classes; just another 6A boy getting licks again. He hit me over and over on the same spot on my right buttock. With many years of practice, he had perfected the art of repeatedly striking the same spot. I expected he would stop after four or five blows, but he kept going, and in my agony, I lost count of how many times he hit me.

I knew he wanted me to cry out from the pain; my classmates knew that if you cried out loudly with lots of drama and tears after a few of his blows, he would stop. Crying out was a form of supplication to the teacher, a way of reflecting to him and to the class the level of pain and suffering brought upon yourself by your transgression, and a plea for his mercy. But crying out was also a concession of guilt that justified the beating. With each blow, my face contorted in agony, and I grit my teeth to suppress the urge to scream. I struggled to hold fast to my dignity and refused to make a sound. With each blow, I squeezed my eyes more tightly shut to suppress any tears, then opened them again. But I began to fear that I would not be able to stand the beating much longer. I began to shake all over uncontrollably on my knees. He stopped and pointed to my desk. I got up slowly from my kneeling position and returned unsteadily to the hard wooden desk. I was unable to sit and supported myself partially on my still trembling forearms.

I stared directly at him. Other than the unbearable pain that kept me from sitting, I felt nothing: not fear, not anger, not remorse, not relief, nothing. But something had changed. He seemed smaller, an ordinary man, not the man I had admired. And I was no longer afraid of him.

From the street below, car horns beeped. Someone yelled loudly for a taxi: "St Ann's?" The coconut vendor's donkey brayed a brief low moan as if he'd heard the beating and wished to protest: "Even donkeys never get treated with such cruelty!" These street sounds, normally suppressed by the background hum of school activity, had become audible because the entire second floor, standards 3 through 6, had gradually fallen silent as the beating progressed.

He would not look at me. He took his white handkerchief from his pocket and wiped the sweat from his brow, face, neck, and throat. He straightened his tie, then took his jacket from the back of his chair where he had placed it before delivering his flogging. He carried on with the afternoon's lesson. The somber faces of my classmates made it clear that they knew he had gone too far. They said he hit me sixteen times. But that was likely an exaggeration.

A few weeks later, as we approached the end of the term, a formal school assembly in place was announced over the school's public address system. When everyone was quiet, the Headmaster began calling students up to the stage, reading from a list in his hand. This was often the start of a serious disciplinary action for a severe transgression. Mine was the third name called. I was nervous and fearful as I walked towards the stage. But based on the names of the first two – they were top performers, not underachievers like me - I clung to a sliver of hope that this was not a disciplinary action, not more licks. The upbeat atmosphere and the pleasant demeanor of the teachers alluded more towards pomp and celebration than punishment and shaming.

Nevertheless, I remained apprehensive. Eight of us were called up, all from Mr. Bradshaw's class. Seven of the eight were among the school's bright boys. I was in unusual company. I was confused and felt out of place, like the only cockroach at a barnyard hens' party. My friends were rambunctious and adventurous, not quiet and studious like the other seven.

With an uncharacteristic show of pleasure and self-satisfaction, the Headmaster announced that he had been informed by the Ministry of Education that eight students from St Johns Boys RC School had done exceptionally well on the island-wide College Exhibition Examinations (the competitive exam for placement in secondary schools). By ranking within the top one hundred students, they had upheld and enhanced the honor and high reputation of the school. These eight students would all be placed in the best secondary schools and would attend free of charge. The exams had not been multiple-choice; handwriting and organization of work contributed significantly towards final marks, so I had not been optimistic about my results. In fact, I was dreading the release of the results and the shame of having failed.

The first student, Jerry, was ranked third among the nearly twenty thousand students across Trinidad and Tobago who took the exam (loud applause). I knew Jerry was bright, but I never realized he was *that* bright. The second student, Dan, had placed twelfth (more applause). Larry McIntosh (me) had placed twentieth (more applause). I was now nervous and apprehensive for a different reason; I was not used to being congratulated or even approved of, let alone being fussed over like one of the teachers' favored bright boys, some of whom had not done very well. I didn't know how to react. I hadn't really done anything to merit all this fuss and was growing increasingly uncomfortable. I just wanted to get back to playing "rescue" (a form of tag) with my friends at recess, even though it was against the rules and could result in licks. The Headmaster continued his proud speech. I shifted and fidgeted nervously, eager for it to be over. Mr. Bradshaw stood to our right with his hand on Jerry's shoulder, smiling broadly. I'd never seen that kid get licks for any reason. And I'd never before seen Mr. Bradshaw look happy.

At lunchtime, I sprinted around to the side of the school building, chasing after my friends. Mrs. Walsh, the kindergarten terror, stepped out into the schoolyard through a side door. Expecting a scolding for running recklessly across the schoolyard, I instantly slowed to a walk. As I was about to go past her, she grinned and spread her arms wide. "Congratulations! We're all so proud of you." I wriggled out of her arms and ran away.

Independence

I started secondary school in the top class of one of the best high schools in the country. I placed 20th among the nearly twenty thousand students taking the secondary entrance exams. This left me confused and anxious. I knew I would not fit in with a class of studious bright boys and teacher favorites. My idea of hell was sitting in a class of bright know-it-alls and teachers' pets and being called on by the teacher. My throat would dry up, my mind would go blank, and my discomfort would be obvious to everyone as I waited to be embarrassed by the teacher.

Thankfully, the use of licks was rare at St Mark's College, and harsh beatings were never used. Starting out in Form 1-A Special, the top First Form at St Mark's, the sting of the heavy leather straps from my years at St John's Boys School still resonated through my 12-year-old body. I was unable to relate to my new teachers in any way that was constructive or productive, or helpful. It would have required an exceptionally dedicated and persistent teacher to penetrate the wall I had constructed to protect myself psychologically from the violence that was a normal part of each school day at St John's Boys. I respected and admired many of the teachers I had at St Mark's. But after all the floggings and shaming at St John's Boys, I could not imagine that any teacher, especially those I admired, could take an interest in me. I continued to keep my interactions with teachers to a minimum.

At St Mark's, the role of underachiever served this purpose; they wrote me off early and expected little from me. I was quietly attentive in class, never intentionally disruptive or undisciplined. Whenever possible, I sat in the back and tried not to be called on. I learned as much as I could while avoiding interaction with the teachers. Once outside the school walls, I hung out with my friends or pursued my real passion, music, largely without direction or instruction.

As I matured into my mid-teens and beyond, I redoubled my efforts to do my homework assignments on time. In the days before computers, having good penmanship was almost as important to a good education as mastering English and Mathematics. Although I learned to write legibly, nothing I wrote by hand ever made a good first impression. I would get out of bed at 1 AM and struggle for an hour or two to make my homework assignment look presentable, only to have it rubbished by the teacher because it looked like it was carelessly done. By the time I got to the fourth form (roughly equivalent to the 11th grade), I had all but given up on homework again. Even with assignments that weren't at all difficult or challenging, I would stare at my empty notebook page for an hour or more and could think only of the shaming that would result from whatever I might put on paper. Sometimes I would do the assignment and pretend I hadn't done it just to see how I measured up with my classmates. Form 4A Special was reserved for the most gifted students. Following in descending order, were Form 4 Special, Form 4A, 4B, 4C, and 4D. Form 4D was the class for the most un-gifted, the incorrigible underachievers, a group of boys who were not expected to achieve anything or amount to anything, plus a few whose parents were so wealthy that they would never have to worry about their future. By this time, we had largely given up on our teachers, and they had given up on most of us. It would be a rare teacher indeed who could look forward with enthusiasm to teaching this class.

Mr McMurray was one of the young Irish Catholic teachers in training for the priesthood. In Form Four D, he taught us English. He seemed to have a genuine desire to help us become better at English. I sometimes felt that Mr McMurray was becoming a priest only because it was expected of him, not because he wanted to. He was a slim young man with a delicate boyish look and glasses that sought to make him look serious and scholarly. His hair was dark, his eyes green, and his face pink. He had the faint wariness of someone who has endured too much disapproval. It had not occurred to me then that this was something he and I had in common. He seldom laughed or smiled like the other Irish Brothers. He tried to maintain a serious professional expression. But his feelings were revealed even more powerfully through subtle unconscious facial changes. His face grew bright red when he was angry. When he was pleased or felt he had impressed the class with the range or depth of his knowledge, he paled briefly, his eyebrows shifted slightly, and his face relaxed a bit. When he was angry or embarrassed, his eyes grew moist, his nostrils flared, and he looked menacing as he struggled to hide his feelings, to appear immune to embarrassment, while he formulated his response and, sometimes, his revenge.

The more sensitive a teacher was to disguising taunting and baiting by the students, the more likely he was to be a target of it but also to believe that he was being targeted when he wasn't.

I eventually became tired of the creative ritual of providing a new plausible excuse for not having done my homework. On the spur of the moment, one sunny morning, I decided to be honest, to not lie. When Mr. McMurray asked for my homework assignment, I said I hadn't done it. He asked, "What's your excuse?". I said I didn't have an excuse. I expected he would send me to after-school detention as my punishment, and that would be it. He said sternly in his strong Irish accent, "You haven't turned in your assignment; what's your excuse?"

I was surprised and confused. I said, "Sir, if you really want an excuse, I can give you one – I forgot to take my textbook home, or I had food poisoning and was sick all night, or we had an electrical failure – but I'm trying to tell the truth because it's the right thing to do; I don't have any excuse". I thought he would be pleased that I had chosen to tell the truth as we were taught to do in our religious instruction classes. But I could tell by his expression that he was livid. He was silent for a few moments. Behind his eyeglasses, his green eyes were slightly more moist than normal. He then said something to the effect that I was rude and obstreperous (you don't forget a word like that) and continued to scold me for a few minutes. He assigned me to do "long penance", the school's designation for ninety minutes of detention after school. I felt he would have preferred to give me a severe flogging if he had that option.

I just couldn't understand teachers. One of my close classmates would console me by saying, *"He just doh like your head!"*

Many years later, I realized that telling the truth that way was an affront; he was personally offended, maybe even hurt. Providing a plausible excuse was the established ritual for acknowledging the authority of the teacher to assign homework and the student's duty to comply with that assignment. Even if you simply failed to make any effort to do the homework, you were expected to respect the senior/subordinate, teacher/student relationship by giving an excuse. In doing so, you acknowledge your *responsibility* for the assignment and profess your *intent* to do the assignment had the excusing situation not prevented it, thus properly recognizing the authority of the teacher. It wasn't that hard. But to just blurt out your refusal to do the assignment was a slap in the face of the teacher. To him, it was like saying, "I don't care about your stupid assignment". As I grew older, I began to see that the teaching profession has its challenges and that even a very capable and committed teacher can find a student infuriating without the student understanding why or even being aware of the effect he is having on the teacher.

A few weeks after that incident, our homework assignment from Mr. McMurray was to write an essay on the first anniversary of Trinidad's independence from Britain. My mother had been highly active in the independence movement at the community level. She attended all the community meetings and often went on marches demanding "Independence Now!" She sometimes gathered me and my siblings around the radio to listen to debates in the new Parliament; the authoritative rhetoric of the new Prime Minister, Dr Eric Williams, full of incisive analysis and historical references aimed at the highly educated but also peppered with common street language to connect with the masses; the fire and outrage of Opposition Member Lionel Seukeran, conceding no deference to the Prime Minister as he held the government to account in his unique rhetorical style.

Independence, the rejection of foreign colonization, was something I cared deeply about. Writing about it was not homework for me; it was an opportunity to express the way I felt about the ills of foreign domination and the confidence I felt in the ability of the people of Trinidad to manage their own affairs. I set out my thoughts in my best penmanship – it still looked like I wrote it using my toes – and turned it in on time, secretly hoping against all odds for something better than a failing grade. At the next class, Mr. McMurray announced that he had selected the two best essays to read to the class. The first one was much shorter than mine and, to me, a bit short on substance. He did a brief critique and pointed out what might be done to improve the document.

He began reading the second essay, and I realized, to my shock and amazement, that he was reading my essay. I wasn't used to getting positive or constructive attention from teachers, so it made me nervous and wary. What was he up to? Even if I had written a decent essay, he wouldn't waste his compliments on me, even if it meant favouring a lesser effort from a more promising student.

Coming from another voice, an Irish voice, my essay sounded polished and grown-up. I kept my eyes down. There had to be a catch. He read the entire essay, then paused for effect. He then said to the class the following words: "Obviously taken verbatim from a book". He paused again, then turned to look directly at me, and with no perceptible physical change to his face, managed to communicate withering derision, disgust, even mockery. Seeing my shock and confusion, his disdainful expression shifted to a smirk of self-satisfaction.

My mind raced as I tried to see beyond the surface. He must have known that my essay was not up to the standard of a published author. If he didn't, he had no business teaching us English. What was he up to? Rather than give me a decent grade, he had found a way to give me a failing grade – for plagiarising. He had taken his revenge on the rude and obstreperous boy.

How could anyone have written a book on the *first year* of independence and have it published by the first year anniversary? My essay had references to recent events and quoted lines from speeches made no more than a week or two before. How could they have come from a published book? I remembered the words I'd recently discovered in the poetry book we were required to study for his class, words written by

William Blake nearly two hundred years before: *"Listen to the fool's reproach! It is a kingly title"*.

There was nothing I wanted to say to this priest-to-be from Ireland that he might understand.

I had grown up amidst the passionate struggle for independence from Britain. I remember being taken out of school at age seven with all my schoolmates in our dress uniforms to line the streets, sweating profusely under the tropical sun with our miniature British flags as we waited to wave and cheer as some visiting British royal drove by in a shiny black royal car. I waved and cheered but never saw who I was waving and cheering for. I also remembered the fiery political speeches and the marches and demonstrations against British rule. I didn't understand all the issues being debated. But even as a child, I knew that people deeply resented being considered subservient to foreigners who lived a privileged life on our island, above the laws intended primarily to protect their privilege and keep the locals in check.

In Trinidad, the descendants of the enslaved Africans and indentured Indians far outnumbered the colonial rulers. The greatest fear among the British rulers must have been an uprising by the masses of people of colour. To avert this existential threat, the English rulers labelled any tendencies towards independent thinking and leadership, especially among young people, as a regression to the uncivilized and savage behaviour of "lesser peoples" that had to be eliminated. Their "civilizing" process was built into the education system. It started in early childhood, from the first day at school. NO TALKING! The colonizers needed obedient, compliant subjects who would never think of challenging authority. This was even more important than education, and The Strap was the instrument of enforcement. The beatings my classmates and I had received in school were intended to mould us into proper obedient subjects of His Majesty. Mr Bradshaw's brutal flogging was not out of concern that my failure to do homework would cause me to fall behind academically. No, my stubborn refusal to do homework showed a tendency toward the worst transgression of all: persistent disobedience, the refusal to submit to authority. That is why at age twelve, I was treated to one of the worst beatings seen at St John's Boys School.

When I got home, I showed my mother the essay and told her what had happened. Mom kept that essay until the day she died at the age of 86.

Three years out of high school, I would witness first-hand the tragic effects of the US government's misunderstanding of the Vietnamese rejection of neo-colonialism and their struggle for independence on their terms.

Coming to America

The Pan American Boeing 707, taking me to the US for the first time on 20th September 1965, was diverted from New York to Washington DC because of weather. We were taken from there to New York in busses. My older brother had arrived in New York three weeks earlier, and we enlisted in the US Army together on 27th September 1965, one week after I arrived in the US. My parents wanted us to pursue a university education. But that would be a financial strain on them, and they had done more than enough already. I had no confidence in my academic ability. It was time for me to pull my own weight. The Army held opportunity, direction, purpose, and adventure.

I quickly discovered that the underachiever mold into which I had been relegated by my teachers in school was breakable. The Army Officers and Sergeants did not care about my bad grades from a school in a place they'd never heard of. They didn't care that I was ridiculed because my handwriting looked like "*crapaud* going to church", and as a result, I seldom did homework. They had their own methods of determining what I might be capable of in the effort to win a war. During those first few days of in-processing, we spent many hours taking a series of mostly multiple-choice tests designed to assess our knowledge and aptitudes. To my great surprise and elation, I did well above average on these initial assessment exams, well enough to be eligible to apply for flight school! Back at St Mark's College in Trinidad, I'd been so frustrated at my inability to do well at school that I never even attempted some of my final high school O-Level exams. I had become convinced that I had no aptitude for academic achievement. Now, for the first time, I dared to think that maybe I had learned something in school after all. Based on my performance on these initial military assessment exams, the Army classified my education level at two years of university. Still, partly in a state of disbelief, I immediately filed my application for flight school. Then it was off to the daily grind of Army Basic Military Training.

The training sergeants pushed us to excel and convinced me to accept no externally imposed limits to what I could achieve. I found a new determination to succeed no matter what. Although they screamed at us relentlessly, day after day, I never felt the fear I'd lived with daily in primary and secondary school. I discovered that I could do more than I ever thought I could. Shackles I didn't know I had were thrown off like the scab on a healed wound. I left my old self behind, vowing never to look back. I would pursue my new-found dream of becoming a US Army Aviator.

A few months after completing basic training, I received formal notification that I'd been accepted for helicopter flight school and that my start date was still several months away. The dream was becoming a reality. In December 1966, I received my formal written orders to report to Fort Wolters in Texas to begin helicopter flight training. I was going to be a US Army pilot!

To fight a war in a dense jungle, the US Army needed helicopters capable of lifting a fully equipped infantry squad. The Bell Helicopter Company responded with the HU-1 (Helicopter Utility-1), which quickly evolved into the UH-1 Iroquois, named after one of the many societies that lived here before Columbus and other Europeans arrived, as all US Army helicopters are. Thankfully, the HU designation had already entered Army speak as the HUEY, and Iroquois was reserved for formal use in official army documents.

A Huey could lift two pilots, two door gunners, and seven fully equipped infantrymen far enough on a load of fuel to make it useful as a combat assault vehicle. Ten of these helicopters could take a light infantry company into battle without the need for roads and bridges. The Army's mobility was no longer constrained by the limits of its ground vehicles amid the muddy tangles of Vietnam's rugged jungle terrain. The Army's combat infantry units now had air mobility. With this new tool, the incredibly powerful US military would surely crush the Vietcong and North Vietnamese. The Army bought thousands of Hueys from Bell Helicopters and rapidly expanded its capacity to deliver trained pilots to fly them. The war in Vietnam became the first Helicopter War.

The US Army Warrant Officer Rotary Wing Aviator Course (WORWAC) was a combination of Officer training and Flight training. It was the most difficult challenge I had faced in my life to that point. Every day required a new resolve to succeed, as the training officers pushed us to the breaking point in their efforts to ferret out any weaknesses in our mental or physical stamina. At first, the training regimen seemed cruel and sadistic. In the beginning, many of us felt we would never make it, and many didn't. But as graduation began to seem achievable, we began to appreciate the value of the incredibly high standards of discipline, stamina, and perseverance we had been forced to attain.

After little more than a week of flight training, with all of seven hours in my student pilot's logbook, my flight instructor had me land the helicopter after completing a few circuits around the traffic pattern. He got out and told me to take it around the pattern. I picked up to a hover a bit shakily – the helicopter felt different without the weight of the instructor in the other seat – and took off as I had done over and over for the past week and a half. I turned crosswind, climbed to pattern altitude, and turned downwind. Once established on downwind, holding airspeed, altitude, and rpm steady, I spontaneously burst out laughing at the sheer incongruity of it: a high school underachiever least likely to become a US military pilot was doing a solo flight in a US military training aircraft! The engine noise dipped a bit as my rpm drooped slightly. I refocused and made my approach and landing. The instructor got in, and we continued with the training session.

On the way back to our quarters, the bus pulled off at a hotel with a swimming pool. My buddies took off my jacket and boots, lifted me by the arms and legs, swung me back and forth a few times, and threw me into the pool. For someone accustomed to water temperatures in the eighties, hitting the 37-degree Fahrenheit water was like an electric shock. As I headed for the edge of the pool, my muscles quickly grew weak, and I wasn't sure I would make it. Spurred on by the excited cheering and the adrenaline, I managed to get to the edge of the pool and pull myself out. The guys quickly threw towels around me, and we reboarded the bus, the shock of the near-freezing pool erased by the sheer elation at completing the first major milestone on the road to becoming an army aviator. The dunk in the pool after the first solo flight at Ft Wolters, Texas, was a flight school tradition best experienced in August rather than February.

Graduation from US Army Flight School was a major triumph in my life. I had done it. Against the odds, I had gone from high school failure to fully qualified Warrant Officer Rotary Wing Aviator in two years. Our graduation ceremony was a euphoric event, not just for me but for the entire class of over two hundred new Army pilots. But for me, there were also moments of sober introspection. I had finally left the old underachieving self behind, and this seemed to be trumpeted to the world by my Warrant Officer's dress blue uniform and Aviator's wings. But I knew that this was also a new beginning and that major challenges lay ahead, both external and internal. I was yet to discover that for many years to come, I would occasionally be haunted by feelings instilled and reinforced during childhood and adolescence; that I wasn't good enough, that my efforts weren't good enough, that I hadn't done well enough, that I didn't belong among those considered to be the best.

I hoped, more than anything else, that my girlfriend would consider me worth waiting for.

Deployment

A frigid wind swept into the crowded room, bringing with it the screaming of the jet engines; someone had gone out and left the door open again. "Shut the goddam door!" the First Sergeant barked coarsely from a nearby room. A young soldier scrambled up and slammed the heavy door, helped by the howling wind. It was late December 1967; the Kentucky winter was impatient. I sat propped against my army duffle bag, amazed at the massive scale of the operation that had been unfolding over the past few hours. Outside on the tarmac, the big four-engine C-141 military transport jets maneuvered around each other in the dark, sounding tense and irritated like giant alley cats sizing each other up. Their high wings and tail, designed for ease of loading and maximum lift, made them seem like predatory raptors about to attack. In the distance, we could hear the ferocious roar as, one after another, the silver Air Force transports charged down the nearby runway and climbed into the night.

The largest-ever deployment of US soldiers into a combat zone by military airlift was underway. The 3rd Brigade of the 101st Airmobile Division was being deployed from its base at Fort Campbell, Kentucky, to a new home just north of the US Air Force base at Bien Hoa, Vietnam, to join the ongoing war against the North Vietnamese and Vietcong fighters.

Thousands of soldiers and tons of equipment and weapons were being loaded onto Air Force transport planes and moved to the III Corps region of South Vietnam, the region that included the capital, Saigon.

My unit, B Company, 801st Maintenance Battalion, waited at the military airfield for our turn to board an aircraft as the planes kept coming to the tarmac, loading up, and heading out again. Even as this unprecedented military operation unfolded, half a world away and unknown to us, the North Vietnamese and Vietcong were feverishly preparing a rude welcome scheduled to erupt about a month after our arrival, with the audacious goal of final victory over the South Vietnamese and mighty US military.

Because of the logistical complexity of the deployment, we had been brought to the airfield several hours early. Apart from our Company Commander and his Executive Officer, there were only eight officers in our unit, compared to fifty or more in the Air Assault companies. I was the new guy at B Company, having joined the unit upon graduation from helicopter flight school just a few weeks before. The other officers were older and seemed to have known each other for a while. They were welcoming and courteous, but we usually ran out of small talk quickly, in part because of my natural social reticence but also because of my discomfort at being the only one who didn't know how things worked at B Company or which NFL teams were favoured to be champions. The atmosphere at this maintenance unit was quite different from an Air Assault Company with its platoons of gung-ho combat pilots.

Quickly becoming "one of the guys" was never one of my strong points. I was eager to start flying in a real helicopter company, but the helicopters and supporting equipment had already been packed up and shipped out. Everyone was ready and waiting for the big deployment. There was no time or need for new pilot orientation; there wouldn't be much to do until we got to the Nam. So, for me, there was none of the normal cockpit interaction by which pilots developed their level of professional respect for each other. In addition to being the new guy, I held one other distinction: I was "the black guy", the only black officer in B Company.

My elation at making it through nine months of flight school had been dampened by my discovery that all my buddies had been assigned to front-line Air Assault units of the 101st, and I was the only one from my group assigned to the aviation maintenance company. I had graduated in the upper half of my class, well above some of those who would soon be flying air assault missions. At the Fort Campbell Officers Club, I still hung out with my flight school friends after hours, but I was nagged by the sense that I had been considered not quite good enough for the top units. I didn't know that many of them felt that I was the lucky one.

A few weeks earlier, I had sat with a group of friends on the patio of the Screaming Eagles Officers club at Fort Campbell. It was Happy Hour; the club was crowded, and spirits were high, bolstered by the anticipation of our imminent deployment to Vietnam, where we would be part of the inevitable victory. Above the laughter and revelry, the voice boomed out across the club, unintentionally calming things down for a moment. From where we sat, we couldn't hear what was said, but it was clear that someone was being severely chewed out. Only an extreme faux pas could produce such a severe public reprimand. Things quickly returned to normal, and my group carried on with our conversation. A minute later, three more friends from flight school came over and joined our group. One of them patted me reassuringly on the shoulder. "You OK, Mac?"

"I'm great! How you guys doin'?"

"We're cool, man; that guy's in a world o' hurt. Hey, how 'bout another beer?"

I never found out who "that guy" was, but I found out what he did. He was with a group huddled near the entry door to the crowded club, and like everyone else, he was talking at the top of his voice. In his build-up to the punch line of his joke, he used a racial slur. He hadn't noticed that the Group Commander, a Colonel, had entered the club and was standing right behind him. There was one other black officer in the crowded Club. He was closer to the door than we were and may have heard the offensive language. The Colonel spun around and dealt with the issue in a manner befitting his reputation as an ass-kicker. The offending officer was ejected from the club.

I still felt new to America and often missed the point of jokes or other references – including some racial slurs - that were obvious to everyone else. I also sometimes grew tired of being a curiosity and having to explain, yet again, where Trinidad was and what life there was like. As the long wait for our aircraft dragged on into the night, I found a quiet corner where my thoughts drifted forwards to what lay ahead – flying soldiers into battles – and backwards over the improbable circumstances by which I found myself heading off to a war in which many thousands of soldiers had already been killed, including many helicopter pilots.

When I first arrived in the US on 21st September 1965, I was completely forward-looking. It was time to grow up, to put Trinidad behind me, and take responsibility for making my own way. Becoming an Army Aviator while adjusting to a new culture had required intense focus and commitment; there had been no time for looking back. Now, with soldiers milling around and the jet transports screaming outside, I felt, for the first time, a deep longing for my friends, the music, the beaches, the laughter, my girlfriend's lovely smile, and warm embrace. Would they all still be there when I got back from the war? Would I ever see them again? Was I doing the right thing? How had I ended up in this strange place on a cold dark winter night?

A Sergeant came over to the senior officer in our group. "Sir, if the officers are ready, I'll escort you out to your aircraft". I jumped up and slung my duffle bag over my shoulder, glad that the hours of waiting were over and we were finally on our way. As we followed him to the door, another Sergeant barked: "Group 49, on your feet! Form up over here!" The enlisted troops formed two rows in the corridor as the officers headed out into the freezing wind, searching the confusing maze of bright lights on the dark tarmac for our aircraft. Someone waved us over, and we climbed aboard one of several C-141s waiting with engines running. As we entered the aircraft from its rear ramp, I realized that although the aircraft was the size of a modern jet transport, it was no airliner. This was a no-frills military cargo workhorse. Several rows of seats had been fitted to a section of the floor to accommodate our small group. Other than that, this was a cargo hauler. Both forward and aft of us, military equipment covered in cargo netting was stacked to the ceiling and strapped tightly to the aircraft's floor. Without the plush interior of an airliner, the noise level of the engines and systems was deafening, even for someone used to the high-decibel screaming in the cockpit of an Army Huey helicopter. There was no chance of conversation without headphones, which we did not have. The aircraft climbed out, and we settled in for the long flight.

Part 2: The Surprising Limits of Superpower

Tet

We touched down at Bien Hoa airbase in Vietnam around 9 AM and trundled sleepily off the aircraft, squinting into the bright morning sunshine. We formed up military style on the dusty tarmac and then loaded onto military busses that would take us the short distance to our Company compound. B Company, 801st Maintenance Battalion, quickly settled into our new home on the north side of the sprawling US Air Force facility.

Custodial maintenance around our compound was performed by a team of Vietnamese workers, all women, who came in daily to keep the officers' quarters and other facilities clean. As I gradually got to know some of them, I tried to get a sense of what their lives were like. Except for the language, they seemed no different from the people I had grown up with in Trinidad. But many of my fellow soldiers considered them to be inferior people. I should not have been surprised at this, but I was. The Vietnamese workers quickly realized that I was not a "typical" US Army Officer and were as curious about me as I was about them. They wanted to know everything about Trinidad and were surprised and pleased to learn that many of my friends in Trinidad were East Asian and looked just like them.

My first job as a pilot in Vietnam entailed logistic support flights, such as delivering spare parts and equipment to front-line helicopter units and flying their helicopters back to our company when they were due for major maintenance. During that first month, I got only a few flight hours each week, and I began to feel that my development as a pilot might suffer due to the slow pace of flying activity.

In the final week of January 1968, we kept getting rumours of an impending attack on our area, but they didn't seem credible. The Tet Lunar New Year would be celebrated in a day or two. Tet was the biggest holiday in Vietnam, and for the last few years, a ceasefire was observed by the warring parties over the Tet holiday period. The North Vietnamese and Vietcong had already announced the truce. Our Company area was part of one of the larger US military complexes in Vietnam. It would be all but impossible for the Vietcong to mass enough fighting units to mount a serious attack without being detected beforehand. There was a village east of the Bien Hoa base quite close to the fence beyond the eastern end of the runway, and the rumour was that Vietcong fighters had been infiltrating the village at night, pretending to be family and friends gathering for the Tet celebrations. But no one believed that Vietcong fighters would be so crazy as to attack one of the largest US bases in Vietnam.

On the afternoon of January 30th, our Commanding Officer returned from a meeting at Brigade Headquarters. He was clearly irritated; he'd been directed to set up defensive positions around our company perimeter. He was sure there was nothing to the rumours, and anyway, we were practically an extension of the Bien Hoa Air Force base, so even if we got a few mortar rounds, the Vietcong weren't likely to mount an assault. But we had our orders, so our helicopter crew chiefs and door gunners dug foxholes and used sandbags to set up five machinegun positions facing to the south and west of the company area. There were other US units to our North and East, so we were not exposed from those directions.

As one of the most junior officers in my company, I was assigned as duty officer for the night. This entailed making inspection rounds of the company compound every two hours till 6 AM. I set my alarm clock and grabbed a snooze after my 10 PM rounds. At midnight, everything was calm and quiet. On my 2 AM check, I chatted briefly with the two guys at the first machine gun position. It was a beautiful clear night, and there were as many bright lights at the Bien Hoa Base as on any other night, indicating business as usual. As I started moving towards the next defensive position, one of the guys said, "Sir, do you think anything's gonna happen tonight?" I looked back at them, squeezed into their foxhole with their M60 machine gun, "Nah, not really, but stay alert just the same." I took two steps towards the next position and saw an object streak from east to west across the night sky, making a beautiful bright orange arc from the edge of the village towards the middle of Bien Hoa Air Force Base. There was a huge explosion as it slammed into the base and was quickly followed by two more 120-millimetre rockets. Bien Hoa Air Base was under attack. It was the start of the Tet Offensive.

I sprinted back to the Company orderly room to raise the alarm, but this was unnecessary; the sound of the explosions had everyone scrambling for flak vests and steel helmets. The Executive Officer (2nd in Command at the Company) screamed at me as he headed for the armoury, still only half dressed. "Are those guys out on the perimeter?"

"Yes, Sir, I was just out there with them."

"Ok, keep 'em out there till I get there."

I ran back towards the farthest foxhole as machinegun fire erupted from the direction of the village. I saw the two of our soldiers come charging towards me out of the darkness. I yelled over the growing noise, "What happened? Where're you going?"

"We need ammo. We don't have any ammo."

I couldn't believe it. "They put you out there with no ammo?"

"Yes, Sir, we're just going to the armoury to draw some ammo."

I ran back with them. By this time, there was a group of soldiers crowded around the Executive Officer as he struggled with a collection of keys, trying to find the one that would open the lock on the armoury door. He yelled over his shoulder, "Get these guys back out on the perimeter."

I said, "Sir, they have no way to defend themselves."

He screamed, "We'll bring the goddam ammo, just get them back out there. GO!"

We raced back out to the perimeter and watched the chaotic situation down at the air base as the explosions and gunfire continued. If we came under a direct attack, my Officer's sidearm was all we had for protection.

Our company compound was on a slight rise, so we had a clear view of the massive Bien Hoa Air Base. There was a firefight down near the runway; the perimeter may have been breached. We could see the tracer rounds, but we couldn't tell the friendlies from the Vietcong. It seemed like the VC were trying to fight their way onto the eastern end of the Bien Hoa runway. If they succeeded, they would be just a few hundred yards south of us. Every so often, several bright red tracer rounds zipped low over our heads from down by the runway, and we ducked behind the sandbags. But we didn't seem to be the main target. Rockets and mortars were hitting the air base, and now there were buildings and aircraft on fire.

Someone emerged from the darkness with a couple of cans of ammo for the machine gun. The enlisted troops were also being issued their M16 rifles and full magazines. The perimeter was soon fully manned, and we searched the darkness for whatever might be coming our way. We didn't want to be shooting at our own troops and drawing their fire in return. The gunfire coming in our direction gradually became less frequent, but the firefight continued down by the main runway. There were many fighter bombers and large cargo transports based at Bien Hoa, and they seemed to be the Vietcong's objective. As the night wore on, we saw several huge explosions as the Vietcong attacked a large ammunition depot at Long Binh, a few miles east of us. It became clear that the attack was not limited to a hit-and-run strike on the Air Base.

At first light, a pair of the new Cobra helicopter gunships showed up overhead and began attacking Vietcong positions just outside the eastern boundary of the Bien Hoa air base. We could see anti-aircraft machinegun fire being directed at them from the village as they broke from their attack runs. The dawn sky was a soft translucent rose-tinted blue as the Cobras circled around to start another attack run. I thought to myself: an army battle tank is as ugly as what it does, but the most lethal military aircraft are often the most beautiful.

As the morning wore on, it appeared as though the initial assault had been repelled, and we were no longer in imminent danger. I shot a couple of reels of super-8mm film, ducking low at the sound of incoming small arms fire that would randomly erupt from the direction of the village. When there was enough light to ensure that the main runway was useable, a pair of F-100 fighter bombers came roaring down the runway towards us with their afterburners shooting bright orange and blue flames from their tailpipes. Loaded down with bombs, they just managed to get airborne at the last second, skimming low over the village. When they had sufficient speed, they climbed out steeply only to circle around and return in a steep dive, sending their bombs into an area just beyond the end of the runway. The shock waves from the bombs exploding so close to us seemed to shake the earth itself. They were bombing just a few hundred yards from where we were. They were bombing the little village.

The gunships and the bombing seemed to have the desired effect. By mid-morning, the tension eased as it became clear that the worst was over. But we continued to hear sporadic machine gun fire all morning and into the afternoon, so we kept our flak vests and steel helmets on and stayed on high alert as we gradually returned to normal duties.

At around 11 AM, I noticed a group of six Vietnamese women in excited conversation in an open area of our compound. These women, some still quite young, did a range of duties on the compound, from administrative office duties to custodial work to helping in the mess hall kitchen. By now, we were getting word of the extent of the Tet attacks across the country, including the attack on the US Embassy about thirty miles away in Saigon. Many villages had been pillaged by the Vietcong, so I was a bit surprised to see the women turn up for work as normal. Some were very animated as they spoke rapidly in Vietnamese, with hands and arms flying in all directions. As I approached, their urgent alarmed expressions quickly softened into smiles as they greeted me pleasantly in English. "Hello, Sir. How are you today, Sir?"

I smiled in return and asked how they were. Still smiling, they said they were fine. I asked if they had had any problems last night. Several of them started talking at once. "Many VC come last night. Yes, make big problem, kill many people." One young woman who worked around our officers' quarters pointed to one of her friends. "VC come her village last night. Kill many people, kill old men." Others took up the story. "VC take her brother go fight with them. Her father very sick, say no, boy very small, er, young, boy very young, still go school. VC kill her father, take boy go fight with them". As they related this, they all continued to smile nervously as if they were simply describing a violent scene from a favourite movie. As the gruesome story unfolded, I was momentarily thrown into confusion because of their smiles. Which was real, the story or the smiles? Maybe a bit too slowly, my smile decayed as the horror of what had happened became clear. Just hours ago, their villages had become a living hell, a nightmare come to life. I didn't know what to say. I said I was deeply sorry, and feeling completely inadequate and a little silly, asked if there was anything I could do; would she like to go home? She spoke softly for the first time, "No, no, Sir, I work. I like work here, no problem." her voice soft without the sparkle of excitement in the other women's voices. She was taller than the others. Still smiling, she brought a small white handkerchief to her nose, sniffed once softly, her pain for an instant breaking through her smile, and took it away again, clutching it tightly to herself. This was the first and only outward sign of her grief and distress. As I walked away, they closed in a circle around her. I looked back at the group. She was taller than the others.

Those smiles – incongruous and dissonant in the immediate aftermath of such horror and loss – would come back to me at odd times over the years. After much reflection, I realized that the smiles were a reflex, an automatic expression used in the presence of the dominant foreign military power in their country. The smiles were meant to indicate friendliness and deference, pleasant acceptance of the power difference, a way of stating up front, "We are good guys - you're the boss". The smiles had nothing to do with how they were *feeling.* The absence of a smile might be interpreted as resentment or hostility towards our presence and our dominance. That power difference was a barrier, a limit to the range of our human-to-human connection. Was I just an agent of colonial occupiers, like the British soldiers in Trinidad when I was a child? I needed to know that we were helping these people, that we were part of the solution and not part of the problem.

Her young brother was now the enemy.

I couldn't stay behind while my peers were out on the front lines, taking the fight to the enemy. I would always be haunted by the thought that I had not been good enough. I didn't want to spend my year in a logistics unit hearing stories about the war as if I had never left the US. I wanted to do what I'd been trained to do, take our troops into battle and pull them out again. The previous day, one of the 101st Division combat assault helicopter units just next door to us had made an assault onto the roof of the US Embassy in Saigon as it was being attacked by the Vietcong. That's where I belonged, not sitting on the ground waiting to take spare parts out to the guys doing the fighting. But more importantly, I wanted an education, to learn about humans at war from the inside. From childhood, we read the comic books and saw the movies; stories of heroics and atrocities, winners and losers, the good soldiers always winning, and the bad soldiers always being defeated in wars. But how do we really behave when the constraints of civility are loosened or removed completely? Do we tell the bad stories along with the good? I wanted to see for myself and form my own opinion.

The next morning, I went to see our Commanding Officer. I wanted a transfer to a combat assault helicopter company. The CO asked with some concern if I was sure that combat assault was what I wanted. I was sure, and I said so. His expression indicated he thought I must be crazy. Two weeks later, I was transferred, not to one of the recently arrived 101st combat assault companies, but to one of the most experienced combat assault helicopter units in Vietnam, the 117th Assault Helicopter Company based at Long Binh, not far from where we were at Bien Hoa. I didn't know it yet, but I would be replacing a 117th pilot who had been recently killed in action.

The 117th had been flying combat assault missions in Vietnam since the beginning of the war and had earned a strong reputation for its skill in air assault operations. On arriving at the unit, I had only a week or two to prove my skill and judgment as a pilot, or I would be rejected. The 117th was given some of the most challenging combat assault missions. Competent but mediocre pilots posed an unacceptable risk to mission success and to the lives of the 117th pilots and crews and the soldiers they carried into battle. I was relieved and elated to be accepted by the 117th and began my development as a combat assault helicopter pilot.

Jungle Operation: Tay Ninh

Our diamond formation headed northeast past Nui Ba Den (Black Virgin Mountain), flying at the base of the midafternoon clouds out of range of small arms fire. My door gunner remarked on the way the mountain pouted from the wide flat landscape like the breast of a reclining woman. Looking over my shoulder from the number two position in the formation, I could see the smiling face of *Little Annie Fannie* painted on the nose cone of the number four helicopter rising and falling gently in the late afternoon breezes. As our flight of four Huey "Slick" helicopters headed for the final extraction of the Special Forces (SF) team from a small clearing that served as the Landing Zone (LZ) in the dense jungle, everyone was calm but alert. It was dangerous work; these SF teams always seemed to encounter enemy units much larger than their twelve-man teams, even when we put in two or three of their teams. Still, we liked the challenge of snatching them from the closing jaws of the Vietcong units following their quick hit-and-run interdiction raids. We were many miles from any villages or hamlets, so there was no chance of causing civilian casualties. And it was far more rewarding than flying boring courier missions far away from any combat operations.

The region from the northern outskirts of Tay Ninh City to the Cambodian border and beyond to the Ho Chi Minh

Trail was mostly uninhabited jungle, providing an excellent point of entry into South Vietnam for fighters from the North. There were rumors that enemy units were massing in this area in preparation for another Tet-style offensive. The mission of the Special Forces teams was to gather intelligence on this activity. The jungle in this region was so dense that trucks loaded with supplies could be driven for long distances without being seen from the air. Going after the enemy on foot or in vehicles would entail high casualties and a lower probability of success. But helicopters could leap-frog the difficult terrain and place our soldiers in a good position to take the fight to the enemy. The Army had purchased thousands of helicopters and trained a steady stream of pilots to fly them. We were now putting that theory into practice.

The Ho Chi Minh Trail was the main resupply route from North Vietnam to fighters in the South. We had already made two extractions of Special Forces teams from this triple-canopy jungle. Our two-gunship escort was still in the area, waiting to provide protective cover for us as we went in for the final lift. Both times we had drawn fire from the Vietcong, both on the approach and on the climb out. Somehow, these Special Forces teams seemed to have aggravated every enemy fighter within a ten-mile radius. This region, close to the Cambodian border and the Ho Chi Minh Trail, harbored many more enemy units than the teams had suspected. The faint puffs of smoke we had seen near the edge of the landing zone on the last lift had come from Vietcong AK-47s less than 50 meters away. My crew chief had even seen some muzzle flashes. I felt certain we must have taken hits. But all four helicopters reported systems normal, and the birds handled perfectly. I could only attribute the Vietcong's poor marksmanship to the fact that they did not use tracer bullets (ammunition that burned bright, making them visible) which would help them hit their targets but would also reveal their position to our gunners.

Under such intense automatic weapons fire, the normal procedure would have been to call in artillery and tactical air strikes to silence the positions. But this was enemy territory, triple canopy jungle for miles around in every direction. If an attempt was made to pinpoint his position, he was nowhere, the jungle empty and peaceful. But if a chopper flew over between 300 and 1,000 feet, he was everywhere, the jungle hostile and deadly.

Despite the risks to our aircraft and crews, we had to get that last Special Forces team out of there before nightfall. There was at least one battalion of Vietcong and North Vietnamese regulars (300 – 400 soldiers) near our landing zone (LZ). Against such odds, the small SF team had little chance of holding out through the night. The Tet Offensive earlier in the year had jolted and embarrassed US Commanders. They realized that the Ho Chi Minh trail was even more important to the North Vietnamese war effort than they had thought. The trail ran outside South Vietnamese territory but was close enough in places to allow North Vietnamese units to get within striking distance of key targets. To the North Vietnamese, the city of Tay Ninh was a key gateway for attacks on the South Vietnamese capital, Saigon, and several other important towns and US bases.

Nui Ba Den - *Black Virgin Mountain*

The audacious Tet offensive launched by the North Vietnamese and the Vietcong in January 1968 had been more than a wake-up call for the US military; it was a surprise punch in the nose from a grossly underestimated enemy. Now, just a few months later, another buildup of fighters and supplies was underway in the dense jungles of Cambodia just across the border north of the city of Tay Ninh. US Army Special Forces were given the mission of going into the jungle to gather intelligence about what the enemy was up to and to disrupt their operations. After Tet, US forces would not be caught by surprise a second time.

A flight platoon of the 117th Assault Helicopter Company was assigned to support the SF teams using four Hueys and a 2-gunship escort. We packed our bags and flew our four Hueys and two gunships up to a base near Tay Ninh, allowing us to get to the SF target areas within a half hour or less. Now, the SF teams we had put in the day before made a desperate call for us to pull them out. They were being attacked by a large enemy force and could not hold out much longer.

"Flight go trail; Lead starting descent." (The flight leader was referred to simply as "Lead". Everyone else used their position in the flight to identify themselves, such as "Two" or "Seven".) Lead's voice was calm and clear. Our crew chief cleared us to the left, and we slipped into the number 2 trail position directly behind Lead as we began the 3,000-foot descent to the treetops. That descent would take about 90 seconds, and we would stay on the treetops for the last three miles to the LZ. Over this hostile jungle, flying was done on the deck as close as possible to the treetops or above 2,000 feet, and the time spent getting from one level to the other was kept to an absolute minimum.

We leveled off with our skids skimming the treetops, flying a comfortable distance on Lead. The thick vegetation was a green blur beneath us as we maintained a high cruise speed to minimize our exposure to enemy units on the ground. I was reassured by the thought that if anyone could see us from the jungle floor, we'd be there and gone in a flash. Lead made gentle turns to avoid the areas where the vegetation became sparse enough to make the ground visible and make us visible to anyone on the ground. Then he rolled smoothly into a 40-degree bank, dipping his blades close to the trees. We banked right and stayed with him.

"Lead starting deceleration." We were too low to see it, but we were on our short final approach to the clearing, where the SF team waited to be picked up. I made a quick check of the instruments and threw a reassuring glance and thumbs up to the crew chief and gunner. They never saw me; their eyes were glued to the jungle below. "Lead slowing through 40 knots." Without warning, lead disappeared into the trees. We continued to slow our forward speed. Then it suddenly appeared ahead of us; a clearing in the jungle just large enough for the four Hueys to get into. As we crossed the tree line and sank into that hole, we were greeted by the familiar sharp staccato of AK-47 rifle fire coming from the Vietcong.

"Lead, this is Three; we're taking fire, taking fire! I think we're hit!" As our skids touched the ground, Lead lifted and started out with his troops.

"Lead's coming out. Can you make it out, Three?"

"This is Three; I'm touching down behind Two. Everything seems to be OK".

"Lead, this is Sidewinder Eight; break right when you hit the tree line".

The Sidewinder gunship crew had seen where the enemy fire was coming from and was directing the flight away to allow them to use their rockets and miniguns on the enemy positions. The gunship team had covered us on the two previous extractions. Their firepower was the only deterrent sufficiently effective to make the extractions possible. Now the two gunships, low on fuel, flew at minimum power to stretch their time on station.

The Special Forces scrambled aboard in a couple of seconds. "Two's coming out." We eased off the ground and began the agonizingly slow climb to the brink of the clearing. The pop-pop-pop of AK47 fire greeted us from very close. Our two M60 machine guns responded immediately as our crew chief and gunner zeroed in on the enemy position. The Special Forces fired their M16s out the open doors as we climbed away. "Two's out; breaking right; taking fire from the left and right in the LZ."

"Two, this is Lead; you alright?" Before we could respond: "Lead, this is Three; I'm losing fuel fast. It's all over the floor!"

"This is Lead; can you make it out, Three?"

"We're not staying in this hellhole; Three's coming out."

"This is Sidewinder Eight; we got you, Three; come on out. Take it easy."

"Three's out. Lead, I just got my low fuel warning light!"

"Roger, Three; set 'er down; pick a spot and set 'er down!"

"Three, this is Two; there's a pretty good area at your two o'clock, about 300 meters."

"Roger; I've got it; I'm taking her in. Cover me, Sidewinders."

"We're with you; we'll have you out in a minute."

There had only been three loads of Special Forces left to be picked up. The number four aircraft had been brought along as a cover ship in case something went wrong. This decision now paid off in full as we shifted seamlessly to a rescue and salvage operation.

"This is Four; I'm going in to get them".

The Aircraft Commander of the lead ship was our Operations Officer. He was also our Command-and-Control

Officer for these Special Forces missions. It was his brilliant tactics that enabled us to insert these reconnaissance teams into the heart of enemy-infested territory and extract them again at a moment's notice, often from the very jaws of an enemy trap. He now resumed his role of Command and Control, and his cool easy tone instilled confidence where it may have ebbed for an instant.

"This is Lead; Roger Four, just get the crew and head for home base. I'll get the radios (to keep the encrypted radios out of enemy hands). Three, don't forget your logbook."

"This is Three; I'm on the ground. No injuries to personnel; no further damage to the aircraft; going off the air at this time."

On the ground, the Special Forces troops on board the damaged helicopter quickly spread out into a defensive perimeter. They were 500 meters from the LZ, where they had just been picked up. The Vietcong weren't far away. A helicopter and crew would be a rich prize. But from the floor of the dense jungle, they may not have seen the bird go down.

Back at the base camp, Sidewinder Seven, the gunship team leader, had been monitoring the radio traffic. Two of his four gunships had been shot up and needed maintenance. As soon as it became clear that a ship was down, he scrambled the team and headed out to the location in the damaged gunships.

"Two, this is Lead; what's your position?"

"We're orbiting at 1,500 feet."

"As soon as four gets the crew, take your troops in as a security force."

"This is Two; we're on our way."

"Four's coming out with the crew."

"This is Lead; Roger Four. Head for home base and have them get a reaction force ready to go."

"Four, Roger."

We took our troops in, and as we climbed out, Lead went into the LZ to get the radios from the downed bird. It was critical that those radios not fall into the hands of the enemy. We established an orbit at 2,500 feet and called our home base, Warlord Control, at Long Binh. We briefed them on the situation, so they could work with higher-level headquarters to expedite the recovery of the downed bird. The radio traffic increased tremendously as everyone seemed to be calling at the same time. To ensure that critical messages got through, we climbed another thousand feet and acted as the communications relay for the operation.

By this time, our fuel was becoming a concern. We would be well into our 20-minute reserve before we got back to our operations base at Tay Ninh. We didn't have much time left on station. I mentally assessed the grim options facing us as nightfall approached. We had three ships available to put in a reaction force to secure the downed bird through the night. It would take quite a force. The Vietcong would go to great lengths to destroy a wounded helicopter sitting in their own backyard. If only we could get a Chinook out here before night closed in, and the enemy with it. The big tandem-rotor helicopter could easily lift out the Huey and take it back to our base. But that possibility seemed remote. Already the shadows stretched way out to the east, shrouding the lower portions of the forest landscape in darkness. Time was not on our side. It would be a rough night for the security forces.

Unknown to us, Lead had already been arranging a rescue operation. On a separate radio channel, he had activated a recovery team to rig the downed Huey to be lifted out, and a Chinook was already on its way to the site. They were in a race with the setting sun.

I began to get worried about Lead. He'd been down there almost four minutes now. From the air, the site had looked like an open area in the middle of the dense jungle. It turned out to be covered with elephant grass up to six feet tall in places, making it difficult to get around on foot.

I looked at our fuel gauge. This was going to be very close. We orbited for another minute. "Lead, you alright?"

"Roger; Lead's coming out. Cover me, Sidewinders."

We're with you, Lead."

The Vietcong had wasted no time getting there. As Lead crossed the tree line, they opened fire from his 12 o'clock position. "Lead taking fire! Breaking right, Sidewinders, breaking right!"

The Sidewinder's rockets blasted the enemy position seconds after they had opened up on Lead. The gunship pilots followed up with a volley of fire from their twin miniguns.

"You alright, Lead?"

"Lead, Roger. I think we took a couple of hits, but the bird feels ok. I'll have to check her out when we get on the ground. As he climbed out, we fell into formation behind him and headed for Tay Ninh.

By this time, Four had dropped off the downed crew and had refueled at Tay Ninh. "Lead, this is Four. What are your instructions, over?"

"Looking good, Four. Stay in the air for radio relay and head out to the downed bird. Coordinate with Pipesmoke (the Chinook helicopter) and guide him in if he gets there before I do. I may have taken a couple of rounds getting the radios out of there. I'll have to shut this thing down and check her out."

As Lead touched down at the base camp, the gaping crowd that gathered around his chopper, staring in disbelief, confirmed his suspicions: 14 bullet holes, one of them right through the engine combustion chamber! How was he able to stay in the air? He would never have made it out with a full load of troops. A quick glance at the punctured skin of the aircraft was enough to dictate his next course of action. Out of the cockpit, before the blades had even stopped, they grabbed their gear and hopped into the cockpit of 208, one of the Warlords' backup ships sent up from Long Binh. They cranked her up and were off again, leaving a crowd of ground troops and Vietnamese civilians to marvel at their bullet-riddled ship.

We refueled and shut down at the Tay Ninh base camp to await the decision to either insert the reaction force or extract the security force now guarding the downed Huey. A close inspection of our ship revealed only one bullet hole in the main rotor blade. We had been very lucky so far.

An excited soldier burst out of the operations tent sprinting towards us and frantically rotating his hand above his head, the signal to crank her up. "The Chinook's only a few minutes out from the downed ship. Head on out for the security force extraction."

We whisked old reliable 562 into the air as fast as we could, anxious to be doing anything but sitting on the ground at a time like this.

It was twilight now, and in the twenty minutes we would take to get out there, it would be a full night. I wondered if the

Chinook was being harassed by the Vietcong. As we passed Nui Ba Den Mountain, we heard over the radio that the Huey was about to be lifted out. The big Chinook would be a vulnerable and tempting target as it hovered over the Huey in the near darkness of falling night in the jungle. But the next radio call was not the urgent MAYDAY we all feared. The Chinook was calling clear as he headed for the early stars with his precious cargo hanging securely from a sling beneath the Chinook. The crew of 562 let out a yell of joy like kids at a football game. We had snatched this valuable prize from the clutches of the Vietcong without a minute to spare. The suppressive fire laid down by the Sidewinders and the security team had prevented the enemy from attacking the Chinook or the salvage team as they rigged and lifted out the Huey. Now came the final challenge, extracting troops under attack by the Vietcong at night.

When we arrived at the location, Four had already climbed out with his shipload of the Special Forces security force. The night was a confusing maze of flashing red and green lights as the Sidewinders continued to maintain their vigilant orbit above the site. We established altitude separation to avoid a mid-air collision, and Lead started in for his load. In the darkness, it was nearly impossible to pick out the LZ, let alone a safe landing spot, from the surrounding jungle.

"Lead, this is Four; go into the South and watch out for those little trees in there; it's tricky."

With the LZ covered in tall elephant grass, it was impossible to pinpoint the exact location of the ground troops, even with the landing light and searchlight on. When Lead was on short final, one of the Special Forces on the ground began to guide him in using his FM radio. With some hasty course corrections and a crazy flare at the bottom, Lead made it in safely. I hoped we could do the same. To roll it up and try to get into that unprepared spot at night on our very last lift would ruin a perfect operation. Lead's ingenuity and courage lighted the way for us – literally.

"Two, this is Lead. We'll sit here with our landing light on to guide you in. When you're on short final, we'll get out of here, and you can shoot to our spot." This was a leader we would follow into hell without a moment's hesitation. His landing light made him an easy target for the Vietcong. But without it, we would simply be sinking into a black void, hoping not to hit anything on the way in. We started in with Lead guiding us on the radio. He had turned sideways so he could see us silhouetted against the starry sky as we made the approach.

"Looking good, Two, keep coming." We began to decelerate.

“Ok, Two, slow her up.” 40 knots; 20 knots.

“Ok, Lead; we can take it from here.”

“Roger. Lead’s coming out.” As he lifted out, we turned on our searchlight. The elephant grass rippled like waves on a lake under the rotor wash. We were a little fast, but thanks to Lead, we landed right on his spot. The troops were on board in a flash.

“How many do you have, Two?”

We made a quick check. “Two’s got seven.” The last thing we needed was to leave a man in that LZ.

“Two’s coming out.” We eased the ship up into the blackness, anticipating an eruption of enemy fire. As soon as we were sure we had cleared the trees; “Two’s out.”

“Roger Two. Smelling like a rose. Let’s go home and get some hot chow and a shower.”

As we fell in behind Lead and climbed away from the jungle, the sky was clear and filled with a million stars; there was nowhere else in the world I wanted to be.

That night, after dinner, I began to write down everything that had happened that day. I never wanted to forget what we had done in Tay Ninh, Vietnam, on the Fifth of June 1968.

Doreen

At our Long Binh base on the night before one of our combat assault missions in September of '68, Specialist Jim Cavanaugh, Huey helicopter technician, and door gunner headed to the enlisted "club" where the crew chiefs and door gunners hung out to check for mail and have a few beers with his buddies at the end of another day of flying. Jim was tall and lean and often looked and sounded as if he'd just walked off the set of a Western movie. He opened a letter from his fiancée, a beautiful tall Texan country girl with long legs and piles of blonde hair whom everyone felt they knew because Jim raved about her all the time, and carried her smiling picture in laminated plastic around his neck on his dog tag chain. Whenever he sat behind the M-60 machine gun mounted in the door of the Huey helicopter, a pair of bright red bikini panties were stretched garishly across the top of his flight helmet, panties that he claimed were Doreen's. As Jim read the letter, his grin faded, his face turned to flame and then to ash. His big hands trembled. Everyone but the most recent arrivals knew that he'd been hit with a "Dear John" letter. His beloved Doreen had found someone else. The laughter and chatter ebbed slightly as those closest to Jim focused their attention on their drinks.

"Goddamn!" Big Jimmy Cavanaugh slammed his fist down on the table. His beer can tipped over. The drink trickled softly onto the floor. Without another word, he slinked off to his hooch like a wounded predator to endure in solitude the loss of his precious Doreen to another man and the flaming rage of his inability to do anything about it. The excitement of his return to her, getting closer each day, had made him almost oblivious to the daily drudgery of the war. As things at the club gradually returned to normal, the platoon sergeant went to check on Cavanaugh.

It could happen to me; the thought suddenly materialized in my mind as if it had been silently incubating there. It was my biggest fear, more than being shot down or killed in a ground assault, losing the woman I loved. I pushed the thought away...

At dawn the following day, as our crews prepared the ten troop lift and four gunship helicopters for that day's combat assault missions, the loud, raucous Texan, always good-natured and foul-mouthed, was sullen, silent, coiled up inside himself. His helmet was bare. No photo hung around his neck. Everyone talked around him and left him alone; war is hell. Next to being killed or captured, a Dear John letter was feared most by everyone who had someone they hoped to return to.

We took off from our base at Long Binh, a few miles east of Saigon and the sprawling air base at Bien Hoa – ten troop carrier "slicks" with two-door gunners each, escorted by four heavily armed gunships – and headed south to work with a battalion of the 9th Infantry Division operating in the Mekong Delta. At around 8:30, we picked up an infantry company – seven grunts on each of the ten slicks – near Dong Tam, a major US base in the Mekong Delta. By this time, I was a seasoned Aircraft Commander flying the number four ship in the flight of ten. Our mission was to place the infantry company into a remote region of the Mekong Delta near the Cambodian Border, a region previously untouched by the conflict and about which little hard intelligence was available, at least to our flight crews. As far as we knew, the village was not known to harbor any significant Vietcong activity, so organized resistance was not expected. This would be a cold insertion; no one would fire unless we received enemy fire. But if we did come under fire, all twenty door gunners would open fire with their machine guns to suppress enemy fire until we delivered the troops and were out of range of enemy guns.

Lieutenant Frank Anderson (not his real name) had only recently been assigned to lead the formation of ten Hueys. He tended to take the flight much too close to the huts and structures of these small hamlets and villages, and this made the flight crews nervous and edgy. Maybe his aim was to maximize the element of surprise and impress our superiors with his daring leadership, but this was not the way the 117th Warlords normally did our air assaults. It was a dangerous gamble that previous formation leaders had learned to avoid.

We preferred to land in the open and let the troops approach the huts as they were trained to do.

"Flight go trail". As the ten helicopters slipped in one behind the other, I became mildly irritated because it looked like he was about to do it again; he was lining up on the narrow dirt road that ran through the little hamlet with a row of huts to the left of the road and livestock pens about 40 yards off to the right. Maybe he had intelligence from Special Forces teams in the area that the little village was secure. I hoped that one of those huts or rice stacks would not turn out to be concealing a machine gun bunker. But there was something else that was strangely calming and disturbing at the same time; there were no bomb craters. Wherever we flew in Vietnam, the countryside was pockmarked with bomb craters of varying sizes from so many years of continuous bombardment. Was this a safe area with friendly villagers or a haven for enemy fighters?

From the cockpit of a helicopter, the approach to a natural landscape has the effect of slowly zooming in on the scene, the splendor of the wide delta landscape with its green and brown checkerboard rice paddies stretching out to the horizon gradually changing to a close-up view as more and more local detail becomes discernable. As the flight leader set up the final approach, we were suddenly flying into a beautiful pastoral scene, as if we had been magically transported to a different place and time.

With my co-pilot flying this leg of the mission, I could, for just a moment, let myself absorb the special beauty of this part of the country. Off to our right was an old man with a stringy gray beard and a ridiculous round colonial-style khaki police hat with a wide brim, carrying a pair of overloaded baskets hanging from the ends of a sturdy bamboo supporting bar, which bounced up and down on his shoulder as he moved quickly along the rice paddy dike in the rhythmic dancing gait used by his people to carry their things for thousands of years. And off to our left were two women about ten feet apart, dressed in their traditional black "pajama" outfit and conical straw hats, lifting their hoes high overhead and bending from the waist to dig the blades in, then turn up the heavy chunks of rice paddy mud. They remained focused on their task as if ten noisy menacing war machines were not descending uninvited into their world just forty yards away, clattering down in formation, louder and louder like giant flying storm troops, their heavy rotors slapping and tearing at the quiet morning air, sending out shock waves that the women would feel in their skulls and teeth, in their bellies, and up through the ground like the trampling boots of soldiers as big as dragons.

As we slowed for our landing in trail formation on the narrow dirt road, there were six little huts to our left about ten yards back from the road. To our right, some water buffalo stood motionless in the mud with horns back and snouts in the air, looking like sculptures of themselves. Some pigs rushed about their pen in panic, probably squealing their heads off. Lead took the flight slowly forward along the road to ensure that all ten helicopters would have enough room to land. As we drifted forward to our touchdown, a little girl no more than four or five years old ran out and stood wide-eyed on the front landing of her home, a tiny straw hut on stilts just ahead of us to our left. Then a little boy, a year or two older, ran out and stood next to her. A pair of arms quickly reached out from low down near the floor and pulled them back into the tiny bamboo and straw hut built on stilts that kept it above the water when the monsoon came, and the Mekong River flooded the paddies. Bits of straw blown from the dry paddies and the thatched roofs swirled around in the downwash from the helicopters as we hovered past the hut where the little girl and boy had stood. Rectangles of green and brown rice paddies stretched away into the distance, out toward the Cambodian border, fringed by strips of palms and shrubs that ran along the ancient dike lines like unkempt hedges.

As we settled onto the dirt road, the ugly staccato of gunfire from the first one, then both of our machine guns, jerked me back into the war. Our two door gunners were firing their M-60 machine guns, the bitter voices of the weapons overriding the familiar noise of the rotors and turbine engine. The quiet little hamlet erupted into the thunder and savagery of combat as twenty M-60 machine guns on ten helicopters delivered "continuous suppressive fires over the entire area and periphery of the Landing Zone". (These are the words that were used in our training courses.) Someone must have drawn enemy fire; the LZ had "gone hot". All twenty machine gunners were laying down suppressive fire to protect the flight until it was safely away from the LZ. Rockets from the gunships began exploding all around the flight, hitting those places where gunship pilots believed the enemy most likely to be hidden. Some rockets were hitting dangerously close to our helicopter. The troops were off the helicopters in a few seconds, and we were lifting off again. They hit the ground, firing their M-16s. We pulled maximum power, and the flight of ten, much lighter now, scrambled up and away from the dirt road like a flock of ducks surprised by a hunter.

The eruption of machine gun fire and rocket explosions was over in no more than twenty seconds.

As we climbed away from the LZ, the rotors sounding soft and hushed in the quiet aftermath, each aircraft commander checked in tersely on the radio with just his sequence number to ensure that any distress calls would not be interrupted; "Lead's up". "Two". "Three's up". "Four"... The calls continued until all ten aircraft had reported in OK. The southern drawl of the gunship platoon leader came up on the radio; "Any y'all see where the fire was comin' from?" No response.

With everyone accounted for safely, I turned to my two door gunners. "You guys alright? Did we take any hits? What the hell happened back there?" A brief silence: then the crew chief spoke up. "The LZ went hot; one of the guys must have seen something". As the flight banked into a climbing right turn away from the LZ, I twisted around from my left seat position and looked behind and below us. I saw only burning, smoking rubble scattered around the quiet place where the residents of the little hamlet had been going about their daily business less than a minute ago. The political allegiance of the villagers, whatever it might have been through the days of their quiet lives, was certified forever by the circumstances of their death: they were the enemy. The infantry would take another body count and report another battle won. The "enemy" had been taken by surprise. Someone in an office somewhere would report another battle won.

Air assaults were our business, and we worked hard to be one of the Army's best combat assault helicopter units; we did not do screw-ups. We knew that a peaceful-looking village could be harboring a well-equipped Viet Cong force. We had brought out dead and wounded US soldiers from such encounters and had even lost aircraft and crews to the heavy enemy fire coming from what initially seemed like a quiet little village. But this felt different. This felt like a major screw-up. No one seemed to know who had seen or heard the enemy fire.

Our flight of ten landed at a designated secure staging area, an open field several miles from Dong Tam. We shut down the helicopters to check for battle damage while we waited for our next mission. That mission would depend on what the infantry company encountered on the ground. The image of the destroyed hamlet, an image I'd seen for maybe less than a second, kept hovering in my mind. There had been a woman running between the burning huts. Maybe there were other survivors.

Lt. Anderson, our flight commander, got out of his helicopter and walked back to where Jim Cavanaugh sat hunched over his machine gun on the number eight helicopter. I wanted to talk to the Lieutenant about the dangers of landing so close to the huts, but I said nothing to him as he went by, looking angry and purposeful. As I began to check my aircraft for hits, a small group of pilots and crewmen gathered around

Cavanaugh and the Lieutenant. Jim's forehead rested on his large hands as they cupped the grips of the weapon with its still-warm muzzle pointed toward the ground in the stowed position. I couldn't hear what was being said, but it was clear that the Lieutenant was angry. He climbed back into the cockpit of his aircraft, put on his helmet, and called for the Operations Officer to send out a replacement door gunner and have Jim Cavanaugh flown back to see the Flight Surgeon.

As we waited for our next mission, we went through the usual routine of checking every inch of our helicopters for battle damage following a hot mission. I wondered whether Jim had lost it, had blamed the war and the Vietnamese for the loss of the girl of his dreams, and could no longer contain his rage. A Huey arrived and took Cavanaugh away, leaving a fresh door gunner to take his place. There was no time or space for feelings of discomfort or confusion or for thoughts of the gentle faces of the two children in the little hut. That would come years later.

Standing on the roof of my helicopter to check the rotors for damage, I could swear I heard a woman's voice in the distance. There it was again: "Hey, G-I!" I spun around, and incredibly, about sixty or seventy yards ahead in the shade of a small tree were two young Vietnamese women, one in a bright blue top, the other in bright green, both wearing silky white slacks that fluttered in the morning breeze. "Hey, GI, I give you good time!" "Number one good time!" This brought on a round of raucous laughter and commentary from the 117th crewmen and some of the pilots.

"Look at them nasty gook whores."

"Them gooks got every disease you can name, and some even the doctors ain't heard of yet".

I had seen the two figures on the road in the distance after we landed but hadn't given them a second thought.

"Hello GI, I give number one hand job, blow job too! Make you velly happy."

The troops continued to cling to the moral high ground.

"You touch one o' them gooks; your dick will fall off before you get back to base, man". Loud laughter. This banter went on for several minutes, and I began to lose interest. Suddenly, one of the women pulled her pants down to her knees and gyrated in our direction, her little patch of pubic hair clearly visible in the bright morning light, before quickly pulling them up again. "Hey GI, I give you plenty happy-happy!" Without another word, a little line of helicopter crewmen and door gunners headed purposefully towards the two women, first two, then two more, then a procession in single file. There was a deep bomb crater on the far side of the tree where the women stood in the shade. That improbable venue provided a degree of privacy and served as the place of business for the crewmen unable to resist the charms of the young women.

Just then, First Platoon (five helicopters) was ordered to head to Dong Tam to refuel and return to the staging area. Responding in disappointment to the call, a few of the men broke from the line and returned to their helicopters. When we returned about forty minutes later, the two young women, with their morning's windfall earnings, were walking briskly back down the road to wherever they had come from. We learned that the pair had been brought back to the staging area to continue their brisk business behind the closed doors of the cabins of two of the helicopters.

Before I could begin to frame the muddled questions and conflicting emotions swirling in my head regarding all that had happened already that morning, another urgent mission came crackling over the radio. Fourteen turbine engines whined, fourteen helicopter rotors turned again, and the flight was up and away.

Over the rest of that day, we placed two other infantry companies into LZs in the same operational area and pulled them out again without incident. When we returned to our home base at the end of the day's operations, Captain Shultz, our Platoon Leader, went in to report to the Company Commander. He learned that Cavanaugh had already been reassigned. No one knew where he was sent. I never saw Jim Cavanaugh again, and no one seemed to know what happened to him.

That night, there were lively discussions as to whether Cavanaugh had saved the flight from an ambush or had precipitated an unintended atrocity. Many took the position, "Better safe than sorry". But the absence of battle damage to any of the helicopters belied the ambush theory. At such close range, enemy fighters could not have missed.

We spent the next two weeks working with infantry units of the 9th Infantry Division in the Mekong Delta. They were great guys, but their operations often seemed to be poorly planned. Or maybe the enemy in this area was exceptionally skilled at dealing with the US air assault tactics. We lost more people and aircraft working with them than we did with anybody else. The infantry was searching for Vietcong and North Vietnamese units that were mounting brazen nighttime raids on the large base at Dong Tam. We would pick up an infantry unit early in the morning and put them into the area they wanted to search; they'd shoot first if they got nervous, or they'd buy stuff from the farmers and give candy to the kids if they felt safe. Then we'd pick them up and take them to another area, and they'd search again. But they weren't finding what they were looking for, and they often seemed relaxed, even bored, when we picked them up. But sometimes, when we went in to pick them up at the end of the day, the Vietcong would appear from nowhere, and we'd have to pull them out under heavy fire. In the delta, unlike the jungles north of Tay Ninh, we were unobscured targets for the Vietcong fighters, while they seemed to be able to melt into the mud and the rice paddies and simply vanish.

Around five o'clock one afternoon, we lifted off from our staging area to pick up the infantry battalion for the last time that day and take them back to their base. On our way there, we got a call that they were under attack and taking heavy fire. These infantry guys had been searching the area all day and found nothing. Suddenly they were under attack by a well-organized force. As we were touching down for the pickup, the sun was low in the sky. I saw bright red tracer fire leaping up from the lush green rice field no more than twenty or thirty yards away, closer than I'd ever been to the source of enemy fire. The infantry battalion had grown complacent and had allowed the Vietcong to sneak up on them through the rice paddies. The Vietcong had perfected the art of becoming invisible in the rice paddies. By tucking rice stalks into their clothing and staying partially submerged, they could not be seen if they moved very slowly or stayed still. The soldiers seemed panicked and disorganized as they scrambled through the deep mud to get to the helicopters. Some were getting stuck in the mud and being hit right beside us. The door gunners did their best to suppress the fire from the closest attackers, but we began to take hits.

Two lifts were required to move the battalion - two infantry companies. We went out with the first lift, and several of our aircraft had been hit. We dropped the first company off and headed back out in the fading light to get the other company with only eight ships, which meant we'd be coming out overloaded. As we came in for the second lift, there was a spectacular orange-red sunset painting the sky to the west, but darkness was closing in on the ground. As we touched down, it was clear that our guys on the ground were much better organized. We weren't taking nearly as much fire as the first time around. It must have been a sneak attack by a small Vietcong force.

We were the last ship in the flight of eight as we started to lift out. The climb out was agonizingly slow because of the extra guy or two on board each ship. Then, as the number seven aircraft rose above the horizon ahead of me, I saw, silhouetted against the pink sky, a guy hanging from the helicopter skid, holding on to a machine gun. We couldn't see him until they got high enough above us for him to be silhouetted against the pink sky. I got on the radio, "Seven, you've got a guy hanging from your skid!" Then I saw the M60 machine gun fall. A few seconds later, he just fell off from about fifty or sixty feet up.

"This is Eight; we lost a guy from seven". The mission commander, who was controlling the whole operation from a couple thousand feet overhead with a senior infantry commander, responded immediately. "Do **not** break formation. We'll have to come back for a third lift; I'm not sure we got 'em all."

We made it back to the staging area and dropped off the troops. With rotors turning in the falling darkness, the flight waited for the flight leader's call to head back out to the LZ. After a few minutes, the flight leader got out of his aircraft and went into the command bunker. We sat there with eight rotors turning for ten very long minutes. Then Lead's voice came up on the radio from the Command bunker and told us all to shut down. But no one did. We all just sat there waiting to go back out with our engines and rotors droning mournfully in the darkness. For me, there was something deeply horrifying about leaving that poor guy out there on his own. I kept seeing him lying flat in the mud with death waiting somewhere out of sight in the darkness. I couldn't make the image go away, and I didn't know why. We saw terrible things all the time, but this affected me deeply.

Our flight leader came out of the command bunker and got into his aircraft. We brought the rotors back up to flight speed in preparation for takeoff. He explained on the radio that only one soldier was unaccounted for, the one who had fallen off the number seven aircraft, and that the infantry Colonel in overall command would not risk valuable aircraft and crews in a dangerous night mission to recover someone who was almost certainly already killed or captured. And even if he wasn't, the chances of finding him from the air at night and then getting to him and getting out again without being shot down were close to zero.

We hated working with these infantry commanders. A Special Forces unit would never leave a guy behind like that. We found out later that Lead had gotten into a heated argument with the Colonel about leaving the guy behind. It was only after being threatened with a court martial that he had finally given the instruction to shut down.

The next morning at dawn, our lead aircraft took off, escorted by two of our gunships, and headed for the landing zone. When they got to the LZ, they made a low pass over the area at a slow cruise speed, and incredibly, they spotted the soldier on their first pass. He had completely camouflaged himself in mud, and they would never have seen him had he not stood up and waved as they went by about fifty yards from where he was. As they came around to set up their approach, he waved his arms wildly, probably yelling his head off. He must have thought they hadn't seen him; he was doing everything he could to attract their attention. But he also attracted the attention of an enemy fighter. They never heard the shot; they just saw him lying down in the mud and thought he was concealing himself from any Vietcong that might be in the area. When they landed to pick him up, he was already dead. He'd been shot through the head. He'd survived out there all that night, only to be killed moments before he was about to be rescued.

The gunships shot up the area but never found the sniper.

The news brought a surge of anger and frustration among the 117th pilots and crews. We felt sure we could have gotten him out if we'd gone back right away. At the end of the day, as the temperature drops, the helicopters can lift a bit more. But years later, I would realize that the Colonel had probably made the correct decision. We would not have found the soldier at night unless he revealed his position to us with a flashlight or flare. The Vietcong would have found him and, under cover of darkness, would probably have fired on the helicopters. In daylight, they knew better than to reveal themselves to the gunships.

At least one enemy fighter stayed in that rice paddy all night in the hope of killing or capturing the American soldier or finding his body and his machine gun.

We were well-trained soldiers doing our job with pride. Our business was to fight the battles, not to question their purpose. In the quiet of the night, in the minutes before you fall asleep, the questions you're not supposed to ask come at you softly. Will all this killing achieve a higher purpose? How many more people must we kill to achieve our objective?

That night I lay on my bunk in my little cubicle back at the 117th, listening to soothing sounds coming from my new Pioneer speakers with 15-inch woofers – Nancy Wilson's voice being caressed by the strings of a large orchestra. The music seemed to take me to another state of being. I heard no lyrics, no subject and verbs, no story or meaning. I just floated in the beauty of the sound. The more peaceful I felt, the more my inner conflict and confusion rose to the surface. As the music played, a question presented itself to me. If I had been a soldier in Hitler's army, would I have participated in some of the ugly atrocities that had become normal for so many of those soldiers? Would I have shot innocent civilians or defenseless prisoners of war in the pursuit of victory? My instant reaction was, No. I could never do that. I couldn't comply with such orders. Immediately, a second question arose in my mind, as if it was somehow being put there: How do you know that you couldn't have done those things when your fellow soldiers, your buddies, and your team members were doing them casually and routinely, and being rewarded for doing them? After a few moments of reflection, I realized I didn't know; I didn't know that I did not have in me the same capacity for ugliness and hate as those ordinary soldiers who committed terrible atrocities during World War Two. How, then, could I ensure that I would never become consumed by hate and rage and resort to callous cruelty? What rule could I use to guide my behavior in the swirl of so much ugliness and destruction?

I thought to myself as the beauty of the music enveloped me like a soft blanket; I'm just an army helicopter pilot, not a philosopher. But I still have an obligation to protect and preserve my humanity. From what? From whom? It was more complicated than that. I had to protect one part of my humanity from being overwhelmed by another part of my humanity. I had begun to see that the savagery of war was an inherent component of human competitive behavior, an inherited survival trait that must have provided some advantage over hundreds of thousands of years of the struggle to survive. Still, it seemed to me you do not counter human ugliness by using more human ugliness. If I devote my mind to being more vicious and hateful than the enemy, I will not only unleash the monster that lies dormant in all of us, but I will also make the world a more vicious and ugly place and demean the collective legacy of humanity. If I direct my mind to seek out something beautiful in every situation, no matter how ugly it seems, not only will I find it, but I'll also add to the supply of beauty and peace in the world. That seemed to make some kind of sense to me. It may well have been complete nonsense, but it became a kind of life raft for my sanity and humanity. I fell asleep feeling thankful that I was not in the infantry, that I was not one of those getting off the helicopter to kill or capture Viet Cong soldiers.

For the rest of my life, I would wonder whether the Vietcong fighter who waited all night in the mud to shoot the soldier who fell from the helicopter may have been motivated by the loss of family and friends a few weeks before in the little hamlet not far away that had been destroyed in a combat assault mission that may have gone wrong because of a Dear John letter to Jim Cavanaugh from beautiful Doreen.

Dragons and Monster Cows

It wasn't a dream. It started out that way, but what woke me was the memory I'd lost as a small child. I sat up and swung my legs off the side of my bunk; 1:30 AM. A pair of fighter jets from Bien Hoa roared low overhead. The whole thing seemed to pop out of my subconscious all at once, with all its detail and context, not like a dream, but as if it all had just happened. What could have triggered these long-buried memories from early childhood? I heard the familiar sound of explosions in the distance, too far away to be of any concern. Is that what triggered these memories? I checked that my flak vest and steel helmet were close by.

My siblings and I stood among the crowd on the sidewalk at Bengal Street and Western Main Road in Trinidad with our mom. It was Carnival Tuesday, 1951. I was almost four years old. One after another, the carnival bands slowly came by with their masqueraders in bright costumes, all moving in sync with the rhythmic Steelband music. Before each band appeared in the distance, there was the faint sound of the rhythm, just the *Boom-Boom* of the bass pans and the cling-clang of the steel percussion section. Those sounds, produced from discarded and repurposed oil drums, meant that another band was approaching. The bands were on their way to the big Carnival competition in the Savanna, the giant park on the North side of the city. Even at four years old, I was fascinated by the sounds of the steel drums, especially the deep rhythmic rumble of the bass drums. Letting go of my mother's hand, I stepped into the street to see the band in the distance. I could see colourful banners and feathery costumes fluttering in the sunny midday breeze, but they were still too far away to see any detail.

Then I saw something else. Halfway between us and the band, there was a massive scaly creature, half walking, half crawling towards us. I stepped back onto the sidewalk and grabbed my mother's hand. "Mummy, look, something's coming. What's that?"

"It's just a man playing a dragon; they're always part of the Carnival. Don't worry, it won't hurt you, just stay back a bit from the street". She pulled me back a little. I peered around her at the dragon. It was huge; a great lizard head with massive pointy teeth and fiery eyes and scales all over and a long thick tail, as thick as the coconut tree across the street. Then I noticed that it was chained. Two handlers were holding its chains, strong men with big muscles, one black like my dad and the other light-skinned like Mom, on opposite sides of the street five meters behind the dragon. The chains clanked rhythmically along the road surface as the handlers and the dragon moved in synch with the music. The band slowly drew closer. Another man, light-skinned and shirtless, danced several yards ahead of the dragon. He took swigs from a rum bottle and taunted the dragon.

As they reached a few yards from where we were standing, the dragon, with a loud roar, suddenly reared up and flew into a rage, trying to break free from the chains. Flapping its great wings, it clawed at the air and bared its teeth, careening from one side of the street to the other as the handlers struggled to restrain it. Puffs of smoke sprayed out from its nose and mouth. I screamed and grabbed my mother's skirt, trying to pull her away as the creature's tail flailed and slapped down on the roadway close to where we were standing on the sidewalk. Children were running away. But the adults were laughing even as they shifted backwards away from the fearsome monster. Some were clapping. A few yards beyond us, the dragon's wild tantrum subsided. The chains and the two handlers were too strong. The dragon gave up and resumed its rhythmic dragon dance up the street on its way to the Savanna. There was a round of applause from the sidewalk spectators. I felt ashamed for having been scared. But I was still afraid of the dragon. *Boom-boom-boom,* the steel pan music drew closer, a welcome relief from the terrible dragon heading to its lair at the Savanna.

But as the band came closer, it brought more scary creatures; huge spiders, giant scorpions, bats with wings that stretched from one side of the street to the other, shaggy goats as tall as the giraffes in my storybook, and great monster cows with giant colorful heads, dancing on their hind legs, bowing and lifting their heads, searching the crowd and threatening everyone with their long menacing horns. The band of monsters slowly drifted by, all heading to the Savannah. As the steelpan sections drew close, the spectators recognized the calypso they were playing, and some began to sing along:

Bredda Willie, Meh-eh-eh,

Meh-eh-eh,

De Preacher in de band

With a candle in he hand

For de Ram Goat Baptism

The collection of scary creatures shuffled past us in sync with the steelpan music. My uncle Ricky said that after carnival, they hide in the Savanna and come out late at night looking for naughty children who didn't listen to their parents. A wild group of blue and black devils scampered around the street, looking freshly burnt in the fires of hell, gyrating and shaking their scraggy horns and tails, threatening everyone with their pitchforks as I peeked in terror from behind my mother's skirt. As they moved on towards the Savanna, my uncle Ricky's favourite band came by, and he sang the chorus loudly as he waved to his friends:

Who dead? Canaan!
Who Canaan? Canaan Barrow!
Canaan Barrow went to Town
And a Red Army Bad-John lick 'im down!

The Savannah is a wide expanse of grass more than two miles around. A road and a wide sidewalk ran all the way around the park. Sprawling Samaan trees and smaller ornamentals grew around the outer edge of the park near the sidewalk. Except for a grandstand at the south side of the park and a small walled cemetery near the middle, the entire surface was grass. To a four-year-old, it seemed vast and easy to get lost in, so when we were taken for a walk by the Savanna, I never ventured far from the sidewalk on my own.

At night it was transformed into the source of a little boy's nightmares. There were streetlights along the sidewalk, but beyond the glow of those lights, the Savannah was a black void. This void was the home of dragons and devils and giant bats. Every scary thing that could be conjured up in a child's mind roamed that dark place at night, kept at bay only by the glow of the streetlights. The trees concealed giant monsters as they swayed in the wind. Formless creatures prowled around in the dark, waiting to pounce on anyone who ventured too deep into the park and take them away. And worst of all, the hungry monster cows. Huge wide cows with tigers' claws and lions' teeth roamed around in that dark Savanna at night. That's what my uncle said. You wouldn't see them in the dark. But they could see you! During the day, they hid in their lairs under the grass.

One came up our street one night. I heard the clip-clop of its feet and saw it coming when I pushed the curtain aside and tiptoed to see out the window. It stared at me and shook its horns. I ran to my mother; "Mummy, Mummy, the cow is coming to get me."

"There's no cow out there," she said. A loud, mournful bellow filled our house. It sounded to me like a cow's way of saying, "I'm coming to eat you!"

I clung to her skirt and jumped up and down close to tears. "Mummy, it's coming, it's coming!"

She said, "Why does that man let his cows roam around the streets at all hours of the night?" That night I dreamed that a tiger was lying in the street outside our house, but instead of stripes, it was the color of a black and white cow. I woke from the dream in a panic, certain that the tiger cow still waited there for me. They can see in the dark and swallow a small child whole. You could scream loudly in the tiger-cow's belly, and no one would hear you or ever find you again. That's what my uncle had said, and it was true.

The end of Carnival was the beginning of Lent, the sombre Christian penitent season from Ash Wednesday to Easter Sunday. My parents had taken the family out for a Sunday afternoon drive. After a stop for pows at Kong Chow's and ice cream cones at the Dairies, the final stop on this exciting outing for the five kids was a nighttime walk by the Savannah across from the grand and stately Governor's residence and botanical gardens. My siblings and I played at scaring each other and running back to our parents for safety. *"De boo-boo man comin'! Run, Run!"* Squeals as our fright swung from make-believe to real and back again. We tried to catch fireflies and dared each other to step on ants' nests to see if the ants would wake up at night. We played to see who could go furthest away from our parents before getting scared and racing back to safety. My older brother went under the Savanna railing and dared us to follow him into the dark void. He was always so much braver than the rest of us. We found prickly Ti-Marie weeds and tried to make them close up their leaves while avoiding their sharp thorns: we sang: *Ti-Marie Ti-Marie, close yuh door, police comin' to hold yuh.*

Eventually, it was time to return to the car and head home. I was intrigued by the way my shadow would almost disappear directly under the streetlight, then get longer and longer as I moved further and further away from the light, making me taller than the grownups. I stopped to investigate something crawling along the sidewalk. I wanted to ask my brother what it was. I got up, turned around, and saw someone get into our car and close the door. I ran towards the car. The car drove off and disappeared down the road into the darkness.

Feelings of primal fear and terror; my family was gone! They didn't want me. I was alone. Every scary thing in that Savannah was now coming for me. I jumped up and down in panic, too scared to scream or cry because the monsters might find me. I thought I saw a huge cow staring at me out of the darkness. I didn't know where to go or what to do. My mind seemed to freeze. Would they come back? Were they gone forever? What would happen to me? The dragons were coming for me! I didn't know where to run, where to hide. I don't remember what happened next or how long I was left there in the dark. There was no sense of passing time, only pure terror and panic. Eventually, a car stopped. Was it my family, or was it someone coming to take me away? Someone opened the door—my sister. I ran to the car and jumped in. She closed the door. I shrank into the corner of the back seat. I was scolded for always wandering off and not doing as I was told. "You mustn't run off like that; you're always off in your own world somewhere." I was relieved, confused, and ashamed for having been bad. I just wanted to go home.

The clarity of the sudden memory and accompanying feelings alarmed me. Until that moment, I had had no memory of being left at the Savanna. The fear and the terror must have been too much for a small boy to carry around. I sat on my bunk, breathing heavily as I tried to figure out what brought these long-buried memories to my consciousness so many years later. After what seemed like hours, I drifted back to sleep.

In the morning, as I got dressed to go out on the day's missions, I remembered. Before falling asleep that night, I had been seeing the sweet faces of the little girl and the little boy in the bamboo and straw hut in the picturesque village out in the Mekong Delta.

Black and White

With no actual experience of racist persecution or deprivation, I arrived in the U.S. in September 1965, at age 18, lacking the subtle codes and cues that allowed Americans of different races to work with each other without straying across the invisible but well-established boundaries between them. After a week of life in New York City – not enough to really get a feel of the place – I had enlisted in the Army and was shipped off to basic military training at Fort Dix in New Jersey. Most of the other trainees were white, but I encountered none of the manifestations of American racism that I had read about back in Trinidad. That would come in my next assignment on completion of Army basic training.

My older brother and I had enlisted in the Army together under a system known as the Buddy Plan. This meant we would be kept together during our three-year commitment unless we chose to follow different paths. On completion of Basic Training, we were assigned to attend the helicopter maintainers school at the Army Aviation Center at Fort Rucker, Alabama. Unlike in basic training, we were now allowed to relax and socialize when off duty and to go off base and explore the surrounding towns. This was the Alabama of Governor George Wallace, who was elected by the people of Alabama using the campaign slogan: **Segregation Today –**

Segregation Tomorrow – Segregation Forever. I had no desire to experience life in such a cruel and backward society. I never left the safety of the Army base – black people were still being lynched with impunity in Alabama in the 1960s. I was forced to recalibrate my understanding of what constitutes a modern human society to include hatred and barbarism.

We quickly made new friends and learned that there would be a dance party at the Fort Rucker Army Service Club on Saturday night. Service clubs like this provide entertainment and relaxation for lower-ranking soldiers, mostly young people like me. My brother and I could hardly wait. We came from a country where partying was a normal part of growing up, and Carnival was weeks of partying topped by a huge annual two-day street party that excluded no one. We had both played music in bands at parties and clubs and had enjoyed a vibrant teenage nightlife.

Bursting with excitement and anticipation, we arrived at the Fort Rucker Enlisted Men's Service Club to the sounds of pulsating '60s party music. The main hall had been set up as a large rectangular dance floor with lots of seating at tables along the sides. Above the seating area were spacious balconies with additional seating and a bird's eye view of the dance floor. No one was dancing yet, but we could feel the energy building. We decided to scope out the scene from the vantage point of one of the balconies.

As we settled in, couples flooded onto the dancefloor to the sound of the Rolling Stones and the Beatles. We checked out likely prospects and waited for the right moment to head downstairs and find a dance partner.

Then it happened. James Brown came screaming from the big speakers, the rhythm sexy and irresistible, the horns urging him on. Gyrating couples filled the dancefloor with a release of pent-up youthful energy. Wait. No. For ten or fifteen seconds, we stared, speechless, in disbelief. Then we looked at each other and burst out laughing, drawing the bemused attention of those closest to us. We simply could not believe what we were seeing.

Before the James Brown number came on, only white couples had been dancing. We hadn't even noticed that. Now, to the sounds of James Brown, only black couples filled the floor, and they had all been sitting below our balcony on the opposite side of the hall from the white couples. We laughed so hard that folks nearby stared at us, wondering what the joke was. We stuck around for another thirty minutes or so, long enough to confirm that this was a racially segregated event, even though there were no signs or barriers in evidence; none was needed. This was still Alabama, and everyone knew the rules. We headed back to our room in the barracks in a state of amazement and disappointment. This was not a party but a mockery of the idea of partying. I was still new to the U.S. and still full of admiration for my new country. But I knew that I could never bring myself to accept what seemed to me like such a gross distortion of natural human relationships. It might be the norm in American society, but it would never be normal to me. I simply knew better. I vowed never to lose my love for the richness of the human family in all its amazing diversity.

As my brother and I became friendly with some of the African American servicemen stationed at Fort Rucker, we began to get glimpses, through their eyes, of what it was like for a black person to grow up in the American South; to have your mother and sister raped by the police; to have the police invade your home and reduce the father you respected and admired to a grovelling mess, to appease the police and protect his family from them. Some of their childhood experiences were so horrific I could only conclude that had I grown up in the southern U.S., I would either be in jail or dead at the hands of the police or other white racists. Some of these guys had *seen* lynchings growing up and even knew people who had been lynched in the early 1960s. Today in the early 2020s, amid the realistic possibility of the unravelling of democracy and civility in America, being black in a white supremacist society can feel intolerable. But 2022 is a single milepost in a journey that began centuries ago when millions of African people were first captured and shipped in chains to the U.S. to be sold as lowest-cost producers of the goods that would help to transform America into a rich and powerful country.

Starting from a position of zero power, with a status in many ways beneath that of draft animals (people may have neglected or mistreated their mules, but they did not despise them or derive pleasure from killing them), how did the African American people survive, persevere and progress to their current status of diminished citizenship in the white society that grew fat not only from the wealth produced by the ancestors of today's African Americans but also by stealing all their wages for hundreds of years? Completely cut off from their social, cultural, and religious support systems, how were generations of black people able to hold on to their sanity and move forward with their lives? What gave them hope? What invisible strength sustained them through such overwhelming adversity? Over time I developed a deep admiration for the resilience, perseverance, and dignity of African American society in the face of intolerable insult and abuse at the hands of their tormentors.

These early glimpses into America's dark underbelly served to prepare me to navigate the distorted American social landscape. So, I was neither surprised nor alarmed by my later encounters with fellow soldiers who lived the sublime illusion that their whiteness conferred on them, among all peoples of the earth, a position at the pinnacle of humanity; the status of Superiority (whatever that means).

Bill Conway

Bill Conway fancied himself a Proud White Man, but he lacked the meanness of spirit and subtle flicker of glowering menace that often betray the most pleasant and dangerous racist bigots. He was basically a nice guy who grew up in Alaska among racist white people and had learned to regard all non-white people as inferior to people like him. He detested the Vietnamese and wished only for a foot of snow to blanket their entire country and kill them all. But he didn't know what to make of me. A hard-core white supremacist would have no such confusion. For a racist bigot, dark skin is the entire story. As it was for the slave trader, the Jim Crow mayor, and the lynch mob, everything else about a black person – a pilot, a janitor, a doctor, a garbage collector, a university professor – is meaningless trivia.

I didn't fit any of his preconceptions about black people. I was the only black pilot in our flight platoon. I didn't sound like the African American stereotype (many African Americans don't), and I was completely at ease with the other pilots, including him. He was intrigued by the fact that I never freaked out when I overheard the occasional N-word slip from his mouth during the telling of his many jokes. He was confused by this black guy who flew helicopters and played and sang country songs in the officers' club at night to the delight of all the good ol' southern boys in the 117th. (In Trinidad at that time, U.S. country music was not associated with racism in the southern American states and was played on local radio as much as any other type of music. It is still a favourite music among black people in some parts of the Caribbean today.)

A group of 1st Platoon pilots stood near my cubicle discussing the best places to go on *R&R* (Rest and Recreation). The conversation was about the relative merits of tourist attractions, nightclubs, restaurants, and girls in Japan, Thailand, the Philippines, Singapore, and Malaysia. I joined the group, eager to hear from the guys who had already been to one or more of those places. The lavishly embellished stories sounded like the closest thing to heaven, and I struggled to decide where I should go when I eventually became eligible for R&R.

Suddenly there was a loud, angry outburst from Bill Conway, who was overhearing the conversation from his cubicle: "I'm gonna get me a WHITE woman!" he shouted from his cubicle. "I hope I never see another slant-eyed gook woman, goddammit! I'm going to Australia!" Instead of "white", he said "HWAAT", the way Ku Klux Klansmen say it when they march through the streets shouting, "HWAAT POWER". He stepped out of his cubicle, red-faced and angry, and discovered that I was part of the group. He struggled to force a smile, projecting instead a strained mixture of bravado and embarrassment. Had he simply said, "I like Australia for R&R; I prefer Australian girls", there would have been no reaction. No one would have been made uncomfortable. But because his outburst was so strong and because it wasn't a joke, no one knew what to say. They were waiting to see how I would react.

It seemed to me there was an undercurrent of fear in Bill Conway's outburst. His social comfort zone was extremely narrow, and he seemed scared of straying beyond its boundaries. To consort with a non-white woman, no matter how interesting or desirable she might be, would tarnish his credentials as a proud white man. His outburst was a way of rebuking the group (minus me) for betraying their race. After a brief pause, he returned to his cubicle, and we went back to discussing the best places to meet girls, the best restaurants, and the best tourist sites and experiences in each of the various R&R countries.

Not every white officer was so clumsy about revealing their racist views. But accidents did happen. As he walked into our officers' quarters, one of second platoon's pilots, apparently in response to a comment or question I had not heard, blurted out loudly, "Yeah, they finally got the son of a bitch". He saw me just as he finished the statement and walked quickly past my cubicle. It was 2nd April 1968. Later that day, I learned of the profound tragedy he had so crudely referred to: the murder of Dr Martin Luther King. Here in Vietnam, I was learning more about my American countrymen than I had in America. I did a further recalibration of my perceptions of the society that I was now a part of and the one in which I grew up.

On the morning of one of my days off from flying, I was asked to report to the Operations Officer. Captain Dillard's demeanour on inviting me into his office made it clear that I was not in any kind of trouble. After some initial pleasantries and small talk, it became clear that, for him, the matter was somewhat delicate. Bill Conway and I had joined the 117th around the same time. As co-pilots, we never flew together on the same helicopter. I had recently been promoted to Aircraft Commander, and Bill was due to be signed off as A.C. by the Instructors within a day or two.

In our unit, co-pilots flew from the right seat. A.C.s flew from the left seat. Most co-pilots are a bit unsteady when they first make the switch to the left seat, but they usually settle in quickly after a flight or two with one of the Instructor Pilots. But Bill seemed to be getting worse with each flight in the left seat, and the Instructors were concerned that he might have to spend some more time as a co-pilot, or worse, that he might be transferred to another unit. The Captain wanted to try the unusual step of sending Bill out on regular single-ship missions for a day to see if that would help him to settle into flying from the left seat. This was risky because Bill was not yet signed off by the Instructors to fly regular missions from the left seat. The Ops officer wanted to know if I would fly with Bill Conway as his co-pilot. He thought I might help to calm Bill down, and he was confident that I could handle the situation if Bill had difficulty controlling the aircraft. But he wouldn't insist if I didn't want to. I told him I had no problem with Bill. I would fly with whoever I was assigned to fly with. He thanked me and said he considered it a personal favour to him. He was taking a major risk that could turn out badly for him.

We took off the next morning with Bill in the left seat. It was immediately apparent that he was having difficulty controlling the helicopter. His whole body was tight and tense. In an effort to force the stubborn machine to do his bidding, he gripped the controls much too strongly and over-controlled the aircraft with tense, jerky movements. He seemed to have regressed to his early days in flight school. As we approached our first landing site, he was really messing up the approach. I calmly talked him through it but did not touch the controls. We hit hard on the landing but not bad enough to cause any damage, something I would not have allowed. He was red-faced and sweating, clearly embarrassed. I said to him, "Hey, we all have a bad day now and then. Why don't we go around and try the approach again together?" He exhaled deeply, releasing a good chunk of the tension in his body. Then he looked at me and smiled nervously.

I knew he was a good pilot, so it was just a matter of getting him to relax and rediscover that he knew how to handle the machine. By the end of the day's flying, Bill had found his groove again and was flying like a normal 117th pilot. The next day, he passed his A.C. check flight and was signed off as an A.C. by the instructor. He had no further problems flying from the left seat.

One of the older pilots asked me in his deep southern drawl what I thought of Conway. I said I thought he had a few quirks but was basically a nice guy. He thought for a moment, then cocked his head to the side and said, "You know, Mac, some o' y'ur nicest people are some o' y'ur biggest haters", then lifted an eyebrow for emphasis.

The change in Conway's attitude towards me was very subtle, but I had no illusions about who this guy was. We were both Aircraft Commanders now, so I would not be flying with Bill Conway again, or so I thought.

Later that year, a detachment of the 1st Platoon of the 117th was again directed to deploy to the Tay Ninh area for three weeks to support a Special Forces Team working in the jungles North of Tay Ninh. We had worked there with them before and looked forward to working with them again. Their missions, though always dangerous, were well-planned and executed. We drew enemy fire almost every day but seldom had casualties, either among the S.F. teams or our crews, because of the low-level tactics we used over the dense jungle. We often discovered bullet holes from enemy fire in one or more of the Hueys.

In some cases, our maintenance crews would apply temporary fixes, and we'd be in the air again the following day. But if the damage was considered too serious for normal missions, a crew would be assigned to ferry the damaged Huey back to our base at Long Binh at the end of the day and return that night or very early the next morning with a fresh aircraft. This was done on a rostered basis, so we all had our turn at these ferry flights.

On a dark rainy evening at about 7 PM, I lay on my bunk in our tent, smoking a cigarette, still in my boots and flight suit after a rough day's flying (I stopped smoking in my twenties). The air felt soggy and heavy in the leaky tent. All four aircraft had taken hits that day while pulling an S.F. team out of the jungle under enemy fire. One of the birds had serious damage to the airframe, and there was some concern about whether it was safe to fly. Our Platoon Commander awaited the assessment from the maintenance crew.

Rain blew in under the tent flap, along with noisy black and brown crickets that screeched loudly, making it hard to catch a catnap. The children in the area loved to catch these crickets and eat their nutritious hind legs.

From another section of the field tent, I could hear raised voices over the noise of the downpour. I'd been hearing them for some time, but they seemed to be getting heated and contentious. I went to see what the commotion was about. The group consisted of the Platoon Commander and five of the pilots, including Bill Conway. As I approached, Captain Shultz, the Platoon Commander, turned to me and said, "You can relax, Mac. You don't have to go. It's not your turn, and anyway, you're not a co-pilot". He assumed I had heard what the argument was about. He was clearly upset and paced back and forth uncharacteristically as if struggling with a difficult decision.

I turned to the group, "What's going on?"

Bill Conway was angry. He yelled, "Those maintenance guys are full of shit! There's a freakin' storm out there, more like a damn hurricane. That aircraft is broken. It could come apart in the air just like that with no warning". His face was bright red, and the veins in his neck stood out. He turned around and stormed away. One of the guys pulled me aside. "It's Conway's turn to fly the aircraft back with one of the co-pilots. He thinks it could come apart in the air, and he may have to set it down in the dark and the rain if it starts to vibrate on the way back".

I said, "They'll be empty. He just has to take it easy on the way back. Why's he so upset?"

"He's refusing to go unless you go with him."

"What!? Conway!? You're joking, right?"

Captain Shultz, our Platoon Commander, stepped up. He said in a firm, clear voice, "We need four aircraft for this mission. He's refusing a direct order to take that aircraft back and bring another one up here. We've all done it; I've done it; it's part of the mission. If he doesn't go, he'll be grounded, court marshalled, and never fly in the Army again. I mean it, goddammit. He's got ten minutes to decide". The Captain checked his watch.

I headed back to my bunk. As I walked away, Captain Shultz said, "Like I said, Mac, you do not have to go."

I returned to my bunk and listened to the rain as I lit another cigarette. It had eased up a lot, and the sound was now soft and soothing. There was some risk that things could go wrong, but our maintenance guys knew their stuff. This was our job; this is what we did. We flew the easy, fun flights, and we flew the high-risk missions. The technicians would not have signed off the aircraft for a one-time ferry flight back to base if they weren't confident it was safe to make the trip. They had even checked by phone with the Bell engineers in Saigon. But Bill was genuinely scared; that would be an added element of danger on the flight. Things could go downhill fast unless there was someone in the cockpit who could keep him from going into a panic.

I needed a moment to think about the safest way to make the flight. A small part of me didn't mind seeing Conway in this predicament, but I quickly recognized in myself the slippery allure of pettiness and spite. I pushed the thought away and focused on the flight.

From some angles, a Huey can look a bit like a giant tadpole; a bulging head and body housing the cockpit and cabin and a long sturdy tail with the little rotor at the tip. That little rotor keeps the helicopter from spinning out of control when hovering or at low speeds. The long tail section (tail boom) of the Huey is attached to the main airframe by just four bolts. One of those bolts had been destroyed by enemy fire along with the attachment structure. The greatest stress on the remaining three bolts would be when hovering, especially during hovering left turns, as the tail rotor counteracts the powerful forces trying to turn the helicopter in the opposite direction to the main rotor. If the crew could get the thing into forward flight with the least amount of power, they should be able to make it back to base. They'd also have to get around the rainstorm at night to avoid the turbulence, which would put additional stress on the tail boom. And they would have to avoid the danger areas where the Vietcong might use them for night target practice. All this with restricted visibility and minimal navigation aids. They wouldn't have the usual landmarks to guide them. They would have to rely on dead reckoning, airspeed, heading, wind speed and direction, and time, back to basics. If the three bolts failed at any point along the way, the chances of survival were zero.

As my cigarette burned down, I thought about my upbringing in the Valley in Trinidad and my exposure to such a rich diversity of human social and cultural norms. I realized that I was exceptionally privileged, and Bill Conway was a severely deprived individual. He really was an ok guy; it wasn't his fault that he'd had such a narrow upbringing. I wondered what it would be like to grow up where all the people you knew looked like you, felt the same way you did about everything, and felt scared and threatened by everything or anyone different. I really couldn't imagine such a banal existence.

Conway often hung out with some of our most experienced and competent pilots, and they, in turn, basked in his adulation. He could have asked one of them to go with him. But he was not just scared of the danger posed by the damaged aircraft and the bad weather; it was more than that. He knew that if he lost his nerve and had trouble controlling the helicopter, the whole unit would know about it the next day unless I was in the cockpit with him. I had never revealed the problems he'd had learning to fly from the left seat. If things got rough on the flight, it would remain between us. I was the only one he could trust to protect him from the possibility of humiliation.

Bill's ten minutes were almost up. I grabbed my flight gear and walked over to where he was sitting, frightened and dejected, on the edge of his bunk. "Ok, Bill, let's go."

Eagle Trap: Bad Day at Ben Tre

Early on the morning of 18th September 1968, our flight of ten troop carrier Hueys lifted off from our base at Long Binh and headed south-west past Bien Hoa and Saigon to work with units of the 9th Infantry Division deep in the Mekong Delta. The mission of the infantry unit that day was to seek out and destroy a Vietcong force that had been operating and training in the Ben Tre region of the Delta, a region with a bad reputation.

At our mission briefing, we were told that the senior ground commander had done a previous tour in Vietnam and favored the use of "Eagle Flights" for this type of mission. Some of the older pilots scoffed derisively at this news. They said that this tactic had been discredited and was no longer used, so we were all skeptical about using a method that had proven to be very costly rather than our tried and tested combat assault tactics. Two of the most senior pilots openly ridiculed the idea, calling it the Flight of the Light Brigade. But on missions like this, the senior ground commanders had the final say.

All over South Vietnam, U.S. Infantry Commanders were frustrated by the elusiveness of the Vietcong. The V.C. picked their own time and place to attack U.S. forces and facilities. When the infantry went after them, they seemed to melt into the landscape, sometimes literally, by disappearing into elaborate underground tunnel complexes. The concept of the Eagle Flight was that our ten Hueys would pick up an infantry company, then split into two flights of five helicopters (1st and 2nd Platoon) and orbit several miles away from the target area at a safe altitude. While we did this, a little egg-shaped Light Observation Helicopter (L.O.H. known as a Loach) would scout the area at a very low level, searching for evidence of Vietcong activity. If the Loach pilot found enough enemy activity to warrant an attack, the ground commander riding in the command-and-control helicopter high above the target area would give the order, a suitable L.Z. close to the enemy would be selected, and one Platoon would take their troops in, swooping down like an eagle to catch the Vietcong by surprise. If the Vietcong tried to escape, the other platoon would then take their troops into a suitable blocking or ambush position. It sounded to me like a comic book fantasy.

When we had worked earlier with the Special Forces teams, we had developed effective tactics to catch the Vietcong off guard. This was certainly not one of them. The Vietcong were a much more sophisticated fighting force than they had been just two or three years before. They had become familiar with the Eagle Flight tactic, and we would simply be signaling to them that we were coming, and they better get ready.

We loaded up the troops, and the two 5-ship platoons were directed to orbit separately several miles apart. We soon began to get reports from the Loach pilot. He said he saw a guy sitting outside a hut reading a newspaper. When the guy saw him, he calmly folded the newspaper, picked up an AK47 assault rifle, slung it over his shoulder, and walked away. He may have had a radio.

This was not good news; it suggested that this was an experienced fighter of high rank who was not panicked by all the helicopter activity. A few minutes later, the Loach pilot reported large numbers of persons moving quickly through the trees and foliage in different directions. Radio traffic in Vietnamese on the ground had increased significantly. Our worst suspicions were being realized; the Vietcong were organized and prepared for our helicopter assault. They were not going to try to escape; they were going to fight.

Unlike most of the sprawling Mekong Delta, this area was not covered by rice fields and dikes. It seemed to be a mix of lightly wooded areas and agricultural orchards interspersed with open green spaces. An L.Z. was selected by the command-and-control ship and marked with a smoke grenade by one of the gunships. The 2nd Platoon was directed to take their troops in, and the first Eagle Flight went swooping in. They delivered their troops without incident and headed back to get another load of infantry. They reported that the L.Z. was what we called a bowling alley, a narrow rectangular shape with trees on all sides affording cover and concealment to the Vietcong; in other words, a good site for us to be ambushed. First platoon was then directed to take our troops to the same L.Z. The troops on the ground reported that they had made no contact with the enemy and were moving into the tree line.

Nevertheless, we remained very uneasy. Sometimes you get the feeling ahead of time that things will not go well. Maybe the Vietcong had a surprise of their own ready and waiting for our surprise. The feeling we got was that this was going to be a bad day.

Suddenly we began to hear frantic calls from the troops on the ground. "We're pinned down about 50 meters inside the tree line under intense machine gun fire! We've got casualties!" Our worst fears began to be realized; the Vietcong had set a perfect trap, and we were about to fly into it. As we set up our final approach, we saw that the L.Z. was actually a plowed field, and the trees were some kind of orchard or cover for crops. Just before touching down our door, gunners opened fire in response to the enemy fire, taking care to avoid hitting our troops from the previous lift. Our troops were off even before the skids touched the ground. They hit the deck using the plowed furrows as cover. We scrambled into the air, and two of our ships reported that they had taken hits.

As we headed back to pick up our second load, we could hear on the radio that the troops on the ground were under heavy attack by a much larger force. We took off with our second load of troops, and it quickly became clear that second platoon was having a bad time of it. We could hear the shouts of "taking fire, taking fire! Lead, my pilot's hit; I may have to set the aircraft down." Three of Second Platoon's five aircraft were seriously damaged, and one pilot was shot in the foot (this was the same pilot who had recently flown into Thien Ngon with me when we took the Air Force guys in. He'd been nicknamed magnet-ass due to his bad luck in attracting hostile fire).

We made our turn to final approach in silence. Everyone knew what awaited us down in that L.Z. Normally with so many of our troops now on the ground, the L.Z. would have been secured. But our guys were clearly outnumbered and facing a well-organized force.

Our door gunners opened fire as we decelerated for touchdown. They could see where some of the enemy fire was coming from and could silence or at least suppress their fire. The troops hit the ground and immediately opened fire. We climbed out as fast as we could, and two more of our ships reported taking hits.

When we got back to the staging area, the situation looked grim. Between the two platoons, we were down to a total of five mission-capable aircraft, and one of those was an extra sent out from our base at Long Binh. I had started out the day as number eight in a flight of ten. I had now become number three of five. Amazingly, only one pilot so far (magnet-ass) was seriously wounded, and two others had minor wounds.

The ground commander was now desperate to get more troops on the ground to join the battle. Our five remaining ships loaded up and headed back to the L.Z. There are rare times on a mission when all hell breaks loose, and the fire is intense, yet you have a calm feeling – an illusion(?) – of being completely secure, as if you're protected. As we turned for our third approach into that L.Z., I had, for the first time, the opposite feeling; the certainty that things were going to turn out very badly.

The door gunners opened fire as we slowed for our landing. On the ship ahead of me, two troops were already on the skids, ready to jump off. Suddenly one of them collapsed, apparently hit by enemy fire. His buddy hit the ground next to him and opened fire with his M60 machine gun. The number five ship went screaming by a few feet overhead. He still had all his troops on board, but there was a spray of fuel coming from a hole in the left side of the aircraft. Our troops scrambled off, and we pulled in maximum power.

"This is Lead; we're taking fire from the right front of the L.Z.!" I was flying straight towards the enemy gunner. I kicked the nose to the left to avoid overflying the enemy fire and to give the door gunner a clear shot in that direction. The aircraft suddenly shuddered and began to lose altitude. There was the sickening sound of the slowing of the whop-whop of the rotor, indicating a loss of engine power. Warning lights were flashing; we were losing lift fast. We were only about 50 feet above the trees. I reduced the rotor pitch to see if I could get the R.P.M. back up by demanding less power from the engine. This increased our rate of descent towards the trees, but the rotor R.P.M. was returning to normal. This meant we still had some engine power, but how much, and for how long? I gently increased the rotor pitch to see if I could keep the thing in the air and avoid going into the trees. The rotor R.P.M. drooped slightly. I set the controls for the best rate of climb and held my breath.

"Three, you're smoking. You're smoking really bad!" That was the number four ship telling me we were on fire. The aircraft leveled off just above the trees and then began a painfully slow climb away from the battle below. Flying so low and slow, we felt like an easy target. I could see the spines of the coconut tree branches as we barely missed them with our skids. I said to my crew chief, "Take a look outside and tell me if you see any flame. I know there's smoke, but let me know if you see a flame."

The number Two aircraft was tracking Five, which had earlier flown over us with fuel spraying from a bullet hole, and number Four was now tracking me in case either of us went down and had to be rescued. Now came the confusion so typical of these desperate situations. Two Hueys closely trailing two wounded birds; one (me) smoking badly and possibly on fire, the other leaking fuel but otherwise ok.

Four came back on the radio, "Three (me), you're smoking real bad!"

Then, "This is Five; we're on fire. We're setting it down."

"Five, this is Two. You're **not** on fire, keep going, keep going!" In the confusion, the commander of the number five aircraft, which was losing fuel from a bullet hole, thought that his aircraft was the one that was smoking and that the fuel might ignite and explode at any moment.

"Three, you're smoking really bad. There's an old runway a couple of miles to the West."

"This is Five. I'm setting this thing down before we go down in flames."

"Five, this is Two. I'm right behind you; you look ok. Keep going."

By now, I was totally focused on keeping the machine flying and preparing for a crash landing. I could not spare a moment's attention to check my heading. "This is Three; just tell me which way to turn to get to the runway."

Four tried to guide me in. "Turn Left." "Stop, turn." "Do you see the runway ahead of you?" I asked my co-pilot if he had the runway. "Yeah, it's about a mile ahead of us."

"We got it; thanks, Four."

The crew chief spoke up, "There's a lot of smoke, Sir but no flames yet."

"Ok, Chief; keep your eyes on it and let me know if there's fire."

By this time, Five had landed in a rice paddy, and the crew was being picked up by Two. As we got within 300 yards of the little makeshift runway, I descended to about 30 feet and held the airspeed at 60 knots. If the engine failed, we would need some airspeed to convert to lift in a flare before touchdown. Approaching the edge of the runway, I descended below 20 feet and began to decelerate. The nose began to veer to the right. I eased in the left pedal to keep the aircraft heading down the runway. The pedal was stuck; it would not move. I pushed harder on the pedal; nothing. The tail rotor control was jammed. We had no directional control at low speed or hover. If we continued to decelerate, the aircraft could spin out of control. I flattened the rotor pitch and eased the nose up for a running landing. The skids touched down, and we slid forward clumsily, veering off the runway to the right like a car with smooth tires on an icy road. Once we were clear of the runway, I bottomed out the pitch, putting the full weight of the sliding helicopter on the skids. With a grating crunch, it slid to a stop just off the right edge of the runway. I immediately shut the engine down, and as the rotor slowed, I heard my door gunner say to the crew chief, "Hey man, check it out, Purple Heart". I looked over my shoulder, and he was grinning like a kid at the circus, with a three-inch gash across his right cheek where he had been grazed by an enemy AK47 round. The crew chief grabbed the fire extinguisher, and we hustled out of the helicopter in case the fire got to the fuel tank.

The right side of the aircraft was covered in engine oil and hydraulic fluid. A bullet had hit the engine, cutting an oil line and puncturing the combustion chamber. The thick smoke everyone had seen was from the spray of engine oil from the broken oil line being burned up by the hot gasses escaping from the punctured combustion chamber. The hole in the combustion chamber accounted for the loss of power. We were amazed that all that oil on the engine deck and side of the aircraft had not caught fire; amazed but elated that we had somehow not gone down in flames.

We were down, and we were safe, for the moment at least. We counted four more bullet holes around the aircraft.

A tired-looking older guy in Army fatigues came walking wearily up the side of the runway towards us. He was somewhat disheveled and carried a bit too much belly for a soldier of any rank. He held his fatigue cap in one hand and pulled his windblown hair into place with the other. I couldn't immediately tell his rank, but his was not a typical Army haircut. He took a walk around the helicopter, observing the damage. He must have seen us coming in with smoke billowing from the Huey like a flying steam locomotive. He came over to me. "Son, did you just fly that helicopter in here?"

"Yes, Sir, I did." He shook his head, smoothed back his hair, put on his fatigue cap, and leaned in to look at my name tag before moving on. That was when I noticed the star on his cap; he was a U.S. Army Brigadier General, probably one of the 9th Division commanders. I hoped he was thinking about who was responsible for this massive screw-up. So far, the Vietcong commanders were getting the better of the day. There were several other damaged Hueys scattered around the small airfield. Some were being rigged to be lifted out by Chinook helicopters.

After about ten minutes, my legs suddenly began to shiver slightly. I was elated, but I could no longer stand. I sat down in the grass beside the runway with the rest of my crew. The surge of adrenaline that had got me through the ordeal was finally wearing off, and with it, the euphoria of our triumph over disaster and of barely saving the lives of my crew and myself. I realized I was exhausted.

My Crew Chief handed me a couple of aspirin. I gulped them down quickly with a swig of water. My co-pilot, 1st Lieutenant Robert Snyder (not his real name), hadn't said much all morning. This was his first combat assault mission in Vietnam, so we didn't yet know each other very well. I tried to reassure him that this was not the way things usually went for us. He seemed ok, but he didn't say much, and I couldn't tell if he was holding it together.

Another Warlord bird made an approach to the runway, and we wondered if they were alright. They landed nearby, and the co-pilot got out and took off his flight helmet. There was a bright red streak across the top of his head where a bullet had removed some of his hair and the top layer of skin from his scalp. He grinned like someone who had just won the lottery, and indeed he had; the prize was living to tell about it. His

Aircraft Commander shouted from the cockpit, "I need a co-pilot". Without a moment's hesitation, Lt. Snyder grabbed his flight helmet and climbed into the co-pilot's seat. The aircraft took off again to rejoin what was left of the 117th Warlord flight. You never forget guys like that.

We had left our base that morning with ten troop carrier helicopters. An additional helicopter had been sent out to replace those that had been put out of commission. By late afternoon only three of the 11 were left flyable. Of those, only one – the Lead ship of our platoon – had not been hit by enemy fire. The Warlords had taken one of their most severe beatings of 1968. Although several of our pilots and crewmen were wounded, no member of the 117th Warlords was killed that day. The same could not be said for the soldiers of the 9th Infantry Division. Our part had been easy; we did not have to close with the enemy fighters in an ugly kill-or-be-killed fight to the death.

My respect and admiration for our infantry grew enormously that day. The ground commanders eventually called in artillery and air strikes to support the infantry. I thought about what was going on out there on the ground and realized we'd had the easy part. We had lived to fly another day. I also thought about the Viet Cong. Only a well-organized and highly motivated unit could deliver the kind of mauling to which we had been subjected. Why were they so much more motivated and dedicated to their cause than the South Vietnamese units we had worked with? Why were they so much more willing to fight for their cause than the people we were there to help?

As I lay on my bunk that night listening to soothing music, one thought went around in my head as I drifted off to sleep: all this slaughter and carnage had to be the worst possible way to resolve a dispute.

Thien Ngon *(Tin Neon)*

Taking troops into battle and pulling them out again was the primary mission of the 117th Warlords. We used ten slicks and at least a two-gunship escort to do our job. But every couple of months or so, we would be unable to provide ten slicks because too many of our helicopters were shot up and being repaired. When this happened, we'd be sent out on single-ship courier missions – taking staff officers from the relative safety of their offices at one of the major bases to visit units in the field or to headquarters at other bases. We would then wait around until they were ready to go someplace else. We generally hated these missions, not just because they were so boring but because we didn't get that much flying time on those days. This was to be one of those days. Or so I thought.

At our early morning mission briefing, the operations officer passed out the mission sheets to the Aircraft Commanders. He handed me a sheet with the date, the mission number, and one line in capital letters:

HEADQUARTERS, II FIELD FORCES: 0700 HOURS

I said to him, "That's just down the road from here; do you know who we'll be picking up or where we'll be going?"

The Captain said, "They'll fill you in when you get there". His attitude and tone made it clear that our question-and-answer session was over. This was quite unusual; we always knew where we'd be going and what we'd be doing when we left our morning briefing. We'd probably sit around at II Field Forces for an hour while some big wig decided where he wanted to go to experience the war firsthand for an hour or two before returning to his air-conditioned offices.

II Field Forces (Two Field Forces) was a very high-level command, probably reporting to one of the top-level commands in Vietnam. They would normally use pristine aircraft from one of the VIP or courier helicopter units assigned to support senior-level commands. Our Hueys were rugged workhorses, scratched, patched, and bullet-holed, not suitable for Generals and their crisply starched entourages. I certainly had no experience flying Generals around. My crew would have to remember to salute and be on their best behavior. I was not looking forward to this mission.

We took off from our base at Long Binh, made a wide right turn, and made our approach to the II Field Forces pad near the Saigon–Bien Hoa highway that ran alongside Long Binh, not knowing what to expect. As we touched down on their helipad, an army Lieutenant in laundered and pressed fatigues came running out, stuck his head in my window, and yelled at us over the noise of the helicopter, "Hotel 3, Saigon. Go to Hotel 3 in Saigon. Here's their radio frequency." He handed me a sheet of paper, waved at us, and headed back into the building in his starched uniform.

This was really getting weird, all this cloak-and-dagger stuff. Hotel 3 was the helipad at MACV, Military Assistance Command, Vietnam. This was General Westmoreland's Headquarters, the highest military command in Vietnam! And why weren't we sent directly there? Why did we have to come here first just to get a bit of paper with their contact frequency on it?

The II Field Forces Air Traffic controller cleared me for takeoff. With a mixture of bewilderment and nervous curiosity, we headed down to the highest US military command in

Vietnam in the heart of Saigon. What could MACV want with a helicopter and crew from a wild and rowdy combat assault company; the 117th at that! When I joined the unit, our call sign had been "Beach Bums," and I had been Beach Bum 10. The Beach Bum metaphor captured the happy-go-lucky attitude of the young Warrant Officer pilots and enlisted crews of the 117th but belied their collective knowledge and skill built up over many years of taking on challenging combat assault missions.

A few weeks after I became Beach Bum 10 (the previous Beach Bum 10 had been killed in action a couple of weeks before I joined the unit), we got a new Commanding Officer who set out to whip the 117th into shape. He didn't last long, but one of his dubious accomplishments was changing our call sign from Beach Bums to Warlords. It's true that, as a unit, we did not fit the image of an Army helicopter company back in the States. But when it came to taking our grunts into and out of battle, we were second to none, and we had the Unit Citations and awards to prove it. So, I felt completely out of place, taking my Huey and my crew to General Westmoreland's Headquarters in the middle of Saigon.

We called into the traffic controller at Hotel 3. He cleared us to land, directed us to a parking pad, and told us tersely to shut down; they were expecting us. We shut down and waited, still not knowing what to expect. After about ten minutes, two guys emerged from an unmarked door carrying a large, heavy blue-grey nylon or canvas bag about the size of a pair of footlockers and, with some effort, heaved it onto the helicopter without a word to any of us. I said, "Wait - WAIT! Hold on, guys; what is this? What's in the bag? Where are we going?"

They went away without saying a word and returned with a second bag and a third member of their team. They wore unfamiliar blue fatigue uniforms with no insignia or other markings. I asked them not to put the second bag on the helicopter until my crew, and I were briefed on the mission. They placed the bag on the ground next to the helicopter and said nothing.

Just then, the fourth member of their crew emerged. He wore the rank insignia of a US Air Force Major, but he looked more like a battle-hardened Army Sergeant. I came to attention and saluted along with the rest of my crew. He went by me and approached my copilot, who was white. As he began to speak, my copilot informed him that I was the Aircraft Commander. He looked around at all the crew members and then said to me, "You're the Aircraft Commander?" unable or unwilling to hide his surprise and disappointment. I said Yes, Sir. He looked angry. He looked like he had been sentenced to do this low-level job because he had pissed off his superiors once too often.

Most of the time, I was just an Army pilot getting the job done, taking care of my crew, and looking out for the guys in my unit. Our lives depended on each other, and we were a tight-knit group. This was one of the rare occasions when I suddenly became aware that I was not just a pilot; I was a black pilot, the only one in my flight platoon.

He pulled a map and some eight-by-ten black and white aerial photographs from a leather folder and began to tell us – finally – what the mission was. He pointed to a spot north of the city of Tay Ninh near what was known as the parrot's beak, an area where the Cambodian Border jutted like a peninsular into a remote corner of South Vietnam. The whole area was heavily forested with a single dirt road that ran from Cambodia south across the border through miles of uninhabited Vietnamese jungle and down to the Vietnamese city of Tay Ninh. This made the area ideal for moving fighters and supplies from North Vietnam down the Ho Chi Minh trail through Laos and Cambodia, then across the border into Tay Ninh and on to Saigon or wherever they were needed. To the North Vietnamese, this road was a high-value asset, critical to their strategic objectives, and they were prepared to fight to get control of it.

I knew the area well. Our Hueys had taken many hits working there with Special Forces teams. There was a joint US/South Vietnamese Special Forces base camp called Thien Ngon next to a runway where his finger rested. There were no buildings, just a complex of bunkers, mostly underground, and a couple of artillery batteries, all surrounded by inner and outer defensive perimeters. The Special Forces teams used this remote camp to go out into the surrounding jungle with their South Vietnamese counterparts primarily to collect intelligence but also to disrupt the North Vietnamese resupply operations.

The runway was about a hundred meters west of the base camp. It had been built by US Army Engineers and was simply a widened and hardened part of the road that ran up to the Cambodian border. The jungle had been cleared for maybe another hundred meters all around the camp and runway, allowing a safe approach and takeoff path for the C-130 cargo aircraft to resupply the camp. The Army Engineers had taken high losses in the effort to clear the jungle and build the runway. In recent times, there had been major North Vietnamese attacks on the Thien Ngon base camp. Despite extensive bombing of enemy bunkers and trenches by the Air Force, no helicopter or airplane had been able to get to the base camp for at least three weeks. A week earlier, one of our guys tried to get in with a Huey. About a mile out, he took a 12.7 mm anti-aircraft round through the rotor mast. He was lucky to turn around and scramble out of there without being shot down.

The Major explained that the camp was positioned beside a main North Vietnamese infiltration route connecting their supply centers in Cambodia down to Saigon and surrounding areas. He pointed to one of the aerial photographs: "They've got 50 caliber anti-aircraft positions here, here, and here."

I said, "You mean inside the tree line?"

"No, in the open, in trenches and bunkers just outside the tree line."

I said, "Major, the Air Force has been bombing that area relentlessly for weeks. If those guys are still dug in with 50 caliber anti-aircraft weapons in the open, there's not much chance of us getting in there."

The Major looked at me with a mixture of frustration and disgust. For a moment, I thought he was going to hit me. Maybe he thought I'd been briefed on the mission and was expecting me to be eager to get going. Perhaps the last thing he expected on his high-value mission was a black aircraft commander who couldn't possibly be of the caliber he requested for this mission. This may well have been the first time he'd seen an African American Army pilot. He looked away and took a few deep breaths as if drawing on an imaginary cigarette. His face was lined and weathered and sad. He may have been an impressive young officer in times past, tough and fearless, hard fighting and hard drinking. But now he seemed rough and worn and tired. Maybe he'd lost too many good men and was just tired of this endless war. I feared he was going to call off the mission.

Without looking at me, as if talking to himself, he said as he looked at the ground, "There's a North Vietnamese regiment, possibly two, in the jungle surrounding that base camp." He paused and looked up at nothing in particular. He appeared to be suppressing anger. "Our guys haven't received any supplies for over three weeks. They're out of water and food, and they're running low on ammo. We've been air-dropping supplies to them at night from C-130s (cargo planes), but the drops aren't accurate enough, and the North Vietnamese are grabbing everything we drop." Now he focused his milky blue eyes on me. "That equipment we just put on your helicopter is to guide the C-130s in at night, so they can make pin-point low-level drops to the base in total darkness. If we don't get this equipment in there, that base will be overrun in the next few days."

It now became clear; this was an Air Force Special Forces team on an extremely high-priority mission. The guys in that camp were probably his guys. If so, he knew every one of them.

After weeks of holding out against impossible odds, he was now their only hope.

I looked again at the markings on the photographs indicating where the anti-aircraft bunkers were, mostly on the West side of the complex. A 12.7mm anti-aircraft weapon can easily knock a Huey out of the air. I said, "Sir, I can't guarantee I'll get you in there, but we'll do our best." But I was thinking, *"A North Vietnamese Regiment? There's no way we can get in there; we'd be shot down before we even got close!"*

They put the second bag on board, and we took off with the four members of the Air Force team and their equipment. As we climbed away from Saigon and headed North towards Tay Ninh and the Cambodian border, I wondered, was I just randomly selected for this mission? Was it just my turn on the pilot's roster? Or had I really upset one of my seniors and was getting one of the dirty jobs? Like most military aviation units, the 117th had its "Top Guns", its pecking order of hotshot pilots. I certainly was not among them. I would have expected a mission like this to be assigned to one of them. I concluded that in making the assignments, the Operations Officer assigned the mission as he would have any other single-ship mission. Tough missions were our job; this is what we did. He may not even have known what the mission was. But this was no time for reflection or speculation. My thoughts turned to the impossible task ahead. I had no idea how I was going to get this team through the ring of fire around Thien Ngon.

We normally leveled off at 2,500 feet for the flight to the Tay Ninh area, but I kept climbing, past 3,000, past 4,000. I had to think of something. I knew that the higher I got above the bomb-cratered landscape below, the more relaxed I'd become and the clearer my thinking would be. As we headed north, the sparsely wooded open savanna surrounding the towns and villages gradually began to change to triple-canopy jungles of the Tay Ninh region. I thought this must be what it would look like to fly from the Sangre Grande region of Trinidad to the rainforests that spread northward from the foothills of the Northern Range. I had spent many happy hours of my youth exploring the forested hills around Petit Valley in Trinidad, and I remembered that very little direct sunlight made it through to the ground, and then only in small splotches of light as the saplings competed for the tiniest sliver of penetrating sunlight. Occasionally, you might hear a plane overhead, but you'd almost never see it through the dense foliage of the canopy. As we climbed through 5,000 feet, the first elements of a plan began to take shape in my head.

The Cambodian border was just a few hundred meters north of the camp at Thien Ngon. We were not allowed to fly across the border into Cambodia, and the North Vietnamese knew this. They would not be expecting a helicopter to approach the camp from the north. Their anti-aircraft bunkers would likely be oriented to the south, east, and west. I leveled off at 7,000 feet. We almost never flew at this high altitude; the air was cool, and the view panoramic. The landscape below looked like a moonscape because of the endless bomb craters as far as you could see in every direction. I thought about what a Huey at 7,000 feet would look like from the ground. I hoped it would seem tiny and harmless. Once we got over the jungle, we should be practically invisible from the ground.

There were two ways to fly over a North Vietnamese regiment in the jungle and hope to live to tell about it: either very high, where their guns can't reach you with any accuracy, or at tree-top level, where only those directly under your flight path might catch a glimpse of you for just an instant as you flash by overhead. We would have to go north of the camp at high altitude and come into the base from the north at tree top level. It was a slim chance, but it was the only chance.

I decided to keep radio contact to a minimum. A few miles south of the camp, I called Thien Ngon. The voice on the other end was unusually excited. "Roger, Warlord 478, it's been quiet here all morning. Do you want us to pop smoke for you?"

I said, "No, no smoke. I'm not sure how I'm going to do this or if I'll be able to get in, but I don't want to tip Charlie off. Keep your eyes and ears open, and don't pop smoke until you see me on the final approach. I'll be staying off the radio from here on in."

My copilot said to me, "He sounds all bright-eyed and bushy-tailed, not like someone who's under siege and about to be overrun".

The attack would come in the dead of night, a barrage of artillery fire, then eerie silence. Then shadows of shadows in the blackness, like the dragons and cows in the savanna at night. Then hundreds of North Vietnamese soldiers charging at the perimeter defenses as the hopelessly outnumbered Special Forces team struggled to throw them back with what little ammunition they had left. Because, despite their desperate pleas for help, no help was sent. No one came to help them. I had to get in there. I had to.

We started a gradual descent and continued North towards Cambodia. We could see where Vietnam ended and Cambodia began because that's where all the bomb craters stopped. I hoped we seemed to the North Vietnamese like a harmless surveillance helicopter. We crossed into Cambodia, and after about 30 seconds, I went into a steep dive and a 180-degree turn back to the south. Getting down from that altitude was taking longer than I anticipated. I pushed the Huey further into the dive and hoped that from the jungle floor, we would be obscured by the triple canopy foliage. As we approached the treetops, I took a bearing to the base camp and checked my heading.

Thien Ngon, Special Forces Camp, looking East toward the treeline, showing the outer pentagonal defensive perimeter, the inner perimeter with a helipad in the middle, and the runway in the foreground.

Flying with our skids skimming the leaves, I remembered that the jungle canopy is not the flat green carpet seen from two thousand feet up, but more like rolling terrain, with little hills and valleys and open spaces. This meant I had to weave left and right more than I expected to stay as low as possible. My simple plan became more complicated; I couldn't just fly a straight course South to the base camp. I increased the rotor thrust until the RPM began to droop just a little, indicating I was at max power and speed. The base camp still hadn't come into view, and I estimated we had drifted left of the course to avoid open areas where we would be more visible and vulnerable to ground fire. This meant we would be approaching more from the east than I had intended. Where the hell was the damn camp? We should have seen it by now.

I banked a bit to the right and said to the crew, "We should start taking fire any time now". As if on cue, we heard the crack-crack-crack of AK-47 fire coming from behind us. The crew chief and gunner responded with their M-60 machine guns. Suddenly I saw the edge of the jungle tree line and the base camp directly ahead of us. We were coming in from the East, exactly what I had hoped to avoid. We didn't know it yet, but we were flying directly into the muzzle of a North Vietnamese anti-aircraft machine gun just beyond the treeline. Because we were so low, we couldn't see him, and he couldn't see us; yet. But he could hear us coming, and he was ready. As I dove over the edge of the tree line, trying to stay as low as possible, a loud explosion jolted the helicopter, and it shuddered as if it had been hit by something big. We felt the force of the impact up through our armor-plated seats. A thin mist or fine dust filled the cockpit and cabin. My first thought was that something in one of the Air Force bags had been hit and exploded. With that split-second distraction and the extra shot of adrenaline, I saw that we were approaching the camp helipad much too fast. I pulled the nose way up and flattened the rotor pitch to slow the Huey and stay low. Someone popped a smoke grenade on the landing pad to guide us in. I couldn't stop; we were going to overshoot. I pulled the Huey into a steep left bank and brought in the power to counter our forward momentum, then leveled the Huey and dropped it onto the landing pad in the middle of the camp. It was a rough landing, but we were in.

As the skids hit the ground, the Air Force guys sprinted flat out for the nearest bunker, leaving their precious gear on the helicopter. The camp artillery batteries and mortars all began firing to suppress any incoming fire from the North Vietnamese. The noise and shock waves from the big artillery guns added to the confusion and chaos. I said, "Chief, kick that stuff off, and let's get out of here." My co-pilot opened his door and started to get out. I reached over and grabbed the back of his flak vest and pulled him back: "Where the hell are you going?"

He stared at me and screamed in total panic, "To the bunker! We've been hit!"

I yelled back, "Sit down and strap in; we're not staying here. Take it easy, ok?"

I saw a puddle of fluid on the aircraft floor near my feet. There was a problem with the electrical system, and warning lights were flashing, but the engines and rotors seemed to be running normally. The heavy guns kept blasting away. I shouted, "Chief, take a quick look around the aircraft and see how badly we've been hit." The crew chief did a quick walk around the Huey. "I don't see anything, Sir. I think we're okay."

We'd made it in using surprise and a lot of luck. The surprise was gone, and we were now pushing our luck. Like everyone else in this hell hole, we were surrounded. The enemy gunners would be waiting for us to leave. I remembered from my crazy dive there was a broken cloud layer at about 1,200 feet. Now that we were surrounded along with the Special Forces at the base camp, there was only one way out of there. I got on the radio: "Thien Ngon, this is 478, heading for Tay Ninh."

"Thanks, 478; great job. Good luck." He still sounded like he was just having a pleasant day from the safety of his bunker. He was probably excited that they would soon be getting badly needed supplies. I thought these guys were truly amazing. I couldn't endure a single day of what they've been through over the past few weeks.

I pulled in maximum power and did what only a helicopter could do; straight up into a vertical climb directly over the camp. The Huey was much lighter now and climbed quickly, yet it felt as if every enemy gunner was lining up his gun sights on our totally exposed helicopter. The base camp controller called: "There's something dripping from your helicopter."

"Thanks for the heads up. Let me know if you see smoke or flames."

I checked the fuel, oil, and hydraulic gauges; everything looked okay. But there was a strong smell and an oily fluid at my feet, and an electrical system warning light was flashing. As we continued to climb, we waited tensely for the enemy fire to start. Seven hundred feet, 800 feet, keep climbing, baby, keep climbing, don't quit on me now. At 1,200 feet, we punched through the broken cloud layer. The suppression of the enemy gunners by the intense artillery fire had allowed us to escape what would otherwise have been a barrage of antiaircraft fire. I pushed the nose over and headed for the runway at Tay Ninh, hoping that the aircraft would stay in the air for 15 more minutes to get us there.

I called the Tay Ninh tower: "I'm pretty sure we've been hit. I needed priority clearance to land". I set up the approach for a running landing in case we started losing power on the way down and couldn't hover. We made it down ok and set the aircraft down on the closest helipad. I left the Huey running and asked the crew chief to see if he could find where the leaking fluid was coming from while I tried to identify the electrical problem. He opened the nose door at the front of the helicopter and immediately signaled me to shut down. We shut everything down, and I went out to see what he had found.

The aircraft battery, which sits in the nose of the helicopter, had been blown apart, along with some other electrical equipment which I couldn't immediately identify. The leaking fluid was battery acid. That was also the source of the mist that had filled the aircraft when we were hit. But there didn't seem to be an entry point for whatever had hit us. We looked below the nose and checked both sides of the cockpit: nothing. Then the crew chief found a single small hole in the fiberglass nose door. We had been hit almost dead center in the nose. Had we been ten inches to the left or right, one of the pilots would have been hit. We were alive by sheer dumb luck.

The search was on to find the bullet so we could determine what type of weapon we were hit with. We checked over the entire aircraft for other bullet holes or marks but found none. To better understand the extent of the damage, the crew chief went to check the aircraft maintenance manual, which he kept in three-ring binders in a pocket at the back of the cockpit center console, along with other aircraft manuals and documents. Lodged in the aircraft logbook, he found an armour-piercing 12.7mm anti-aircraft round. The battery and other electrical equipment had absorbed most of the energy of the projectile. The five-inch-thick package of aircraft manuals and other documents had dissipated the rest.

As we waited for one of our aircraft to bring in a maintenance crew and take us back to the 117th base, my crew and I began to piece together what had happened. I had come over the edge of the jungle tree line in a dive to stay as low as possible. Coming from the east instead of the north, we must have dived directly into the anti-aircraft weapon. But because we were so low and fast, only one round hit us from maybe thirty feet away, and then the weapon was behind us. We were on the camp helipad before he could get his weapon turned around to engage us again. By then, the Special Forces were raining artillery and mortar shells on the anti-aircraft weapons bunkers. They kept up their barrage until we punched through the cloud layer and headed for Tay Ninh at a relatively safe altitude. The artillery and mortar fire from the camp forced the enemy to take cover and allowed us to reach the safety of the cloud layer.

Back at the 117th base the next day, we heard that a major battle was raging with the Thien Ngon camp under relentless attack. The camp had been resupplied with ammunition by the C130 cargo planes and was handling the attacks well, taking only one wounded so far. The number of North Vietnamese dead probably ran into the hundreds. The base camp was very well fortified against a ground assault across the open area between the tree line and the camp. Our gunships had also caught large numbers of North Vietnamese in the open as they attacked the base camp. After a couple of days and nights of fierce fighting, the North Vietnamese called off the attack and melted back into the jungles of Cambodia under cover of darkness. They had suffered heavy losses.

The morning after the battle ended, we were back in the area with several other helicopters from different units. We were now able to resupply the base camp with medicine, food, and water, plus other critical essentials such as beer and ice cream. There were many South Vietnamese Special Forces soldiers at the Thien Ngon base camp with the US Special Forces. Some of these soldiers had families in the Tay Ninh area, and they brought clothing, blankets, cookware, and other such items to be loaded onto the helicopters and taken out to their family members. As we were about to lift off to head out to the camp loaded to the roof with supplies, a young Vietnamese woman ran up to the helicopter and flung a live chicken on board, barely missing the spinning rotor blades. As the thing flopped around with its legs tied, the crew chief informed me that we also had three live ducks on board as well. Presumably, the intended family members would recognize their birds.

Nothing was ever said to me about our successful mission to break the siege at Thien Ngon, which suggested that the mission had been classified. It was as if it never happened. For three weeks before that mission, every attempt to get to the camp by helicopter or airplane had been turned back by enemy gunners, and attempts were made almost daily. We took comfort in knowing that General Westmoreland knew that the 117th had once again accomplished its mission.

Leaving

As the commercial jetliner lifted off the Tan Son Nut runway in Saigon, a loud cheer went up from the servicemen and women returning home to the US from Vietnam. But not everyone cheered. I had arrived in Vietnam a year before, an eager twenty-year-old Army pilot hungry for knowledge and experience. I'd been so excited to go on those early combat assault missions. But over the course of the year, I had seen so much killing and devastation, yet the situation seemed not much different from when I had arrived. I had lost friends to enemy fire; the Vietcong continued to be killed in large numbers and continued to fight with fierce determination; the inevitable losses of civilian lives and property continued unabated. What were we doing here? I had a vague sense that I was not finished with Vietnam, or it was not finished with me.

As young soldiers, we believed what our leaders believed; that if the North Vietnamese prevailed, South Vietnam would be subjected to unspeakable atrocities, mass murder, slave labor, concentration camps, and mass starvation. Totalitarian communism would spread throughout Southeast Asia and beyond, eventually posing a threat to the US. That's what we had been told repeatedly. And we knew such things had happened before in other countries. I had focused on doing my job, on being a good soldier. Now, as I left Vietnam behind and settled into my comfortable airliner seat, questions began to take shape in my mind; questions a soldier ought not to have about where this was going and how it would finally end; larger questions about the human inclination to resort to war to solve problems despite its savagery, devastation, and enormous economic cost. Was the solution becoming far worse than the outcome we were trying to prevent? I didn't know it yet, but I was deeply involved with this beautiful country and its resilient people.

I'd received my wings as an Army helicopter pilot before I'd ever driven a car. Flying helicopters in Vietnam was the only real job I'd ever had. I had developed strong bonds of friendship with some of the other pilots. We were good at what we did and deeply respected each other. I also developed a real fondness and respect for my Vietnamese friends. Climbing away on this plane was like leaving home, not knowing if you'll ever return. Again. Even as I looked forward to returning to the US, not worrying about being shot down, attacked in the middle of the night with mortars and rockets, or captured and tortured, I could feel the gentle pull of Vietnam calling me back.

And where was I going? I really hadn't given it much serious thought. I hadn't thought about the fact that things would have changed for my family and friends. I would have a few weeks left before my next Army assignment. I longed to see my parents, my brothers, and sisters, the friends I'd left behind. They'd be so glad to see me, and me to see them. I would tell them about the war, all the battles we had won, all the crazy things we had done. Surely, we'd go to parties and have a great time. I was still just a 21-year-old kid.

But I mostly wanted to see my girlfriend, Nicole. As the plane climbed to its cruising altitude, I wondered what the year had been like for her. Many young men would have been after her, guys with good jobs, maybe a nice car. I wasn't at all sure she still wanted to see me. I hadn't kept in touch as much as I should have. The guys at the 117th said that sometimes the girls don't tell you in their letters that they've moved on to someone else because if you're killed, they'd feel as if they might have caused it. So, they wait until you get back to tell you that things had changed. The 117th pilots had talked about a guy they knew who went home and found that his fiancé had a new lover and shot them both. Stories of husbands getting home to find that their wives had found someone else and were filing for divorce were all too common. As we headed to the US, I remembered Jim Cavanaugh's rage at losing his girlfriend, a loss he may have blamed on the war.

The fear of finding out she had moved on was growing, and I couldn't say why or make it go away. As I left behind this new world, where I had gained a new self-confidence and sense of accomplishment, and traveled back to my old world, old insecurities, like whether I was good enough for her, seemed to be closing in again. When the situation on a dangerous mission suddenly changed, I always knew what to do. But I didn't know what I would do if my girlfriend had found someone else. Could I be gracious, wish them well, and move on, "See you around, ok, bye." Or would I sink into a depression and take my anger out on myself? I was on a different kind of mission that seemed fraught with danger, and I didn't know how to approach the situation.

About two months before the end of my tour, I began to get the feeling that her letters had changed. I could not say exactly what had changed, but they no longer seemed to connect me to her the way they always used to. They seemed more casual and generic, but I couldn't say exactly why they seemed that way. I was becoming haunted by a growing feeling that I had lost her, despite having no evidence of this. Around this time also, the daily grind of the war was beginning to take its toll; we had been warned by our flight surgeons that this would happen. The daily missions, the smell of wounded and dead soldiers in the helicopter, the sporadic mortar attacks on our base that sent us scrambling for the bunkers, the B52 raids that shook our buildings from many miles away, the sudden burst of enemy machinegun fire as you approached an LZ; it was all becoming a bit dreary and pointless. We were losing our sense of purpose. It was hard to become excited about anything. I wasn't really feeling anything one way or the other. I didn't recognize it at the time, but after a year of stressful combat flying, I was becoming worn out. It didn't feel that way; I just seemed to be bored with everything, and in an active combat environment, that was dangerous. At the time, I made no connection between the growing stress of the war and my fears about the change in my girlfriend's letters. Many years later, it would occur to me that I was the one who was changing. Maybe we both were.

As the plane sailed softly towards home, pretty flight attendants brought us drinks and promised meals later. This was so much better than deployment on noisy military cargo transports. I decided it was time to shape up and get a hold of myself. A 21-year-old US Army officer who has just faced a year of combat operations and been decorated for heroism does not become confused or overwhelmed by emotions. You deal with whatever comes along, no matter what. I told myself I could handle any situation I might face. I "bravely" shoved it all away and gazed at the beautiful clouds below. I thought about how much I loved the sky, how much I loved flying. I had no idea where I was going or what I would do when I got to the US. I would handle whatever came along, I told myself. I'll think of something. Everything would be just fine.

This unexpected swirl of emotions was resolving into anger; at who? At what? At myself, for suddenly finding myself unprepared? I should have given more thought to my return; I should have planned it out. As I listened to the drone of the aircraft's jet engines, I set aside my confusion and let my thoughts drift back to the guys I'd left behind. Were they out on another mission? Was everyone ok? Already, I was missing the action.

I thought of the smiling faces of the pilots and crewmen who would never return to their families. I thought of all the Vietnamese who had lost their family members. Was this really the best solution to whatever the original problem was? As a soldier, I had to believe we would ultimately achieve our goal. I hoped we would. I couldn't imagine that all this effort, sacrifice, and devastation could accomplish nothing of lasting value. What would I say to friends and family members who felt the war was wrong and that we should get out of Vietnam? We can't just get out and leave the Vietnamese to themselves, can we?

Home

Arriving back in the States after a year of combat assaults was strange and surreal. America was a Disney World. The spacious polished airport, the escalators, the glittering shops with everything you could possibly want, the highway packed with a million shiny spacious speeding cars; everything is real yet not real. Everything is over the top. It's all so - nice, even amazing. Of course! This is America. I'm home. But it also felt frivolous and excessive, like coming from the outskirts of the empire to the center of Rome at the pinnacle of its glory. It struck me that I hadn't had that feeling when I'd first arrived in the US from Trinidad.

On arrival at my parents' apartment in New York, it was great to see everyone. But after the rich warmth and joy of their initial welcome, things began to feel transient and a bit awkward, like meeting friends you haven't seen for many years in an airport or train station on their way somewhere else. I didn't yet realize that <u>I</u> had become someone else, someone they didn't yet know. Now that I was back and I was safe, the war for them was this bizarre thing on the television at night that was outside the realm of their everyday lives. They were genuinely happy to see me, but they weren't quite sure how to handle the topic of the war. Should they ask about it? Should they wait for me to bring it up? I soon realized that I was expecting too much, that my family and friends could never understand what I was talking about, what it was like. They were simply happy that I was home and wanted me to know I was loved and valued.

As to the war that was my life less than two days ago, I had no one to talk to about it. I talked about my R&R in Thailand; the floating market, the temples with their giant buddhas, the riverboat trip, and the amazing ruins. These are experiences that can be shared because people can relate to these things. But I quickly saw in my mother's eyes that my clueless attempts to bring the kill-or-be-killed ugliness of a helicopter combat assault into the peace and warmth of a pleasantly furnished living room were an obscene intrusion. The contrast was too stark. The war was a different world, a world that, despite its ugliness and savagery, I still missed.

When I left Trinidad and went into the US Army, I left behind the old persona of a chronic underachiever that I had adopted to keep the teachers away from me. I couldn't know that remnants of those old shackles would lie in wait for me in the shadows of those who loved me the most, my parents, my siblings, and my closest friends. Those shackles now reached out for me from within my mother's loving embrace. They bared their claws at me from behind my father's broad smile of pride in his son. Those shackles threatened to send me into a swirl of confusion about who I was and where I was. I could feel them, but I didn't know what they were or where they were coming from. I wanted to feel like my old self again with my family and friends. But my old self was the shackled, insecure self, and it kept pulling at the new me.

After a couple of days at my parents' new home in New York, I boarded a flight to London, still worrying about the possibility that my girlfriend might be in a new relationship. Would she take me into a quiet room and gently explain that she hoped we could still be friends? Would she say, "I didn't know you were already in London," as she introduced me to her new boyfriend, fiancé, or whatever? It was an unreasonable fear, but it had stalked my consciousness for the past several weeks, and I couldn't make it go away. After clearing customs and immigration at Heathrow, I headed to the nearest phone booth to call her. I searched my wallet for her number. Rising panic; what had I done with it? It must be in my luggage. Nothing there. I was in a strange country for the first time and didn't know where I was going. I'd have to find a hotel. Maybe a cab driver could recommend one. I searched my wallet again. There was a number on a worn and wrinkled slip of paper.

A few weeks before leaving Vietnam, I'd received, out of the blue, a letter from Carol. At around age sixteen, we had been high school sweethearts of sorts for a year or so until she had immigrated to the US. I don't know how she got my address; probably from one of my siblings. She was now studying at a university in London and living with an older family member. She'd heard that I was serving in Vietnam and hoped that I was ok. Maybe when I got back from Vietnam, I could get in touch. It would be nice to catch up. I had tucked her number into my wallet. It would indeed be nice to catch up with her when I got to London to see my girlfriend, Nicole.

I started to call the number Carol had sent me, then hesitated. A small voice deep inside tried to warn me. It was the same voice that told me at Ben Tre that I was in extreme danger, the same voice that had guided me into and out of Thien Ngon through a determined North Vietnamese siege. Now, far away from the high tension of the battlefield, I did not know how to hear and heed the guidance of that inner voice. But I didn't know where I was going. It was my only option. I called the number.

Carol sounded pleased to hear from me. I tried to sound relaxed, but I must have sounded confused. I must not have made much sense. It was 11 PM, cold, and raining. I explained that I had neither a number nor an address for Nicole. She said, "Why don't you come here? Grab a taxi, it'll be great to see you, and you can have a bite and sort things out."

The proper response would have been, "Thanks, but I just thought you might know where she lives. Don't worry; I'll figure it out. Maybe we can all get together for lunch somewhere in a day or two." That would have been the normal thing to say, the correct thing. But that's not what I said. Somewhere between Heathrow airport customs and the phone booth, the last strand holding my clear-thinking, logical mind together had quietly, imperceptibly snapped. What I heard myself say was, "Are you sure that's ok? It's very late." That was the wrong response. That response would derail and destabilize the trajectory of my personal life.

I was suddenly very tired. It was late, and I was cold and wet. In the taxi, I rationalized that maybe Carol might know if Nicole was seeing someone else, or maybe she could find out. But I was no longer in rational control. Instead, I was being carried along by this taxi, this cocoon of evasion and avoidance powered by the return of deep insecurity I thought I'd left behind in Trinidad.

Carol and her aunt were friendly and welcoming, and my spirits began to lift. There was so much catching up to do; we hadn't seen each other or been in touch for at least four years. Those four years gave us much to talk and laugh about and gave me a chance to forget about the damn war. They served me some delicious fish left over from their earlier dinner, and we had wine and coffee and more wine and talked until the wee hours when finally, I crashed.

I had flown from Vietnam across the Pacific to California, then across the US to New York. After two days of disorientation, readjustment, and little sleep, I flew across the Atlantic to London. My circadian rhythms no longer knew night from day. I woke up the next day thinking it was early morning. It was 9 PM. Carol and her aunt had already had dinner and were having a glass of wine. They made me a breakfast of eggs and sausage, after which we chatted and drank wine until they were ready to turn in. I had a shower, then watched their little black-and-white television and drank more wine. I had never been much of a drinker, but by the time I crashed again around 4 AM, I had had more than two bottles of wine through the course of my day. This cycle repeated itself the next day. I was disoriented and exhausted, physically and psychologically, and I felt like I was losing track of reality. I needed to contact my girlfriend Nicole and face reality, whether the news would be joyful or devastating.

Before I could find Nicole, she found me. It hadn't occurred to me that she might discover I was in London. Carol opened the door and let her in, then allowed us some privacy. I think it was sometime in the afternoon, but I didn't know what day it was or how long I'd been in London.

She was angry, deeply hurt, and stunningly beautiful, more so than I had remembered. The sudden sight of her like that, poised and radiant, destroyed any hope I might have had of finding words to explain the inexplicable. My whole being was captivated by her; my rational mind was suspended. What could such a sophisticated woman see in a simple guy like me? Her intense anger surprised me and made it impossible for me to reach her. We had never been angry like that with each other. I searched her face for some tiny space, some crack through which I might make contact. I had no explanation, no answer to the obvious question; what the hell was I doing at Carol's apartment?

I felt small and unworthy of her. I tried to tell myself that it would be alright, she would calm down, and we would talk. But her reality was that of a woman betrayed by the man she had waited all year for. I couldn't lie to her; I didn't know why I was there. Nothing I tried to say would comfort her. I kept a calm exterior, remaining cool and disconnected from my feelings. Inside, I was immobilized and crouching in fear and shame. Outside, I felt nothing. She turned away and headed down the hall to the front door. The quiet little voice that tried to warn me at the phone booth now whispered to me that I had done something craven and cowardly, unforgivable and irreversible. I suddenly wanted to hold her and never let go. This precious woman - to whom in my mind, in my dreams, I was already married and raising small children and throwing parties at our home and going on family vacations together - was gone.

During life in a combat zone, soldiers gradually perfect the capacity to go directly from hostile threat to action, bypassing analysis, emotions, and decision-making. This keeps us alive, but at a cost; we lose touch with our feelings. I was unable to absorb the emotional impact of what had just happened. I stared at the door that had closed behind her. I didn't know what I felt. I was ok. I could handle it. I was a combat-experienced soldier. I could handle anything.

I regrouped and collected myself. An unexpected problem had arisen. I had dealt with it. I was no longer a person who "didn't know what to do". The underachieving high school kid was gone. I could feel myself reaching for the clarity and comfort of my military life. This civilian world felt confusing and hostile. I had only been here a couple of days, and already, I was someone's problem. In the cockpit of my helicopter in Vietnam, I was always in control. I always knew what to do. The war was where I felt needed, valued, and respected. The war was where I felt safe.

The rest of my time in London is a blur. I don't remember how much longer I stayed there. I remember it snowed that winter while I was there and that I drank copious amounts of wine every night and every day. Many years later, I would begin to understand the role my own fears of abandonment and rejection may have played in engineering this horrific outcome. Did I just happen to retrieve Carol's number before Nicole's when I got to London? Had I, unconsciously or otherwise, arranged to have a safety net in the event of Nicole's rejection? In so doing, did I unwittingly bring about the very outcome I feared most? Had I, for a moment, lost my mind?

The next time Nicole and I would hear each other's voices and see each other's faces, and gently embrace, everything would have changed except our attraction for each other. Twenty years will have passed. Twenty years of commitments and obligations, successful careers, beautiful children, and marriages that hadn't worked; all of this plus the implacable expanse of the Atlantic Ocean would prove too much for us to overcome, in seeking, after so many years, a path back to each other. I would forever hate the damn war for what it had done to us.

I flew back to my parent's apartment in New York. The home I had longed to return to had been the house in the Valley in Trinidad, the home that always seemed to be filled with warmth and friends, and good feelings. But it was no longer there. I had not realized that, in my long year in Vietnam, everything that was important to me outside the

Army had changed. The place that had been home wasn't home anymore. My parents had emigrated to the US with my younger brother and two younger sisters and now lived in an apartment in New York which, for me, was not yet home. My two older sisters had married and moved to homes of their own in Trinidad. My girlfriend was now living somewhere in London. Our home in the Valley back in Trinidad had been rented to friends of the family. I had come back from Vietnam to find I no longer had a family in a place called home. Everyone around me seemed happy and fully adjusted to this new reality. So, I acted as if everything was normal for me too. But I was eager to return to the familiarity of military service. Within the predictable structure and culture of the Army, relationships were far less complicated than the frustrating maze I had encountered during my few short weeks of leave from military life. My home was the Army - and Vietnam.

Thankfully, my next assignment soon arrived in the mail: Training Officer at the Army Primary Helicopter Flight School at Fort Wolters, Texas, where I had been a flight student two years earlier. As soon as I got there, I applied to go to Chinook helicopter flight training at Fort Rucker, Alabama, knowing that upon graduation, I would almost certainly be sent back to Vietnam. I'd seen the amazing things the Chinooks did in Vietnam. Flying them was a dream I never thought I'd achieve.

At Fort Wolters, I finally learned to drive, got my driver's license, and bought my first car, a shiny blue Oldsmobile Cutlass with an all-white interior and a V8 engine. My assignment to Chinook school came through in a few months, and I was off to Fort Rucker, Alabama, the place where I'd started my military aviation career as a helicopter maintainer and graduated as an Army Aviator and Huey pilot. Becoming a Chinook pilot brought a deeper sense of accomplishment as well as the renewed self-confidence and pride that I needed. Graduating as a Chinook pilot was a new high. While going through Chinook school, I discovered that two years earlier, during my initial flight training as a Huey pilot, amazing events had swirled around me, of which I knew nothing at all.

The Army and the Klan

To fight the war in Vietnam using hundreds of helicopters, the US Army needed thousands of helicopter pilots. The solution to this was the Warrant Officer Rotary Wing Aviator Course (WORWAC). This nine-month course was a combination of Officer training and pilot training. In the US Army, Warrant Officers are full military officers with all attendant rights and privileges. As officers, they are specialists in a particular field, in this case, aviation, but do not command Platoons, Companies, or larger units, as Commissioned Officers do.

The course consisted of a Primary Phase conducted at Fort Wolters, Texas, and an Advanced Phase at Fort Rucker, Alabama. The first four weeks of the course were intense officer training. There was no flying. It was a high-pressure hardship environment intended to weed out any candidates who showed the slightest inadequacy in mental or physical stamina or who could not accept the extremely harsh discipline for the most trivial infractions. Candidates were free to quit the course at any time, and many did.

Those who made it through those first four weeks were finally allowed some time off from 4 pm Saturday to the same time Sunday. Those with families nearby could go home and return the next morning. As 4 pm rolled around, the two-storey students' quarters, normally quiet and spotless, turned into a madhouse as two hundred tightly constrained Warrant Officer Candidates (WOCs) were suddenly unleashed for the first time in four weeks. Family and friends arriving in their cars caused a minor traffic jam as they searched excitedly for their future Warrant Officer Helicopter Pilots.

A handful of us was left behind, feeling a bit strange in the nearly empty building. Every minute of our lives had been tightly controlled for the last four weeks. Now there was no one standing us at attention and yelling at us from an inch away, checking our uniforms, inspecting our lockers, demanding push-ups for any or no reason. I had no friends or family nearby and knew nothing of the towns around the base. I had nowhere to go. I looked forward to just having some time to myself.

Curtiss Lovell was one of the older students on our flight. He had been a Sergeant in the Army National Guard and reserves for several years, and after a long wait, his application for flight school had been approved. Before starting the 9-month course, he had rented a modest house in a town not far from the base. His wife and three young boys were waiting for him in the family car, and he had fled the building like almost everyone else. Ten minutes later, he was back upstairs, and I wondered what he had forgotten. He passed by my room hurriedly and then came back a few seconds later.

"Hey Larry, aren't you getting out of here?"

"I think I'll stick around, relax a bit, and do some studying."

He smiled a sympathetic smile. "It's been a rough four weeks. We all need a break before the next phase. You can take a run into town, have a look around, get a nice steak dinner."

"I don't have a car or anything; I'll just stick around here. I'll be fine."

"Ok, take it easy. See you tomorrow".

Five minutes later, he was back. "Hey Larry, why'nt you come with us to our place? You can have dinner with us and stay the night. We've got sleeping bags, and we'd love to have you."

"Thanks, Curt, but I'm fine, really. That's truly nice of you. I really appreciate it."

"Ok, how about lunch tomorrow? I'll pick you up around ten, and you can come to have a home-cooked meal with us. I'll be coming in any way to take some things back to the house so you can think about it overnight."

"Ok, great, I'll let you know in the morning."

It was a modest house and a very lived-in home. The front door opened onto the small living room. There were toys scattered around the floor, a few blankets and sleeping bags not yet put away, and some half-finished drinks and beer cans belonging to the three other flight school students who had clearly been there for a while, maybe overnight. Two acoustic guitars leaned against a small, overstuffed lounging chair.

Curt's wife, Elaine, greeted me as if she already knew me. "Hi Larry, come on in. We're running out of chairs, so grab a seat on the floor somewhere and make yourself at home." She threw a blanket or small rug across the room for me to sit on. "The beers are in the fridge right over there, and there's Chivas and Bacardi's on the counter there. When you're ready for a drink, just go get it; no one's gonna serve you here, so make yourself at home."

She was completely disarming, and I was immediately at ease. I said hello and fell in easily with the group. We got to know each other and had a tasty buffet lunch. One of the guys grabbed a guitar and started singing a popular protest song. I picked up the other guitar and played along. Everyone joined in, and more songs followed. Eventually, there was a pause as drinks were topped up. I was asked to play something. Ray Charles' "I Can't Stop Loving You" was popular at the time and easy to play. Loud voices filled the house, and an encore was demanded. The song became a group favourite.

This exercise was repeated every time we got a weekend or holiday off. Other students stopped by occasionally, but the core group developed a tight bond that lasted throughout flight school and beyond.

The second half of flight school, the Advanced Phase, was conducted at Fort Rucker in Alabama. Curt and his family found a house in a residential suburb of one of the towns nearby. As advanced students, we now had most weekends and holidays to ourselves. The tradition of weekend music and fun at Curt's house now resumed at his Alabama home. He lived on a quiet street that sloped downhill and ended in a cul-de-sac with a little roundabout. His was the third house from the cul-de-sac.

One Saturday afternoon, as we turned into his street, we saw a sheriff's patrol car atop the roundabout facing directly up the street towards us. I asked Curt, "Has there been some kind of problem on your street; what's he doing there?"

"Oh no; they just hang out there sometimes when they need a break from catching speeders on the highway." I couldn't tell if he was joking. After a brief pause, he added, "I think they know the guy who lives at the bottom there."

I thought I detected a hint of tension in his voice, but I figured if the sheriff was hanging out on my street, I'd be just a little cautious too.

The friends who were already relaxing at Curt's welcomed us heartily, and we settled in for a night of music and good times. In the wee hours, when we were finally exhausted, the sleeping bags came out, and one by one, we fell asleep in mid-conversation. The next morning as we freshened up before breakfast, Curt's wife Elaine suddenly started frantically stuffing empty beer cans into a closet and getting rid of all evidence of alcohol. As we all pitched in with the cleaning up, I noticed out the window that the sheriff had returned to his previous position. I said to Curt, "Looks like the sheriff's back." He replied, "Yeah, that's why we're cleaning up. This is a dry county. We're allowed to drink inside, but I don't know if we're allowed to serve it to guests, like at a party."

When all evidence of partying was cleaned up or hidden away, we enjoyed breakfast, chatted for an hour or so, then headed back to Fort Rucker. The following weekend when we arrived at Curt's house, the sheriff was there again. We ignored him and went inside. There were two students at the house who I knew from a different section of our large class but hadn't really met before. Our weekend fun time had become a thing, and we usually had a few extra students drop by to join the fun for an hour or two. Like Curt, these two were among the small number of older guys in our class. They had the hard-edged look of Army Sergeants. It turned out they were both Special Forces Sergeants before coming to flight school. In addition, they had both served in Vietnam. The youngsters like me could hardly wait to hear what it was like over there.

I wondered if such hard-core types would enjoy our music. They stuck around till quite late and seemed to enjoy our homemade variety show. Curt invited them to join us for breakfast the next morning, and, to my surprise, they showed up.

The following weekend we all seemed to have things to do, and there was no gathering at Curt's house. We picked up again after that break and carried on our little tradition until graduation, following which we dispersed to our various units, with most of us ending up in Vietnam.

After completing my first year in Vietnam and a brief stint as a training officer at Ft. Wolters in Texas, I returned to Fort Rucker to attend Chinook school. I discovered that Curt had also completed his year in Vietnam and was stationed at Fort Rucker as an Instructor. He and his family lived on Fort Rucker in official Officers' housing. I was in Bachelor Officers Quarters (BOQ). He invited me over for dinner, and I looked forward to catching up. One of the old gang was there, and two other officers I hadn't met before. As Curt introduced us, one of the guys said, "Is this THE Larry McIntosh?" I smiled pleasantly as I waited for somebody to explain. The other guy said, "You're really famous around Fort Rucker – the guy who almost started a war with the KKK!"

I turned to Curt; "What the hell are they talking about?"

He said, "How about a beer, Larry?" He brought us drinks, and we sat at his breakfast counter. He then related this story.

"Remember that sheriff's cruiser that used to be parked near our old house? Well, the sheriff was pretty high up in the KKK. The neighbours had reported that some damn (n-word) was coming into their neighbourhood and staying at our house. The sheriff came to the house and told us we better not do that again. This was a nice neighbourhood, and people don't want their kind comin' round here, blah blah blah. I said I'd bring whoever I damn well please to my house, and that did not include him since I hadn't broken any law. Things got a bit heated, and we yelled at each other for a while. He finally said that I was putting my wife and kids' lives at stake because if that (n-word) came here again, they would blow up our goddam house, and he meant it; burn it to the ground."

I was dumbstruck. "Curt, this is crazy; I had no clue. You should have told me; I still can't believe this."

Curt continued. "I was pissed; Elaine and the kids heard all this. I was ready to go after him right there. Elaine calmed me down, and I slammed the door in his fat face. I called the Captain and told him what had happened, and he said he'd have some guys keep an eye on the place." I grew more and more incredulous as Curt continued.

"I'd heard about this sheriff, and I knew he was just trying to scare me, but I thought I better be on the safe side. There's a Colonel I'd worked for on another Army base before coming to flight school. He knew Elaine and the kids; I figured I'd better give him a call and get his take on it. Well, he was as pissed as I was. He said the guys at Rucker had trouble with this sheriff before, roughing up young black soldiers and throwing them in jail for no reason. He called some senior officers at Rucker, and the word quickly got to the Commandant, the top General at Fort Rucker. Well, that was it. He'd had enough of the Klan. It was bad enough they were messing with his enlisted soldiers; now they were harassing his aviation officer trainees. He decided to put a stop to this crap once and for all. He sent a team of 'emissaries' to carry a message to the Klan; if they so much as laid a hand on you or harassed you in any way, the KKK would have a war on their hands, and (my jaw had dropped) wait, wait, he would not hesitate to put tanks in the streets if that's what was needed to protect his troops and get the KKK to back off."

I don't know if I was more amazed that all this had gone on or that I never caught on, never connected the dots. "So those Special Forces guys that showed up at your house that night didn't just happen to drop by?"

Curt laughed. "We were concerned you might put two and two together and figure out what was going on, but the Captain wanted to make sure we could handle anything the Klan might try, so he asked the SF guys to stop by and keep an eye on things. Look, if we'd told you, would you have come back to the house?"

"No way; of course not. I'd never put your family in danger like that."

This was a sobering moment for me and, at some level, a loss of innocence. Even allowing for some embellishment of the story over the course of a year, this was alarming and depressing. I wondered then, and have continued to reflect since then, how were African American people able to persevere in the face of such hate and oppression. Because I was not at all sure I could have survived one week of what many African Americans in the southern US live with every day of their lives.

Bearcat Library

Preparing to return to Vietnam in August 1969 was a bittersweet experience, with none of the high excitement and curiosity of the first time around. In my confusion and disorientation, I'd managed to ruin my relationship with my girlfriend beyond any hope of repair. I wouldn't fully realize what I had done, the pain I had caused, until years later, by which time it was too late. On the long flight back to Vietnam, I felt very alone, yet very calm. There was comfort in going back to what was familiar and in knowing that I was good at my job and respected for my ability. But was this war becoming my life? I felt estranged from the people who mattered most, my family and my girlfriend.

During the final months of my first year, flying troops into and out of battle had begun to acquire some of the routine and banality of a dead-end job. We just seemed to be doing the same things over and over with no end in sight. Maybe I had become depressed, emotionally numb. If I was depressed, Vietnam had been the cause. Maybe Vietnam would provide some relief from my empty feeling, if only through the distraction of work. The cockpit of a helicopter was the one place where I felt totally in control. I was sad, but I was Ok; I was coming back home. I looked forward to the gratification of doing a job well; that was enough for now.

During my first year in Vietnam, I tried to capture some of the excitement by taking countless reels of 8-millimeter movies and hundreds of photographs. In my second year, I seldom picked up either camera. I was aimless, more reflective, and less of a wide-eyed tourist. But I felt ok. I was always ok.

The Chinook helicopter is an amazing engineering achievement. I've heard it described derisively as a giant flying bathtub, but it's the type of aircraft pilots fall in love with. I just wanted to fly this machine as much as I could wherever I was needed. With each flight, I focused on improving my skills, eventually becoming the senior Chinook Instructor Pilot for my unit.

My assignment was B Company, 228th Aviation Battalion, 1st Air Cavalry Division, based at Bearcat, Vietnam. Bearcat was not far from my previous location at Long Binh, and I would be flying in the same areas in which I had been flying Hueys seven months earlier. Everything was completely familiar to me. Operationally, I was quite at home. Our primary role was logistic support rather than combat assault, moving tons of stuff to where it was needed, almost all of it slung beneath the helicopter—this type of flying afforded a broader perspective on tactics being used to find and destroy enemy units.

Special Forces teams supported by my previous unit, the 117th AHC, had collected intelligence that the North Vietnamese and Vietcong were again massing in the remote jungles North of Tay Ninh, preparing for another assault on the Saigon area, a second Tet-type offensive. These units were well-trained and equipped. US infantry units would require artillery support to engage and defeat them successfully. The standard tactic was to set up artillery fire support bases from which the infantry units would go in search of the enemy. The infantry would then direct artillery fire onto the enemy positions they discovered. But the enemy had learned to operate just beyond the range of frontline US artillery.

Using its Chinooks, the 1st Cavalry Division had worked out a system for quickly setting up an artillery fire support base in the dense triple-canopy jungle. A powerful bomb would be dropped in the target area to blast a hole in the jungle big enough for a single Huey to get in. Going in one at a time, the Hueys would take in a small security team and an engineering team. The engineers would expand the size of the hole in the jungle until it was big enough for our Chinooks to bring in bulldozers and more infantry and engineers. Within a few hours, enough space would be cleared for the construction of a complete artillery firebase.

Modern Chinook preparing to airlift an Armoured Personnel Carrier.

Everything needed at the firebase would be prepared in advance in large nets or other containers and assigned a specific mission number for transport by Chinooks. This meant that we knew how many flights would be required to set up the base and in what order things should be picked up and delivered. Almost all the equipment was set up for quick pick up and delivery using external slings. We delivered every type of military equipment available – artillery batteries and their crews, generators, 500-gallon fuel bladders, drinking water in water tanks, field rations, heavy lumber for constructing underground bunkers, tons of barbed wire for the defensive perimeters, and many tons of artillery shells and other ammunition, 10 and 20-foot steel containers full of supplies, all without having to land except to refuel with engines running. Each load averaged about 4 tons. Two Chinooks flying 15 trips each to the firebase would deliver over 100 tons of equipment and supplies. By the end of the day, the firebase would be set up and ready to take the fight to the enemy, who would suddenly discover that they were no longer beyond the range of US artillery. This approach required us to exceed our maximum flying hour limit regularly.

I flew many more hours in my second year than I had in my first. Chinooks had less exposure to enemy fire than we had flying combat assault in Hueys. But the noise and vibration in the Chinook cockpit were above safe levels, making long days in the Chinook much more stressful than in a Huey. Sometimes after a ten-hour day in the Chinook, it was difficult to walk a straight line on exiting the helicopter. The Commanders tried to avoid sending pilots and crews out two or more days in a row so they could have at least one day to recover. But sometimes, this was unavoidable.

Our overall objectives were not being achieved. We still had nothing to celebrate. We were winning battles, killing a lot more of them than they were killing of us. But so what? Maybe if we kept killing more of them than they killed of us, they would eventually give up. "Ok, we're done. You win." Was that the plan? (Years later, it turned out that was indeed the US government's plan!) But how much more killing would it take? At some point, doesn't the price of winning become higher than the price of losing?

This type of logistical support flying allowed me to better appreciate firsthand the massive scale of the US effort to win this war. An enormous amount of equipment, firepower, and people were being thrown into this fight. Yet it was clear we weren't winning. A year ago, I had been flying soldiers into battle in these jungles. Now here we were, fighting the same enemy with more men and more resources, making little, if any, progress. Why? The mild depression that had settled over me like a shroud on my long flight back to Vietnam began to shape itself into questions. Forget what our leaders say is happening; what is really going on here? Where are the South Vietnamese? Why aren't they as willing to fight for their cause as are the North Vietnamese? Why do we want this so much more than the people we're here to help?

Around this time, I also began to be haunted by the growing realization of the cruelty of what I had done to Nicole in London. No matter how hard I tried, I could not find a reason or an explanation for the way I had behaved. I felt that no amount of punishment could be sufficient for the pain I must have caused. I tried to fly as many missions as I could because flying required complete concentration and left no time for self-recrimination. I would accept any mission without much concern for the danger involved.

As I walked towards the base barber shop one morning, I came upon a small white prefab building that looked to me like an administrative office building. It would have been unremarkable except that it looked out of place among all the military field structures with their olive-green canvas roofs and walls and their waist-high sandbag revetments. As I walked past the building, I noticed a sign near the door that seemed so incongruous it stopped me in my tracks: BEARCAT LIBRARY. The sudden encounter with this fragment of an institution dedicated to quiet reflection, research, and learning, here in the middle of a savage war, made my mind do a backflip in my head. There had to be a catch. Maybe it was just a catchy name for a bar or club or game room, maybe a place to meet girls who had been "vetted". I lingered for a while, debating whether to risk barging in where I might not be welcome.

A soldier came out, and as the door closed behind him, I glimpsed what looked like standing shelves with rows of books. I cracked open the door, peered inside, and entered tentatively. The building seemed bigger from the inside. Rows of shelves stacked with books ran wall to wall. A long table was covered in magazines and newspapers. I stood for a while, absorbing this oasis of civility. A pleasant woman sitting at a desk said hello and invited me to look around. "If you find something you like, you can check it out and return it when you're done". She tilted her head and smiled as if to say, "Yep, it's a real library". I thanked her and started down one of the rows.

I discovered a book called "The Smaller Dragon: A Political History of Vietnam" by Joseph Buttinger. I leafed through it long enough to realize that it was an authoritative history of Vietnam from its early beginnings thousands of years ago to the end of the war against the French in the 1950s. As a young child aged five or six, I'd heard on Radio Trinidad the BBC news reports of war in a place called Dien Bien Phu in Indochina. I remembered because the name had sounded so musical, especially when read quickly in the phlegmatic style of the British news presenters at that time as if it were all one word. My brother and I had laughed each time we heard him say it.

This war did not start with the arrival of American military advisers in 1960 or 61. It started around the time I was born, maybe even before that. I checked out the book and hurried back to my room, forgetting my haircut.

As I read Buttinger's work, I began to see the Vietnamese people with new eyes. I became even more impressed with their resilience and determination and more depressed about our chances of ever "winning" this war. I felt that if US leaders had read this book in 1961, this American phase of the war would never have been started, and all these thousands of American lives and millions of Vietnamese lives would not have been wasted. The Vietnamese had suffered French domination and colonization, followed by Japanese occupation during the Second World War. Vietnamese leaders had helped US pilots fly high-level intelligence missions against Japan during that war. In return, Senior US government officials had promised the Vietnamese leaders that the US would support Vietnamese Independence and oppose the recolonization of Vietnam by the French after the end of World War II war. But when that war was over, the US reneged on this commitment and supported the French effort to recolonize Vietnam by military force. To the Vietnamese leadership, this was a devastating betrayal. They would no longer seek or expect help from rich Western democracies. They resolved to take up arms and rid their country of foreign occupation. For the North Vietnamese and Vietcong, this was the continuation of a war against recolonization, a war for independence.

The first step in this process was political action, the education of the population about their history, with the objective of inspiring them to embrace the struggle to achieve an independent, unified Vietnam. I had experienced the unstoppable force of the drive for independence by a population inspired to believe in themselves and their right to self-determination. I remembered my mother's passionate commitment to the anti-colonial independence movement in Trinidad, a much smaller country. She had become an organizer, helping to rally the community to support the non-violent independence movement. If this movement had been forcefully suppressed by the British, I doubt it would have remained non-violent.

As I read Buttinger's work, the answer to the question that haunted me through my school years – why all the beatings and shaming of children? – began to reveal itself. It was written in the tightly spaced bomb craters that littered the South Vietnamese countryside in all directions. Those violent beatings were meant to mould us into submissive subjects who would never choose the path that was taken by the North Vietnamese and Vietcong. *NO TALKING! You must do as you're told if you want to grow up to be good British Subjects.* Now, outside our military compound, I became conscious of the faint rumble of distant explosions that never stopped for very long, day or night. Instead of licks with a leather strap, disobedience, and defiance were being treated to a truly lethal punishment: heavy artillery and B52 bombers.

Even so, even as my understanding of the war deepened, and I realized there was much more to the war than we were told, I still "knew" that it was only a matter of time before we achieved our objective. The North Vietnamese and Vietcong could not hold out much longer against America's vast firepower and superiority in the air, on the ground, and offshore. America was a superpower, too powerful to be thwarted by little North Vietnam and its supporters in the South, no matter how committed they might be to their cause. I still believed in the honour and integrity of our leaders. I still accepted that our cause was just.

Op Tempo

By early April 1970, our military and political leaders seemed to have run out of new ideas for achieving victory. They now appeared to be searching for a way out that might be made to look like something other than abject failure. In the meantime, we fought on, as good soldiers do, to the bitter end, still believing (hoping?) that our leaders would lead us to a free and happy South Vietnam living in peace with its neighbour to the north.

Word around the B Company Longhorns compound at Bearcat was that something big was being planned by the generals and their bosses. Maybe our leaders had decided to strike a final overwhelming blow that would bring an end to the long conflict. This type of rumour popped up from time to time and quickly faded when the rumoured event failed to occur. But this time, on our daily missions, we also noticed an increasing number of add-ons and urgent missions. Normally, at our 6 AM mission briefing, the aircraft commanders (ACs) would each receive a mission sheet containing a list of 4-digit mission numbers and a brief description of each load, the pickup and drop-off points, and the radio call sign and frequency for pickup and delivery. As the day wore on, it was not unusual to receive a few additional missions by radio. But of late, we were getting many more additional missions, including more frequent Tactical Emergency (TAC-E) calls, and flying even more hours than before. There was a definite increase in the operational tempo, especially around the Tay Ninh area near the border with Cambodia.

The TAC-E designation meant that troops on the ground were in a battle and in urgent need of additional supplies, usually ammunition. These TAC-E missions took precedence over everything else, so we would immediately divert from our normal missions to deliver whatever was needed and then return to complete our interrupted missions.

Like B Company, the other two Chinook companies that made up the 228th Aviation Battalion - A Company Wildcats and C Company Crimson Tide - were flying longer than normal hours, and the flight crews were feeling the stress. We were putting more artillery fire support bases into the jungle north of Tay Ninh near the Cambodian border and moving them to a new location every week or two, sometimes only a mile or two from their previous location.

The Vietcong and North Vietnamese were not happy about these US firebases within artillery range of their jungle camps just across the border in Cambodia. They mounted savage assaults against the artillery bases. But after so many years of this war, the 1st Cav Division knew how to build well-fortified fire bases in the middle of nowhere using Chinooks to quickly deliver everything needed to function effectively and to repulse the most determined ground assaults. The North Vietnamese lost hundreds of men in their attempts to breach the defences and overrun these fire bases. As far as I know, they never succeeded.

On a day of this high-intensity flying, touching down only to refuel with engines running, we got an urgent mid-afternoon call to pick up a high-priority classified item at Tay Ninh and take it to a base about 40 minutes away. When we got to Tay Ninh, the classified items had been loaded onto a three-quarter-ton army truck and covered tightly with a tarpaulin. The truck looked like an old WWII-era vehicle that had seen better days and had been pressed back into service. We had no idea what was on that truck. Whatever it was, it looked like two truckloads had been piled onto one truck and strapped down tightly.

The hook-up man on the ground climbed atop the truck and held up the sling, indicating that the load was ready for pickup. The sling was attached to the truck by four clevis bolts, two on the front bumper and two at the back. We hovered over the truck, guided by the crew chief laying on his stomach and looking through a door in the floor of the helicopter directly over the cargo hook. As we hovered inches above his head, the hook-up man slipped the sling onto our hook. He quickly jumped off the truck and scrambled away with our gritty rotor wash sandblasting his bare back. As we lifted the truck into the air, we realized that even for a loaded three-quarter-ton truck, it was heavier than normal.

We climbed out and cruised along smoothly at three thousand feet over flat savanna terrain pock-marked everywhere with bomb craters. About twenty minutes into the flight, the helicopter suddenly jerked violently. The instruments all read normally. I called back to the crew chief: "What was that, Chief?"

"We lost the load, Sir." We immediately entered a 180-degree turn to see if we could see the impact site. The hook safety switch was still in the SAFE position, and neither of us had touched the hook release switch. The crew chief came up to the cockpit holding the lower end of the sling with a small piece of the truck bumper still attached. The sling was intact and still attached to the hook. The crew chief had pulled it into the helicopter. The weight of the loaded truck had caused the bumper to fail at one attachment point, immediately overstressing the other three points and sending the truck and its classified cargo plummeting from three thousand feet. That sling and the chunk of the truck bumper were critical proof that we had not dropped the truck by mistake. Had we done that, the sling would have gone with the truck, and we'd have been in serious trouble.

We circled around the cratered landscape of grasses and scrub bushes searching for anything that looked like a smashed truck or debris from whatever was on the truck, with no success. We called our base and told them what had happened, emphasizing that this was not due to any error on the part of the crew. A few minutes later, we were told to return directly to base and submit a report.

Upon landing at our home base, we delivered to our Commanding Officer our brief report accompanied by the sling with the chunk of truck bumper still attached.

We then went across to the officers' club to get a cool drink in the hot mid-afternoon. The Maintenance Officer sat at the bar with his back towards us. No one else was in the club on either side of the bar. He was a bit older than most of the other pilots, maybe early thirties, over six feet tall, a pleasant sort, but ran a tight ship. He knew everything there was to know about a Chinook and was highly respected by all the pilots. I asked how things were going and took a seat a few feet to his right. He said nothing. I looked across at him, and there were tears rolling down his face. He took another sip of his drink.

He was not one to break down in tears even if we'd lost one of our pilots or crewmen. More likely bad news of a personal nature. I thought it best to give him some space; I was not someone he would confide in. I hoped it wasn't a "Dear John" letter. As I headed down to the maintenance office to find out what had happened, I ran into one of the pilots who had not flown that day. He said the Assistant Division Commander for Logistics, a General, had flown in on a shiny VIP helicopter and had gone directly to the Maintenance Officer. This was highly unusual. A General would not normally visit our Company, and if he did, he would be met by the Company Commander and his senior officers and NCOs. But the General went directly to the Maintenance Office and had a "discussion" with the Maintenance Officer, which grew more heated as it progressed. It ended with the General shouting expletives before storming out and re-boarding his helicopter.

Early Chinook helicopters like the ones we flew were notorious for their high maintenance requirements, measured in maintenance man-hours per flight hour. From our compliment of sixteen Chinooks, our company was required to provide six every day to support operations in the field. The General said that in two weeks, at least eight Chinooks per day would be required. The Maintenance Officer told him the only way that could be achieved is if the current requirement was reduced to four or five per day to allow additional mandatory maintenance work to be done ahead of time to get those aircraft back out on the line more quickly. He showed the General the big maintenance wall charts that laid out how the work was scheduled to deliver six airworthy Chinooks per day. It showed the dates each aircraft would be in and out of maintenance and the tasks to be completed, projected out up to three weeks ahead. Adjustments could be made for unexpected component failures without affecting the six-per-day rate. But pushing it up to eight per day couldn't be done unless two additional aircraft were made available for maintenance each day for the next two weeks. But the operational tempo was already increasing, and the six per day were being overworked. A reduction was out of the question. Voices were raised, and guess who had the last word? "Get it done, or I'll find someone else who can get it done."

This incident validated the current rumours: something big was being planned, and our Chinooks would play a key part in it. It also made me appreciate that as much as the pilots were being overstressed, the maintenance officer held the most high-pressure job in the company. He and his technicians regularly worked 18-hour days and sometimes worked round the clock to get aircraft ready to launch at first light.

A security force was put in to secure the area where the truck went in with its classified cargo. A small observation helicopter was assigned to help the ground force search for the truck. It took them three days to find the truck. Each day, additional personnel and observation helicopters were added to the search effort. One of the observation helicopters had flown over the site several times without recognizing it. The impact had produced a crater very similar to the many other bomb craters that pockmarked the area for miles around. On the third day of searching, the observation helicopter pilot thought he saw what looked like a piece of debris near one of the bomb craters. He landed several yards away and walked over to the edge of the crater to have a closer look. Just another bomb crater. He was about to return to his helicopter when he thought he heard a faint dripping sound. He peered down into the dark hole and listened closely. Engine oil was still dripping slowly into a pool that had formed deep down in the dark crater. Dirt from the crater had collapsed in on the truck, completely obscuring it and making the indentation look like all the other bomb craters around. He had found the precious truck, and there was no evidence that it had been discovered by the enemy.

We were later told that the truck had been overloaded with tightly packed flak vests and the latest high-tech night vision devices. These devices may have been the reason the load was classified. In the hands of the enemy, these would confer a major advantage that could cost the lives of many US soldiers.

As the tempo of our operations continued to increase, we noticed that enemy activity was also on the rise, and the attacks were more brazen. On the rare occasions that we received direct enemy fire, we immediately reported the location via a designated radio frequency. The response was always swift and overwhelming; artillery fire from all available batteries devasted the area from which the hostile fire came; fighter-bombers were sent in to attack the area with napalm and high explosive bombs; and on one memorable occasion, a flight of B52s had their original mission cancelled and were redirected to the site where the enemy had taken a few pot shots at us. This oversized response was intended as a deterrent. Chinooks were vital to the war effort. The loss of one Chinook was very costly because of the impact on critical logistical support for the troops on the ground. The message to the enemy was clear; do not shoot at our Chinooks.

So, it was as much a curiosity as a surprise when we came under attack during an early morning delivery to a fire support base east of Tay Ninh. As we had done many times before, we approached the firebase with eight thousand pounds of artillery ammunition slung beneath the Chinook. As we came to a hover, arcs of dew spun off the rotor blades in the early morning air. I neither saw nor heard the first mortar round explode; I just saw the soldiers on the ground dive for cover behind sandbags. The next round hit close to the aircraft sending a spray of fine gravel onto my face through my open window as the load touched down. I immediately released the load and went into a full power climb-out. Moments later, one engine shut down, and one of the two main hydraulic systems went offline. We could easily have flown away on the remaining engine and even done an autorotation and running landing if we lost the second engine. But a Chinook cannot be controlled if the second hydraulic system fails. Earlier in the year, a crew lost one hydraulic system just a few miles from our base. They tried to make it back to base on the second system. The aircraft went out of control and crashed when the second system failed, killing the crew. We had to find a place to land.

There was a narrow, paved road about a hundred yards ahead of us. We made a running landing onto the road, and as we touched down, we saw two battle tanks about fifty yards further up the road. Great! We had protection; we didn't have to worry about the enemy fighters closing in on us. As we shut down the aircraft, the two battle tanks took off up the road away from us and disappeared over the hill. Yeah, really great! We suddenly felt like every Vietcong in the Tay Ninh area was racing to be the ones to kill or capture us.

The crew set up defensive positions on both sides of the aircraft using the two machine guns while I confirmed our position over the radio to our base. I then had the crew chief remove the encrypted radios and logbooks as we exited the aircraft and prepared for whatever came next. We made crude foxholes in the ditches that ran along the roadsides and prepared to hold out until help arrived. In the meantime, I tried to diagnose the extent of the damage to the aircraft. Within ten minutes, what came next were two Cobra gunships circling low overhead. You don't feel the pressure of having to fight off the Vietcong with just your co-pilot and two crewmen until suddenly you're no longer on your own. The two Cobras seemed to us like guardian angels. But they were deadly killing machines, and the Vietcong would be crazy to start a fight while the two gunships orbited on station above us.

Twenty minutes later, a Huey arrived to take us back to our base. A recovery crew was already on its way to the downed Chinook. The aircraft was just a couple hundred meters from the firebase where we had been hit by shrapnel from the mortar round. An infantry security detail was on its way from the firebase to secure the aircraft.

Back at our base at Bearcat, we learned that a piece of shrapnel from the mortar round had severed part of a main electrical wire harness that runs along a compartment on the roof of the Chinook. The effect of this was to shut down one engine and the hydraulic system just as if we had switched them off from the cockpit. The recovery crew temporarily repaired the critical severed wires and flew the aircraft back to base, with both engines and hydraulic systems functioning normally.

With everyone safely back at our Bearcat base, we reflected on the increasing aggressiveness of the enemy units in the Tay Ninh area. We wondered if another build-up to something like the Tet Offensive was underway. These guys – the Vietcong and North Vietnamese army – just refused to give up or back down. You had to respect these fighters; they had suffered years of enormous losses to US firepower, yet they fought with high morale and full confidence that they would ultimately prevail against the overwhelming odds.

Night Tactical Emergency (Tac-E)

A few days later, as my co-pilot and I staggered down the rear ramp of a Chinook at the end of a long day in the cockpit, heading for the operations office, I realized I could not quite walk a straight line. We had just returned to base at 8 PM after flying another ten-hour day in the noisy, shaky helicopter, and I felt a bit high as if I could happily turn around and fly another ten hours. Our flight surgeons had warned us that this was a sign that the stress was beginning to take its toll. We were flying more than twice the maximum number of hours per month allowed for Chinook pilots. The doctors said that we would almost certainly experience permanent damage from the excessive amount of stress and noise. They said they had expressed their concerns in a letter to members of Congress. But we felt great and were sure we'd be fine, even as I wobbled a bit as I walked away from the Chinook.

After checking in with the Ops office, I headed for the mess hall, hoping there might be something palatable left from dinner. There was quite a lot left, but that was because so many people decided it wasn't worth trying; it was that bad. I headed for the Officers' Club, where there was always a cold beer and a good choice of snacks.

As I took my first sip of beer and joined the banter at the bar, one of the three Vietnamese waitresses came over and whispered something to me. With the noise of rock music and high spirits in the Club and my ears still ringing from my long day in the cockpit, it took three tries before I began to decipher what she was saying. If I could get her some rice and some eggs from the mess hall, she and the other waitresses would cook a nice meal. I called down to the mess hall; the sergeant said, "Just send her down, and we'll give her whatever she needs". I remembered I had a small, canned ham in my room that I figured might come in handy if I ever needed a break from the mess hall food. This seemed like such a time, so I collected it and handed it over to the waitress on condition that I get a sample of whatever she and the other waitresses were cooking. She beamed an excited grin and promised I would love the meal.

The Vietnamese who worked around our company area had quickly deciphered that I was not a typical US soldier. Within a few days of my arrival at Bearcat, I noticed that they often brought a few fruits to snack on during the day. These were tropical fruits commonly eaten in Trinidad, like *pommecythere* and mangoes that most Americans had never seen – or tasted. I hadn't seen these in years, but when I asked one of the women if I could have a taste, she and her friends seemed shy and embarrassed. They were used to Americans ridiculing their food. I said, "No, no, I love these; please can I have just one? I'll pay you for it." She tentatively handed me one of the fruits, but as I bit into it and my face lit up, they laughed excitedly and chatted in Vietnamese. Then to me, "How you know [Vietnamese fruit name]?"

A long conversation followed, during which I explained that I had grown up with many Chinese and other Asian people just like them. I showed them on a map of where I came from and told them I had many friends who looked just like them, and we all grew up eating those fruits, so they made me feel at home. This is why the waitress felt she could approach me regarding the food.

The beer flowed, the music played, and spirits got higher as the evening wore on. In the midst of the war stories and raucous laughter, the waitress appeared from nowhere and placed a steaming hot meal on the bar in front of me. It smelled heavenly, like home cooking but with an exotic new flavour I've never encountered outside of Vietnam. She had managed to get onions and garlic and a variety of spices and seasonings and turned it all into a gourmet meal. It was incredibly good, my first taste of genuine home-cooked Vietnamese cuisine.

Comment number 1 from my left: "Hey Mac, you're not actually gonna eat that gook stuff, are you; you might be eating some kinda rat or snake or something." The food was delicious, flavoured with garlic and spices and spring onions; I was in heaven. The mess hall, on its best day, could not produce such a tasty meal. I wondered if one of the waitresses had worked at a Vietnamese restaurant.

Comment number 2 from my right: "I can't believe you're really eating that gook crap, man; you must have one hell of a cast iron stomach." I beamed a happy smile as I dug further into the rice and ham and carrots and bits of egg, all in a sauce to die for.

Comment number 3 from my left: "That smells really good, Mac; what is it? You look like you're really enjoying that." I downed another mouthful.

Comment number 4 from my right: "You mind if I have just a little taste of that?" Not at all; grab a fork, and help yourself.

Upon tasting the food, he quietly got up and headed to the small back room where the waitresses had worked their culinary magic using a two-burner electric cooker. I hadn't realized that they sometimes cooked meals for themselves there but kept the door shut to avoid being ridiculed by the officers, who didn't want the women bringing their "gook" food into the club. Before long, several officers were enjoying their meal and complimenting the young women on their cooking skills. So impressed were they that it became a once-a-month tradition at the club to have the waitresses provide dinner for the officers using ingredients from the mess hall.

As the night wore on and the alcohol flowed, someone brought out a guitar, and I played some of their favourites. Drunken singing filled the club, and the requests kept coming. I've always had a limited tolerance for alcohol, and around 11 PM, I finished off the gig with everyone's favourite; "We gotta get outa this place if it's the last thing we ever do". Given where we were, the irony of that last line was completely lost on us.

I went straight to bed and was awakened from a deep sleep by a loud knocking at my door.

"Yes, what is it?"

"Sir, you're needed down at the Operations Office". I checked the time; 0030 (12:30 AM).

"Why, what's going on?" I was dazed and confused. The combination of the excessive flying and the late night at the club had knocked me out.

"A mission came in from Battalion Headquarters; you need to come right away, Sir."

"No, no, no; I flew yesterday. It's my day off. I only just got to bed. Why can't they get someone who's rostered to fly today?"

"Sir, it's a TAC-E, and they're all still at the Officers' Club."

"Damn!" I jumped out of bed and started to get dressed. A Tactical Emergency meant that US troops were in a battle and urgently needed supplies. I would have to save my protests for my return from the mission. "OK, I'll be there in five minutes."

I grabbed my flight gear and hustled down to the Ops Office.

I was greeted by smiling, slow-talking Captain Griffith, our Operations Officer. He had clearly also been woken out of bed, and he spoke even more slowly than normal. "Mac, we er, we just got a call (long pause) from er (long pause) from Battalion." Only Captain Griffith could take so long to say such a brief and urgent statement and still not get to the point. I interrupted him. "I'm not rostered to fly; why didn't you get one of the rostered guys?"

He gave my question some deep thought, or maybe he was still trying to wake himself up. "We just couldn't get anyone else Mac."

"You mean they're all too drunk or too tired to take the mission. Did you tell 'em it's a Tac-E?" He looked like he was about to doze off.

"Ok, Ok, what's the mission? Where're we going?"

He resumed his sleepy drawl; "We got this call from Battalion for a TAC-E. I've got the coordinates right here. Let's see..."

His super-slow delivery was driving me crazy. I couldn't wait for him to finish. "I'm heading down to the aircraft. You can have someone brief me in the air. Who's my co-pilot?" I was already heading out the door.

"We're still trying to find you a co-pilot; I'll send him right down to the aircraft."

As I hurried to the flight line, I saw Captain Davis coming out of the Officers' Club. "I'll be right there, Mac. I just need to grab some gear."

This was really getting crazy. Captain Davis was a Staff Officer at Battalion Headquarters. He came down to our Company once or twice a month to get some flight time and maintain his pilot currency. He had flown with me before, including the time we were brought down by shrapnel from a mortar attack. He outranked me, but in the aircraft, I was in Command. He seemed impressed by my ability – it can't hurt to have a senior staff officer on your side – but right now, he had been drinking all night at the club. This was going to be one hell of a night tactical emergency mission.

As I was about to start the engines, he came hurrying up to the cockpit. "Sorry to take so long, Mac; I had to borrow a helmet from one of the guys. Don't know what the hell I did with mine. Must have left it up at Battalion. Where're we going?"

"Don't know yet. Give Ops a call and get the mission. I'll take off and head north. I'm betting the trouble is somewhere up around the Tay Ninh area.

The battle was near a firebase north and west of Tay Ninh; no surprise there. The infantry was in a firefight and calling for artillery support from the batteries at the firebase. But The artillery batteries were running out of ammunition. Our mission was to pick up a load of artillery ammo at Tay Ninh and deliver it to the firebase, then return for a second load. The sky was overcast, and once we left Tay Ninh with our load, we would have no horizon. We would have to be on instruments until the firebase sent up a flare to mark their location.

As we got closer to Tay Ninh, we discussed how we would divide the high pilot workload involved in flying into a black void with eight thousand pounds of explosive artillery shells swinging beneath the aircraft, a perfect recipe for disorientation and vertigo. We made it to Tay Ninh without incident, and Captain Davis took the controls and hooked up our load. He seemed alert and on the ball, as we left the lights of Tay Ninh behind and headed northwest toward the Cambodian border. Outside the cockpit, there was nothing for our eyes to lock on to. Everything was completely black. The jungle and overcast sky were blended into total darkness. We relied on heading, airspeed, and time to get us to the vicinity of the firebase. We turned off our external lights and traded flying duties every five or six minutes to avoid a build-up of pilot fatigue. The heavy load beneath the helicopter and the lack of any external visual references required intense concentration to maintain control of the helicopter.

When we thought we were within a couple of miles of the base, we made radio contact. They sent up a flare to guide us. Fifteen seconds later, they sent up a second flare. The two flares, one higher than the other, were the only visual references available outside the cockpit. Our eyes instinctively tried to use them as a horizon, creating a conflict between what we were seeing on our flight instruments (reality) and what we were seeing outside (illusion). We decided that the pilot at the controls would stay on instruments while the other would search for the firebase.

As we got closer, the light from the descending flares slowly made the terrain visible, and I made out the outline of the firebase. I gave heading directions to the co-pilot and had him begin his descent. When we were properly lined up for the approach, I took the controls to complete the descent to the dimly lit firebase. As we crossed the firebase perimeter, the downwash from our rotors began to set off trip flares in the barbed wire. These were intended to light up any enemy fighters trying to penetrate the perimeter under cover of darkness. Now we were momentarily blinded by the sudden bright light against our night-adjusted eyes. There would also be anti-personnel mines in the perimeter, and I silently prayed that we wouldn't set one off with four tons of explosive shells hanging below us. We gently set the load down and released it from our hook, then headed for the dark sky. I was silently thankful that I was not down on that firebase in the middle of the jungle, waiting for the enemy mortar shells and the next wave of attacks to emerge out of the darkness.

We returned to Tay Ninh, picked up the second load, and delivered it without further incident. We then made a refueling stop in Tay Ninh before heading back to our base at Bear Cat. On the way there, the clouds began to clear, and I commented to Captain Davis how beautiful the sky looked with so many stars. I got no response, and when I looked over at him, he was fast asleep with his head propped against the half-open window and his mouth open. He stayed that way until we touched down at Bearcat. As he sat up and looked around, I said, "You're home Captain, and thanks. You did a great job".

Stevens

Flying combat assaults in Hueys during my first year, the focus had been on specific battles and searches for the enemy. We regularly drew enemy fire, and our perspective on the war was based on these daily kill-or-be-killed encounters. The logistical nature of our Chinook operations during my second year afforded a much broader perspective on the war. Moving tons of material all over our area of operations every day, it was easier to appreciate the massive scale of the effort and resources the US was throwing into this fight. Yet the Vietcong, despite the tons of bombs dropped on them every day, despite the many battles they continued to lose to overwhelming US firepower, always came back fighting with courage and determination. Everything I'd read about the Vietnamese people was being validated as the war dragged on with no end in sight. After so many years of subjugation and exploitation by the Chinese, the Japanese, and the French, the Vietnamese simply refused to be dominated by any foreign power, no matter the cost.

As the war ground on with no end in sight, I tried to see the war from the point of view of the Vietcong fighters. For them, submission to a foreign power was not an option. I began to see the folly of asking Vietnamese villagers to support the foreigners who just used napalm to incinerate half their village, including their family members and neighbours. As a soldier, I was still fully dedicated to my job and our mission. But the continued destruction and loss of life began to seem doubly tragic as the likelihood of achieving our ultimate objective seemed more and more remote. As we flew our daily missions and played our part in defeating the enemy, we didn't know that our top government leaders had already realized that we could not win the war.

Around this time, and with no explanation, I was asked to report to the Commanding Officer, Major Dolan. I had no idea what I might have done. But nevertheless, I prepared myself to make no excuses and firmly committed to doing better in the future. To my complete surprise, he said he had been getting good reports about me, and he had followed my development and observed the way I conducted myself. He wanted me to apply for a direct commission from Warrant Officer to 1st Lieutenant. He was confident my application would be approved. Relief. Shock. Joy. In roughly that order. I thanked him, saluted, and set about doing as he suggested. After several weeks, the Company was assembled, awards were presented, and I was promoted to 1st Lieutenant. I was being commended as a soldier just as I was having growing concerns about our chances of "winning" the war. But I was now increasingly self-assured in taking a greater leadership role at B company.

I'd been pleased to see Warrant Officer Marcus Stevens join our Company. During my brief assignment as a Tactical Training Officer in Flight school, Candidate Marcus Stevens was one of my students and had stood out because of his willingness to provide help and support to some of the younger students who were having a rough time of it and were in danger of failing. Stevens had been a Sergeant with several years' Army experience before being accepted into flight school. He had a lazy southern drawl revealing his roots in the deep South. I had commended him for his patience and kindness in working with the struggling students. Because of his maturity and strong performance in flight school, he was assigned to go on to Chinook school upon graduation from flight school. I was, therefore, pleased to see him join the ranks of B Company Chinook pilots.

As I sat in the club late one afternoon chatting with one of the other Instructor Pilots, I thought I glimpsed over my shoulder a sudden movement at the bar. The bar was up on a small stage, and the other instructor and I were sitting at a table down on the floor of the club. I looked up to where Warrant Officer Stevens, with his back to us, was chatting (I thought) with one of the Vietnamese waitresses who was tending the bar. Just then, she jumped backwards away from him in response to something he had said to her. The instructor I was chatting with was facing the bar. He said, "Did you see that?"

I said, "What's he saying to her?"

He said, "Mac, he spit at her!"

I stood up and turned around to get a better view. Stevens took a small sip of his drink and spat it towards her. She moved further away. I rushed up toward the bar. "Stevens, what the hell are you doing?" The waitress came forward again as I approached. Stevens quickly repeated his gross action, this time hitting her full on the front of her blouse. She jumped backward again, then bent forward to shake the liquid from her blouse. Stevens spat a small ice cube in her direction. It fell harmlessly on the floor. By this time, I was close enough to see that he was very drunk. I looked directly at him. "I want you out of this club right now!" He looked at me with a slight smirk that seemed to say, "Vietnamese are lower than dirt, so what's the big deal?" and spat another bit of ice in her direction.

"Now! Or you're in serious trouble!" I could feel the anger rising, and struggled to maintain my composure, especially as he was quite a bit bigger and taller than me. He stumbled off the bar stool, almost falling off the stage, and mumbling something about f***ing gooks, drifted drunkenly toward the door and out of the club.

As the minutes passed, I only grew angrier. This was the behaviour of a racist occupier and would-be colonizer, albeit a drunk one. I learned that this was not the first time he had spat at one of the women. I was full of rage. I felt I had to do something, or I would explode. As the newest Commissioned Officer, I was now in charge of the Officers' Club. I went to the First Sergeant and asked him to inform all the Officers that there would be an Officers meeting in the club at 2000 hours (8 PM).

At eight, all officers were assembled in the club. The Executive Officer and Commanding Officer joined me on the stage. The XO asked if he could make a few announcements. When he was finished, he quietly told me that Major Dolan, the CO, would close the evening with a few words to the Officers. With the CO a few feet behind me, I got straight to the point. "An Officer was today observed sitting at this bar and spitting his drink at one of the waitresses doubling as a bartender. I understand it's not the first time this Officer has been seen doing that. I don't care how you feel about the Vietnamese or anyone else, including how you feel about me. These women are employed here to do a job. Everyone who works at this club will be treated with proper respect." - my voice was rising – "These people do a damn fine job as far as I'm concerned. Furthermore, that kind of behaviour is completely unbecoming of an Officer of the United States Army and reflects poorly on all of us. If that's the way you would treat someone because they're different from you..."

The Commanding Officer sensed, with some alarm, where I was going. He stepped forward and said to me in a low voice, "Good job, Mac; I'll take it from here."

In a voice amplified by anger, I said, too loudly, "Sir, I'm not finished", and continued speaking to the group. "If that's the way you see people who look different from you, then you might as well just cut the crap and call me nigger-boy to my face and spit your drink at me!"

I was out of control; Major Dolan stepped quickly to the front of the stage. "OK, gentlemen, let's make sure we conduct ourselves properly at all times and always respect the decorum of the Officers' Club. I have a few announcements; I know you guys are all heavily overworked, and you're doing a fine job out there every day..."

I stepped off the stage with the rage still building inside. To me, racial slurs were still like water off a duck's back. I hadn't been in the US long enough to appreciate how deeply offensive they were. But assaulting someone because of their race was intolerable. That is what Stevens had done earlier. It had left me shaken and confused about my fellow officers. What kind of people were they? Our lives depended on each other every time we went out on missions. Here in Vietnam, I was learning more about the dark underside of American society than I had in my few short years in the US.

I figured I was in trouble with the CO for my outburst, and I really didn't care. But neither Major Dolan nor anyone else ever said anything to me about my little speech. His last words that night were, "Stevens! My office, zero seven hundred hours tomorrow."

As far as I know, the incident was never repeated.

Cambodia

On 1 May 1970, the "Something Big" that we had been expecting for a few weeks finally happened. Our Commander-in-Chief, President Richard Nixon, announced to the American people and the world that we were going into Cambodia. It was the start of the Cambodian Incursion.

Early that morning, several of our Chinooks headed up toward the Tay Ninh area. As the highway leading into Tay Ninh came into view, I saw for the first time a scene that seemed taken directly from a World War Two movie. Heading towards Tay Ninh were miles of military vehicles – battle tanks, armoured personnel carriers (APC), Army trucks of various sizes – with occasional civilian vehicles mixed in. We swooped down low to get a close look at this unusual scene and to be part of the excitement. Troops atop the long military convoy waved excitedly as we flew low overhead. They seemed eager to be taking the fight to the enemy on a scale that more truly reflected the conventional capability of the US military.

Nixon was keen to reassure allies and adversaries that he was not expanding an already unpopular war. He stressed that the US was not attacking Cambodia and described the action as a "limited incursion". Two of those limitations would have a significant impact on our operations. The first was that our footprint on Cambodian territory should be minimal; upon leaving, there should be no long-term evidence of the US military presence in the country. The second was a limitation on time; we had to be out of Cambodia by a date which the President made public. Both these requirements worked in favour of the enemy and put us at a disadvantage.

When going into new areas in Vietnam, US forces would first establish a well-fortified base equipped with one or more artillery batteries to provide artillery support for the infantry. These bases were easily identifiable from the air and included a designated logistics helipad that was free of obstacles that could pose a danger to helicopters. In the Cambodia operation, things were more haphazard, especially in the early phases of the operation.

We received an early morning mission to pick up a load from a location in Cambodia and take it to one of our bases across the border from Tay Ninh. The troops on the ground were discovering large military complexes that included training facilities, a wide range of supplies capable of supporting entire regiments, and huge underground storage facilities full of brand-new weapons and ammunition stored separately. We got to the pick-up coordinates but saw nothing but a green jungle canopy in every direction. We made radio contact and asked them to pop a smoke grenade, so we could find them. After a few minutes, there was still no sign of them, and we began to worry that we were given the wrong coordinates. Then they called and said they could see us circling right above them. We slowed the Chinook and asked them to let us know when we were directly over them. Laying on his stomach and peering down through the door on the floor, the crew chief spotted them moments before they called up to us. They had cleared a couple of large trees to allow us to come in. But the surrounding jungle canopy was so thick that they could only be seen from directly above. The smoke from the smoke grenade had dissipated through the surrounding trees and never got above the treetops.

Jungle bases in Vietnam had the trees cleared back at least a hundred meters from the defensive perimeter, and the logistics helipad was sited and constructed by trained soldiers. The space the troops had cleared for us to come in may have seemed wide enough from the ground but was very tight for a Chinook. We'd have to hover straight down from over a hundred feet up and do it very carefully. With the crew chief looking out the forward cabin window and the gunner looking out the rear ramp, we started down. About halfway down, there was a tree branch obstructing the forward rotor. I asked the crew if we had any clearance to the rear. They said it was tight; we couldn't go any further backwards. Then the crew chief said, "Sir, if you make a 90-degree turn to the left, we may be able to get in."

"Ok, coming left."

"Keep coming, keep coming, ok we're clear to the rear".

Our forward rotor was now clear of the tree branch, and we eased the Chinook down very slowly. As we approached the bottom, we realized we could not land. The ground was very uneven, and there were several fallen trees and four-foot-high tree stumps. This was extremely dangerous for a hovering helicopter. Hemmed in on all sides by dense jungle, it felt as if we'd been sucked into a prehistoric world from which we might never emerge. Then we saw a guy standing on a massive tree stump about thirty feet ahead of us, holding up the sling, ready to snap it onto our hook. He clearly thought we had enough clearance to make that pickup, but our rotor blades would be too close to the trees. We hovered over towards him with the tree branches flaying wildly in the rotor downwash. As we got close, the crew chief began directing us from his position over the door on the floor. "Forward five". The tree branches were flying up and down close to the forward rotor. "Forward three, two, hold, hold, down one, hold, load's on the hook."

"Ok, chief, I'm coming back a bit before I pick the load up". I eased the aircraft backwards a few feet to get some clearance from the tree ahead of us, then brought in the power and lifted the load off the ground. Hovering a few feet off the ground requires significantly more power than a normal cruise flight. A high hover – above fifty feet in a Chinook – requires even more engine power. We quickly did a rough calculation of our power reserve. We would need that extra engine power to lift the load straight up for about a hundred and fifty feet, a manoeuvre that requires far more power than a normal forward take-off.

With leaves and twigs blowing up around us, we turned the aircraft around and hovered back to the spot where we had come in. I called back to the crew, "We clear, guys?"

"Clear right, Sir."

"Clear Left."

"Clear to the rear."

"Ok, coming out."

We reversed the procedure we had used to get in; up fifty feet, turn 90 degrees to the right to avoid the tree branches, then up past the treetops and away.

The crew chief said, "That was pretty hairy, Sir; it's way too tight in there for a Chinook. I think we trimmed a few branches."

I said, "I really don't want to do that again. I'll call ops and tell them those infantry guys have to do better than that. They're not supposed to clear-cut the forest to build a firebase like they do in Vietnam, but if we have to operate into holes like that, somebody's gonna get hurt. Chief, can you see what's in the load?"

"A" Company Wildcats making a pickup from a prepared site in Vietnam. Sites in Cambodia were unprepared.

"Just a lot of wooden boxes."

"Can you see what's in them?"

Our door gunner was a gun enthusiast from Texas. "Those look like AK47s. If they are, I'm gonna get me one. The grunts must have found a big weapons cache down there."

AK47s were like a form of currency in Vietnam. They were in high demand by both US troops and the South Vietnamese.

Somebody was always willing to trade something of value for one of the weapons, especially one in mint condition.

We spent the rest of the day going into other rough man-made holes in the jungle and pulling out loads of enemy weapons and ammunition. In one of these holes, we saw a Chinook from one of our sister companies sitting at an awkward angle on the unprepared ground with tree stumps and fallen trees scattered about. The Chinook, lifeless with its engines and rotors stopped, looked incongruous as if it had been stolen and hidden in this man-made cavern deep in the remote Cambodian jungle. The crew were nowhere in sight.

We dropped off the load of equipment we had brought in, hooked up another load of weapons and ammunition, and headed out. We called back to base at Bearcat and asked about the Chinook asleep in the jungle. They said a crew was on its way to the aircraft but gave no further details. Later that night, over drinks at the Officer's Club, one of the older instructor pilots told the story of what happened, a story we were never able to either verify or debunk.

C Company was based at a location about 45 minutes away from Bearcat. The previous night at their Officers Club, there was a lively session of hangar flying and war stories, a regular pastime among pilots at the club after hours. The topic turned to emergency procedures – what if you lose a generator or get a low oil pressure warning on a high-priority mission – with lively discussions of the options available depending on the specific circumstances. One of the new pilots who had arrived at the unit a couple of days earlier asked. "What if you get a blade strike coming out of a tight LZ?"

One of the more experienced instructors, working on his fifth beer, blurted out, "Pull One and Two to STOP." (i.e., Shut off both engines) The group broke out in loud laughter at the instructor's joke. Rotor blade strikes on foliage at the end of tree branches were rare, but they did happen and generally caused no damage to the blades. In a severe case, the blades might have to be repaired or replaced, but the helicopter flies just fine with minor damage to its blade tips. In no case would the engines be shut down in flight.

But the new pilot completely and tragically misinterpreted the response. He thought everyone was laughing because the answer to his question was so obvious. He thought the joke was on him.

The next day, as they were climbing out of the site where we had seen the ghostly Chinook, there was a sound like the staccato of enemy gunfire. The new pilot said, "What's that?"

It was the sound of the rotor tips slapping leaves and twigs at the end of tree branches. The crew chief answered, "I think we had a blade strike, Sir".

The new co-pilot shouted, "One and Two to STOP!" and, in one swift move, shut down both engines. The instructor pilot did a standard hovering autorotation, but with no clear landing spot at the site, settled onto a tree stump, which punctured the belly of the aircraft. No one was hurt, but a maintenance crew had to be brought out to assess the damage. The maintenance crew determined that the damage was limited to the aircraft's skin. No major systems were affected. After a thorough inspection, they cranked up the engines and gingerly lifted the aircraft off the tree stump, and flew it back to their base.

Incidents like this may well have contributed to an easing of the restrictions that had been imposed on forest clearing operations in Cambodia. But the main reason was probably the sheer scale of the enemy storage facilities hidden beneath the jungle canopy. So vast was the network of equipment, ammunition, and weapons storage facilities that a dirt runway had to be quickly constructed to allow C130 Cargo planes to come in and move the stuff out. First, we lifted in bulldozers and other heavy equipment with our Chinooks to construct the runway. Then we moved hundreds of tons of enemy supplies and equipment from their jungle sites to the helicopter landing pad near the new runway. From there, they were loaded onto the C130s and flown out. This operation continued day after day for weeks.

Heading to my room after a long day in the cockpit, I noticed that our supply officer had sealed up his room using plywood panelling and installed air-conditioning. I had seen pallets of plywood being stored at the back of the aircraft maintenance hangar and assumed they were just for normal base maintenance and upgrade, such as additional offices and other facilities. But an air-conditioned room was a real luxury, and I was curious to know how the supply officer got authorization to upgrade his room. When I asked one of the pilots, he laughed. "Are you kidding me? All those AK47s and Russian Officers' pistols we've been pulling out of Cambodia, they're like gold, man. You can get anything for just one of those. How do you think we got all the plywood and A/C units? We're fixing up the Officer's Club. It's really starting to look nice inside. The sergeants have already done theirs. Everyone's taking at least an AK47 back to the States when they leave. You've got one, right?"

Not being a gun enthusiast, I smiled and shook my head. "Don't worry, I'm fine", I said. He gave me a weird look. "Check with Schriver upstairs; he's got some extras, all brand new."

A few days later, as I was leaving the helicopter after completing another flying day, my crew chief handed me a new AK47. "Where'd you get this?" I asked.

"Don't ask; everyone's got one. Direct from Cambodia. We heard you hadn't got one." Growing up in relatively peaceful Trinidad, I never acquired the American fetish for guns, despite my American military training and combat experience. I kept the thing in my room until, several weeks later, one of the new pilots stopped by my room and was admiring it. He had arrived in Vietnam after the Cambodian operation had ended. He picked up the rifle and caressed it as if it were a priceless artwork. When I told him he could have it, he didn't believe me and handed it back to me. "No, no, it's yours; I've already got one," I said, eager to get rid of it. I made his day. He got his coveted war souvenir.

The tonnage of weapons and supplies amassed by the North Vietnamese in their Cambodian jungle depot began to seem endless. As the deadline for leaving Cambodia approached, the troops on the ground began destroying the supplies in place using explosives. B Company was becoming saturated with AK47s and Russian Officers' sidearms.

"Hey Mac, guess what; 'A' Company's built a swimming pool."

"A what?!" I shouted in disbelief.

"Yeah, it's almost finished. They just need the pump and filter system, and they'll have the only swimming pool in Bearcat."

"How are they gonna get that? It's not like there's a bunch of them sitting in their supply room", I said sarcastically.

"Just like they got the cement and the rest of the stuff to build the pool – from Saigon Sam. A few Russian Officer's 9mm pistols ought to do the trick."

I was still incredulous and chuckled to myself as an image took shape in my head. After a hard day's combat flying, dodging enemy mortars and bullets, you come back to base, grab a quick shower, then do a few laps in the pool. On days when you don't have to fly, you lounge by the pool with two or three female nurses in swimsuits who also happen to have some much-needed time off.

Saigon Sam was legendary among troops serving within reach of Saigon by road or helicopter. It was claimed that Saigon Sam could get you anything you wanted if you could meet his price. For a swimming pool pump and filter system, weapons were not what he wanted. From a Chinook helicopter company, Saigon Sam needed something quite different, something only a Chinook could deliver.

Work had recently been completed on the expansion of the highway that ran east from Saigon past Bien Hoa and Long Binh. A bulldozer, grader, and some other heavy road-building equipment had remained parked in a staging area about fifty yards off to the side of the new, improved highway just a few miles outside Saigon. At ten o'clock one morning, a military "Jeep" from A Company showed up at the staging area. Three of the soldiers went over to where the heavy equipment was parked and began working on one item. Ten minutes later, a Vietnamese police vehicle pulled up next to the A Company vehicle. The Vietnamese cops asked if everything was OK. The 1st Cav driver greeted them pleasantly and said everything was fine. Just then, a Chinook could be seen making an approach to the area where the soldiers were working. The driver of the A Company vehicle explained to the Vietnamese policemen that the Chinook was about to land there. The alert policemen, quickly grasping the situation, immediately moved to stop the highway traffic in both directions to facilitate the operation. As the A Company Chinook came to a hover, one soldier quickly attached a sling to the hook, and the Chinook flew off with a giant Sheep's Foot Roller, a piece of highway construction equipment used for compacting soil during road construction. This giant roller was Saigon Sam's price for a swimming pool pump and filter system. A Company got their swimming pool, complete with pump and filter system, even as the war raged on around them. And Saigon Sam got his Sheep's Foot Roller.

As the time for leaving Cambodia drew close, the situation grew tense. The enemy fighters knew that we'd be heading back across the border soon, and their preferred time for going on the attack was when their enemy went into retreat. In the early days of the operation, they had vanished into the forest, leaving a vast arsenal of weapons and ammunition behind. Now they were returning, making quick probing attacks on our makeshift bases and disappearing back into the jungle.

On the final day of the operation, we received the unusual mission to pick up a load of ground troops from one of the last remaining bases and return them to Tay Ninh. Our Chinook had seats and seat belts for thirty-three troops, but we could easily lift twice that number if the mission required it. A Huey company was normally used to move an infantry company or battalion. Chinooks were used to move equipment that was too heavy for a Huey to lift. It was rare for Chinooks to be used for a troop extraction from a hostile area. But the clock was ticking, and we had to meet the President's deadline.

We arrived over the location, and things on the ground looked very strange. There was no fortified perimeter, no fifteen-foot berm protected by several strands of barbed wire, no bunkers, and no artillery. All the heavy equipment had already been pulled out by other Chinooks. The site had been levelled so that the jungle would reclaim the area in the shortest possible time. But this was crazy; there was nothing that could be used as cover or protection if the troops came under attack. As we landed at the site, the Crew Chief lowered the rear ramp, and the troops prepared to get on board. From my window, I suddenly saw the troops on my side dive to the ground, trying to fit into any small depression they could use for protection. I checked the rearview mirror to get a sense of what was happening. I saw an explosion about two hundred meters directly behind us. Then another about fifty meters closer. The Vietcong were back, and their mortars were walking a direct line to where we were sitting.

"Chief, raise the ramp; we're out of here". As we lifted off, I heard the next explosion, which meant it was dangerously close. The enemy mortar gunner was perfectly aligned with the direction of our aircraft as it sat on the ground. He knew we would land into the wind and that we had poor visibility to our rear. But he didn't know we had a rear-view mirror in the cockpit. His plan was too perfect. Had he been a few degrees to the left or right, I would not have seen the explosions in the rear-view mirror, and we would have been seriously damaged or destroyed by a mortar shell.

As we climbed quickly to a safe altitude, I thought about how often, in this war, the difference between disaster and success comes down to dumb luck. I called our contact on the ground. No answer. We orbited the site for a few minutes and tried again to make contact. Still no answer. We circled and waited.

"Longhorn 238, we've got several casualties here, over."

"Roger. Are you still under fire, over?"

"It's calmed down a bit. We need to get these wounded guys out."

"We're on our way."

We made a rapid descent and landed where we had previously. The troops began loading their injured buddies on board. The smell of severe wounds wafted up to the cockpit. Another mortar shell hit two hundred meters behind us, just as it had previously. "How are we doing, Chief?"

"One more guy, Sir. I think he's the last." Another mortar burst closer in. This must be the same mortar crew. "Ramp up, Chief". I began to bring in the power. "They're just bringing him on now, Sir." I held our position and counted; one, two, three . . .

The Crew Chief shouted, "Ramp's up; we got him." I pulled in maximum power and jumped the Chinook away from the site. As we climbed out, we saw two Cobra gunships coming in to suppress the enemy activity on the ground and allow the remaining troops a chance to be pulled out safely. We headed for Tay Ninh, where a medical team was waiting for us. We dropped off the wounded troops and headed back out to the site with the afternoon sun dropping lower over the Cambodian jungle. We got there just as the last of the ground troops were being pulled out by another Chinook. The enemy mortar had been silenced by the Cobras. We followed them back to Tay Ninh, then refueled and headed for Bearcat.

The Crew Chief came up on the intercom: “Couple o’ them guys was tore up pretty bad. You know, Sir, for the President to go on TV and tell the VC exactly when we’re leavin’ and then order our troops to destroy all their defences before pulling out, that’s just suicide.”

The door gunner chimed in: “Everyone knows we’re in there, he announced it to the whole damn world. So why are we gitt’n good soldiers killed, just so he can say we never went in there? If we’re givin’ up goddamit, let’s just git out and go home. We’re getting our asses shot off every day just so them big wigs can save face. They oughta make some o’ them politicians come along with us and see what they’re doing to their own troops.”

But it was worse than that. What we didn’t know then and would only learn years later was that our decision-makers in Washington had already decided to pull the plug on the US involvement in the war. Those soldiers who had just been torn open by enemy mortars had been sacrificed to allow the US time to devise a respectable exit from the war, and disguise its failure, despite its military superpowers, to achieve its objective in Vietnam.

My co-pilot said sarcastically to the crew chief and gunner, "You know the drill guys, same as always, ours is just to do and die." He paused and glanced at me with a smile, then said, "Between you and me, I think we came too damn close to dyin' back there. You guys did a great job getting those wounded guys out. It could have been much worse. We just do our job and hope we live to tell about it."

I said, "If the President and his advisers knew anything about a tropical rainforest, they would have known there was no need to destroy the bunkers to remove evidence of our presence. A few sandbag bunkers that could have saved the lives of many soldiers would be completely swallowed up by the jungle in a few months. After one monsoon season, you'd never know they'd ever been there."

Within weeks of wrapping up what was hailed as a highly successful military operation into Cambodia, the North Vietnamese and Vietcong had returned and restocked their Cambodian bases across the border from Tay Ninh.

Over three hundred US soldiers had died in the two-month Cambodian operation.

We were now into July 1970, and my second year of war in Vietnam was coming to an end in a month. Going home as a soldier in a victorious army was not something I had ever thought about. My focus had always been on being the best military helicopter pilot I could be. That seemed to me to be the best way to serve my new country as a soldier. Like most Americans, I had internalized the idea that the mighty US military could not lose a war. We were the good guys, fighting to make the world a better place by defeating the forces of evil. One part of me continued to expect that we would achieve our goal and go home, while another part of me was being worn down by the apparent futility of it all. But this did not feel like an inner conflict; the two states existed within me simultaneously, and I felt perfectly normal. Ideology and military indoctrination were in a head-on collision with daily experience and observation. To preserve my sanity and my ability to function effectively, the two were being kept apart in my overstimulated psyche.

The most powerful countries often seem to bend their history and self-image towards their more heroic and uplifting aspirations and away from realities that do not conform to the burnished image they wish to project to the world and to themselves. In support of their leader, many citizens will disbelieve what they observe for themselves and promote as truth what they know to be false. As I reflected on the appalling human savagery that had become normal life in Vietnam with no redeeming consequence, no "Well, at least we ______ (fill in the blank)", I tried to take comfort in the thought that we would never again make a similar mistake. But there were still many advocates of a further expansion of the war; as one reporter put it, some leaders seemed to be saying, we can put humpty-dumpty back together again – we just need *more* horses and *more* men. Others seemed to advocate destroying North Vietnam to save it from communism.

To me, each side in the war had a simple overarching objective: The North Vietnamese objective was to unite the country under their communist system; the US objective was to prevent the North Vietnamese and the Vietcong from uniting the country under their communist system, and "allow" South Vietnam to become a Western-style capitalist democracy. The outcome is a fact of history too well documented to be easily moulded into something that fits comfortably into America's proud narrative. But that fact remains culturally unacceptable to many Americans.

So we don't talk about it. We make great movies about things that happened in the war, and we talk about those movies, the heroes, the great scenes. But we don't talk about the war. We built the Vietnam War Memorial in our Nation's Capital, and we talk about the memorial from time to time. But we don't talk about the war, the terrible war that cost all those lives and gained us nothing. Not talking about the war is the best way to keep it buried in the crypt where so many other unpleasant facts of our history, too painfully incongruent with

America's cherished view of itself, wait restively to be accepted as an integral part of who we are and what we did. The extent to which that effort at denial has been successful can be measured by the extent to which the lessons of the Vietnam War have been forgotten or ignored and the mistakes repeated.

Goodbye Vietnam

My 4:30 am alarm went off, but I was already awake. I got up, took a shower in the Officer's common shower room, got dressed, and prepared to head down to the mess hall for breakfast and the daily mission brief before heading out on the day's missions. Two long weeks to go before heading home. It was still dark outside. I opened my locker and grabbed my flight helmet, flak jacket, bulletproof breastplate, and leather holster with a .45 calibre side arm issued to all officers in the unit. I looked at the weapon for about two seconds, put it back into the locker, locked it, and went down to breakfast with the rest of my gear. I was relaxed, tired – we were always tired – and didn't give the matter another thought. It was as if I'd left my baseball cap behind because I'd grown tired of it.

The Operations Officer stopped in the middle of his mission briefing to the assembled flight crews and said to me, "Where's your weapon, Mac?" I should have been prepared for the question, but I wasn't. I didn't have an explanation. I blurted out, "Oh, it's OK, it's safe. It's locked up."

He waited a moment for the rest of my explanation, then said to the whole room, "You're required to carry your weapon at all times when you're out on missions. I don't want to see anyone going out there without their weapon. You just might need it to protect your ass if you get shot down or..."

I interrupted him, surprising myself with the strength of my response. "Look, Steve, we can spend the day making a Federal case out of this, or I can go fly the Chinook, OK?" I could feel my anger rising from my chest in a rush without knowing why I was suddenly so angry or who I was angry at. I was risking my Army career without knowing why. I was as surprised as he was by my outburst. He chose to go with the second of my two options, closing the subject with "Just don't go out there without your weapon," before continuing with his mission briefing. He knew that his Chinook aircraft commanders were overworked and stressed out. He knew that I gave 100% whenever I went on a mission. I never questioned or refused a mission. He knew I was highly respected by seniors, subordinates, and peers. I was his Standardization Instructor Pilot, the most senior Chinook pilot in the company. My year was almost up; I would be going home soon. He knew I was weary of the futile war, even if I didn't know it.

For the final week or two of my tour, I never carried a weapon, and no further mention was made of it. Everyone except me seemed to understand. It didn't occur to me then that it might have been interpreted as a protest against the war or an act of defiance of military procedures. It was neither of those, and fortunately for me, no one else was stupid enough to follow my example. As my time to leave Vietnam for the second time approached, I continued to fly missions, giving my best to our effort right up to the end. But I was somehow lighter, freer, and more complete without the cold weight of the .45 calibre weapon strapped to my waist.

Many years later, as I struggled to draw meaning and value from my two years of war, I realized that when I had picked up my weapon early that morning, I'd felt silly. Every day and every night, there were Air Force B-52s and F-4 Fighter Bombers, Army heavy artillery, naval sixteen-inch guns, grenade launchers, and heavy machine guns, weapons of every description, all blasting away at enemy targets day in and day out, year after endless year. And I had my little gun, so I could do my little share of the killing.

All this killing may not be the whole story of how wars are won, but it is the part the military plays in the struggle to win. And it had been my duty to play my part if called upon. So how could I have done that, left my weapon in my room? Looking back, maybe I did not have the makeup of the complete soldier. Maybe I was less than 100% soldier. Maybe two years of unrelenting futile war was enough to make me see that I was not just a soldier; I was a person, I was human. Maybe my mind was trying to protect itself. Maybe there was more behind my strange action. The war had cost me the loss of what was most precious to me – the love of my girlfriend, Nicole. Was I striking back against the war itself? The older I got, the more the questions haunted me.

I remembered how at flight school, everyone's dream, including mine, was to become a gunship pilot, the best of the best. During my first year at the 117th, the best "slick" pilots would apply to be assigned to the gunship platoon. The applicants would be put through an extensive evaluation to assess not only their flying skills but their compatibility with the members of the gunship platoon. It was a real honour to be one of the few selected. I never thought of myself as the calibre of the pilot they would consider, and I never thought of applying. So it came as a shock when I was approached by the gunship pilots to join their ranks. This was regarded by all as a special honour, and for most, rejection of the overture was unthinkable. But over four months of combat assault operations, I had seen what gunships did, and my flight school enthusiasm for the role had gradually faded. I used my best diplomatic skills to say how genuinely honoured I was that they would consider me capable of meeting their rigorous standards. I thanked them for the many times they had saved our lives by putting their lives at risk in a shootout with the enemy. But my decision was firm; I would remain a humble "slick" pilot.

Over my two years of war, had the situation required it, I would have killed enemy soldiers. I am thankful that such a situation never arose. Had I been required to do it by my superiors, I certainly would have flown a gunship. But I think that today, I would be a different person if I had.

I was still a fully committed US Army Aviator and Soldier, proud of my two years of combat service in my new country. But through the long lens of many years of reflection and hindsight, I came to see that by not carrying my weapon, even for that short span of time as my year wound down, I may have failed in my duty as a soldier. My unconscious need to protect my sanity had taken precedence over my duty to protect my fellow soldiers.

We kept looking like we were winning even as we continued to lose. We were winning all the battles; didn't that mean that we would inevitably win the war? The US military build-up in 1967 and 68 was meant to be an early version of "shock and awe", or maybe just another in the long history of attempts at shocks and awe that never achieve their intended outcomes. Faced with the full onslaught of the greatest military power on earth, the foolhardy peasant armies of the Viet Cong and North Vietnamese would have no choice but to recoil in the face of overwhelming firepower and accept the terms imposed by the US to save themselves from the full wrath and fury of "the world's greatest superpower". Surely. But they weren't doing that. Maybe they hadn't seen the movies depicting the heroic triumphs of the Americans in World War two. Facing the full force of the US Army, Navy, Marines, and Air Force – the most highly trained fighting force of more than half a million men and women with the best weapons and equipment in the world - they stubbornly continued to fight us as if we were just a rag-tag collection of fighters and they were the superior military force.

Several years after the end of the war, this is what became public knowledge. By the beginning of 1969, even as we delivered daily supplies to our troops battling the enemy, our Commander in Chief and his advisers in Washington could no longer evade the reality that was unfolding and the enormous problem it presented. By definition, the World's Greatest Superpower cannot lose a war to half of a small, underdeveloped country. But that's exactly what was happening, and that reality was incompatible with America's prevailing concept of itself. Either you win the war, or you're not a superpower. A narrative was needed, a closing chapter to the long war, that would not entail, in any form, the use of the verb "to lose" or the verb "to fail."

To any seasoned politician, the solution to this problem would be obvious: if you can't accomplish the mission, rebrand the mission into one you can claim to have accomplished. The mission was changed from preventing South Vietnam from becoming communist to Vietnamization: make the South Vietnamese responsible for "their" war, then get out (and watch them lose the war). The leaders in Washington even managed to preserve the use of the hallowed verb "to win". America was going to win the peace! But the truth that dared not be uttered was nevertheless obvious to all the world; Americanization of the war had been a monstrous failure. America's ability to project its enormous military might against small or weak adversaries anywhere in the world did not guarantee victory and was, therefore, not a fully reliable deterrent. The military superpower was not invincible.

Embodied in the Vietnamization "solution" was the tragic sacrifice of the thousands of additional soldiers and civilians who would be killed and wounded to minimize America's embarrassment for this colossal miscalculation. Our leaders knew, as surely as we did, that we were just delaying the inevitable outcome. The South Vietnamese Army had no hope of prevailing where the mighty US military had failed. But to have any credibility as a strategy, Vietnamization – the transformation of the weak South Vietnamese military into one that could defeat the North Vietnamese and Vietcong - would require years of effort and expense. During those years, the fighting would go on, and many more soldiers and civilians would die, leaving more families to mourn the loss of their loved ones. This would have a profound effect on many of us still fighting the war.

When a battle is won on the ground, and we've killed many more of them than they've killed of us, we are grateful for our victory and mourn the loss of our fellow soldiers. In our quiet moments, the ugliness and carnage of battle are soothed by the knowledge that it moved us one step closer to accomplishing our overall mission, that we've played our small part in keeping our country safe, and that we served with honour. That sense of mission and purpose is part of what holds our sanity together through the savagery of war. But when the mission has been abandoned by our leaders, yet we are required to fight on with no hope of victory, the concept of honour, so vital to our dignity as soldiers, becomes distorted. We struggle to remain soldiers. Because without honour, we begin the slide towards becoming killers without a cause, unwitting mercenaries, killing and dying in battle to buy time for our leaders to weave a shawl, a shroud, a decent suit of clothes in which to disguise and bury our costly sacrifice, our failure, and move on.

That might explain why one dedicated and decorated Army pilot suddenly went a bit crazy and went out on his last few combat missions without his weapon, without knowing why he was doing it or why he felt so much better without the gun.

As the US gradually disengaged and turned the fighting over to the South Vietnamese, it was often said that no one wanted to be the last American to die in Vietnam for a lost cause. Maybe I did not want to be the last American to kill someone for a lost cause.

Once a war reaches a stalemate, and winning it is no longer considered vital to the security of the United States, it seemed to me that the most honorable option is to quickly negotiate a withdrawal and get out. It may be a major embarrassment to a superpower. But it saves the most lives. Delaying the exit to avoid embarrassment only postpones that embarrassment expends more lives and debases the honor, commitment, and service of the soldiers charged with continuing to fight for a lost cause. The best way to end a lost war is to end it as quickly as possible.

A few weeks before deploying to Vietnam for the first time, a group of new flight school graduates, me included, huddled in the lounge at the Officer's Club at Fort Campbell, Kentucky, listening to a senior infantry officer talk about his experiences in Vietnam. It was a special treat for young pilots, and we hung on to every word as he painted pictures of heroic battles, brilliant tactics, and narrow escapes in places with exotic names we couldn't yet pronounce correctly. His descriptions, some amazing, some tragic, held us spellbound, and as his stories built to an excited finish, he said something that would always come back to me. His eyes lit up, and he became animated as he said, "It's the most exciting game you'll ever play. Nothing else comes even close." Then he paused a moment and lowered his head and his voice. His eyes misted over a little; "It's also the ugliest thing you'll ever be a part of." He stood up; we came to his attention. "Good luck, soldiers." As he headed out the door, we knew he was also saying goodbye to those among us who would never return. He was the highest-ranking African American officer I met during my six years, five months, and ten days of active military service in the US Army.

As I prepared to leave Vietnam for what I hoped would not be the last time, I reflected on the resilience and determination of the Vietnamese people. To us, the US soldiers and our allies, this was a killing contest, one we were clearly winning based on the number of enemy soldiers we were killing. But the North Vietnamese and Vietcong were not doing tours of duty and returning to their faraway peaceful homes, as we were. This <u>was</u> their home. There was nowhere to go back to. For them, this was not just a killing contest. They were fighting for the dignity that comes with deciding for themselves what kind of society they would be, even if the core of that fight was among themselves. It might not be the type of society I would choose, but I am not Vietnamese.

I began to see also that, although I had barely made it through high school, my colonial education in Trinidad had achieved one of its key objectives; that I would think so little of myself on leaving school that I could never pose a threat to the colonial status quo. But emigration provided the chance to step into a new self, to go from colonial high school failure to Captain in the US Army, and to see the legacy of colonialism with clearer eyes.

For hundreds of years, Europeans had fought each other to enrich themselves by enslaving African people and exploiting the resources of the "New World", including Trinidad and Tobago and other Caribbean islands. The social and economic aftershocks of that greed-driven upheaval continue to rattle the structures and foundations of those societies today. Arriving in Vietnam for the first time as a 20-year-old US Army Officer, I would naively dismiss the suggestion that the "freedom for South Vietnam" that we were fighting and dying for might include the freedom for wealthy Western businessmen to further enrich themselves by continuing to exploit Vietnam's resources. As my two years of war slowly wound down, there was one thing I knew without knowing how I knew it: The Vietnamese people will not stop fighting us, no matter how many of them we kill, until we go home and leave them to run their country as they see fit.

One of my last Chinook missions in Vietnam was to take a tank of water to a South Vietnamese unit that had not been resupplied with water for three weeks. All supplies sent by road werc being ambushed. The load was a full two-hundred-gallon water tank mounted horizontally on a two-wheeled trailer but tilted slightly towards the rear dispensing tap. It was normally pulled along behind an Army truck. As we lowered the trailer and tank with its precious water to the landing pad, a few hundred South Vietnamese soldiers, some in just a pair of shorts, came running towards us with their plastic bottles, basins, and buckets, eager to get their share. There seemed to be no one in charge. The powerful downwash from the rotors slowed their approach.

We placed the tank of water gently on the dirt helipad, then hovered backwards and upwards to see how this very unmilitary scene would unfold. As the rotor downwash followed us away from the tank, the crowd closed in. The first three or four to reach the tank jostled to be the first to fill their container from the tap, causing some of the water to flow onto the ground. The group of thirsty soldiers quickly turned into a mob, and the pushing and shoving turned into a chaotic brawl. A young lad in bright red shorts climbed atop the tank, threw open the filling hatch at the top of the tank, and began dipping water into his bucket. Others quickly followed, shoving him off the tank and struggling with each other to get to the top to dip their containers into the tank. Five seconds before it happened, we could foresee the tragi-comic ending. With more bodies scrambling up one side of the tank than the other, it teetered on one wheel for a second in slow motion, then crashed onto its side. With the hatch fully open, all the water poured out onto the ground in one great gush.

My crew and I could not stop ourselves from laughing at the painful scene. We had been diverted from an urgent mission because these guys were in desperate need of water. As we returned to resume our scheduled mission, my crew chief spoke up, "These are the guys that's supposed to take on the North Vietnamese and Vietcong after we leave?"

The North Vietnamese and Vietcong fighters had earned the respect of the US military many times over. The contrast with the South Vietnamese army was painfully on display as the brawl continued below us. But the contrast was even more stark where it mattered most – among the top leadership of the two adversaries. The North Vietnamese leadership had cultivated enduring connections with their people. They successfully inspired their people to make the long and painful sacrifices necessary to achieve the common objective. The

South Vietnamese leadership was widely regarded disdainfully by their people as corrupt puppets of the US. The rabble below us reflected no indication that they would give their all to defend their leaders' cause or their country.

The Big RIF

For the second time in my young life, I prepared to leave my new home for what I was sure would be a break of two or three months in the US before returning to Vietnam. The war was becoming a way of life. You returned to the US every year or so for some training and some time with family before returning home to the war. Our supply officer was a career soldier with over twelve years in the Army. When we younger officers would vent our frustrations about the war, he would sometimes say, "Don't knock it, guys. It's the only war we've got." I was beginning to understand what he meant.

I rang the bell to my parents' New York apartment and tried the door. It was unlocked. Everyone yelled SURPRISE! I entered tentatively, unable to make the sudden switch to party mode. Calypso music filled the apartment. Everyone was clapping and dancing to the rhythm, all eyes on me. I put down my bags. The scene was familiar, but I felt strange and out of place. I stood there with a silly grin on my face, not knowing what to do or what to say. A pretty young woman took my hand as she swayed to the music. Tricia was from Trinidad, not far from where I grew up, and she had that carefree, happy-go-lucky spirit that makes some Caribbean people seem immune to unhappiness. She handed me a drink.

I spent a few weeks on leave in New York with family and friends and Tricia. She lived in a nearby apartment in the same building. We saw a lot of each other over those weeks. She knew many of my friends from Trinidad, and I renewed friendships while learning about New York. It was a welcome bit of rest and relaxation away from the rigors and drudgery of army life, but for me, it was a diversion. My heart was in Vietnam: Lan. I met her just two weeks before leaving. After two years in the country, it finally happened – I was captivated. I had to get back to her.

My next assignment was Infantry Officer School at Fort Benning, Georgia, the US Army Infantry Center. I began to learn the formal military theories underpinning the tactics I'd seen employed by the infantry units in Vietnam. I discovered that a Vietnamese language course was being offered at night on the base. I signed up and began to learn the language I had heard almost daily over the past two years. But I also learned that the US was winding down its operations in Vietnam more rapidly than I expected and turning the fight over to the South Vietnamese. My chances of returning to Vietnam were quickly diminishing. My life began to seem grey and meaningless.

Upon graduation from the Infantry Officer course, I was assigned to a Chinook company at Fort Sill, Oklahoma, home of the Army Artillery Center. The operational tempo at the unit was surprisingly low, and there was relatively little flying compared to my unit in Vietnam. I was about to get a glimpse of what post-war, peacetime army life might be like.

Almost everyone in the unit had done at least one year-long tour in Vietnam and seemed to treat their Ft Sill assignment as a sort of working Rest & Recuperation (R&R). Officers and Sergeants worked a loose schedule that often facilitated relaxed lunches downtown and getting to the golf course by mid-afternoon. The inevitable result of this leadership vacuum could be detected on a casual mid-afternoon walk past the enlisted barracks. The smell of marijuana smoke was unmistakable. Being fresh out of Infantry Officer school, I at first found this alarming. But I quickly realized that this situation was not unknown to our superiors. Everyone had done their time in hell and needed time and space to readjust to normal life, spend time with family, and decompress without the pressures of the early starts and late nights that are part of a high operational tempo. We had proved ourselves in high-intensity combat. We did not need to be whipped into shape, at least not yet.

Fort Sill held all the hidden stresses of another new beginning. At work, getting to know everyone was slow going. There wasn't very much flying – other than the odd natural disaster rescue mission - and pilots sometimes struggled to get the minimum flying hours required to maintain their pilot currency. All the officers seemed to have re-established their social lives, and that did not include me. I was once again "The Black Guy", assumed to have achieved my assignment and rank not based on my ability as reflected in my records but to fill a quota mandated by the government.

As the weeks passed, it became increasingly difficult to evade the reality that I was lonelier here than I had ever been in Vietnam. This was a part of America where whites and non-whites still lived apart from and in fear of each other. There were rules about where you should not go if you were black. They weren't written anywhere, but they were real. *Long's you follow the rules, would'n be no trouble.* An evening out in the unfamiliar segregated town in the hopes of meeting new people held more dangers for me than an air assault into a hot LZ.

Tricia suggested coming out to Ft Sill for a long weekend. Why not. Over many cold lonely nights, I had gilded and polished my memories of the good times we'd had together in New York while dismissing my sense that, beyond the fun, the dancing, and the laughter, we really weren't a good match. She flew out, arriving all bubbly and happy with the world. Five weeks later, before anyone could talk us out of it, we were married. The justice of the peace stepped out of the room briefly to snag two people to witness our marriage. It was a joyful time. I pushed my concerns away and allowed myself to be happy.

Then came the big snowstorm over the winter of 1970-71. A state of emergency was declared for several counties in Arkansas and Kansas. Chinook helicopters were dispatched to aid the relief effort in the hardest-hit communities. My orders were to head out to a rural farming community in Arkansas. We landed at a small rural airport. The snow had been pushed up into a kind of berm at the edge of the field. There were several specialized tractor-trailers parked nearby, all fully loaded with bales of hay. We set the engines to ground idle to reduce the downwash from the rotors.

The crew chief lowered the rear ramp, and one of the locals came up to the cockpit. His uniform identified him as local law enforcement. He started talking to my co-pilot, who referred him to me. There was that moment of involuntary hesitation as he looked back and forth at the two of us. I stuck my hand out and yelled over the aircraft noise: "I'm Captain McIntosh, the Aircraft Commander. Should we shut down, or do you know what you want us to do?"

But I could see in our rear-view mirror that bales of hay were already being loaded onto the aircraft. He was the local sheriff. He opened a map and showed us areas that were highlighted in different colours, some red, some green, others blue and yellow. The crew chief brought him a headset so that we could hear what he was saying. He wanted us to take the hay out to these areas. The colours indicated the various owners of the plots. The hay currently being loaded belonged to the owner of the red plots. The red farmer would come to the cockpit and direct us to his land. He would then show us exactly where the hay should be dropped. The Sheriff then removed his headset and went to get the farmer. The co-pilot said, "Disaster relief for cows? I thought we came to help people snowed in or trapped in their cars."

The crew chief said sarcastically, "I guess you'd have to be a cattleman to understand."

Using the map to navigate, we headed out in the general direction of the red farms, with the farmer providing minor course corrections along the way. He was having difficulty finding his way because of all the snow. The landscape was snow and fence lines with a few trees and the occasional barn and farmhouse. We began to see clumps of cattle huddled against fences or around trees, sometimes just three or four together, sometimes a dozen or more.

"There! Over there, those are mine." From the map, it looked like the storm had driven his cows onto someone else's land. We descended and headed towards where he had pointed. "No, NO! Not those, they're not mine. Over more to the right."

Seemed like the same herd to me, but they were probably tagged. As we approached them, the freezing animals, some up to their bellies in snow, began to panic, struggling to stampede but making little progress. The farmer pointed straight down; we were over his heard.

"OK, Chief, start dumping hay." We hovered forward slowly about fifty feet above the snow as the hapless beasts tried to escape the noisy machine above them, some desperately trying to scale the fence.

The farmer pointed and shouted again, "No, no. Not those two; those aren't mine."

I chuckled and looked across at my co-pilot. The crew chief said, "Once there's hay on the snow, and we're not hovering around scaring the piss out of them cows, they're all gonna join the feast."

We flew around and found a few more of his precious cattle, but some were still unaccounted for, and he seemed genuinely distressed. "Look, over there, I think there's some over there," he'd say, pointing. We'd hurry to the spot and find some logs sticking out of the snow or an outcrop of large rocks swept clean on one side by the wind with snow stacked on the other. We investigated everything that might be a cow in the snow. Eventually, we dumped the rest of the bales near one of the larger herds and headed back to the staging area.

The word had spread around the community. There were now several more tractor-trailers piled high with hay lined up along the road. We flew several more sorties, with each farmer trying to feed his animals without feeding his neighbours'. Around mid-afternoon, the locals brought us sandwiches and drinks. A large fuel tanker showed up, allowing us to refuel and continue our search for lost animals.

At the end of the day, with darkness closing in quickly, we shut down and closed up the aircraft for the night. The Sheriff assured us that his people would provide overnight security. Arrangements had been made for us to stay at a local motel. The Sheriff offered to take us to dinner and then to the motel. He invited me to ride in his patrol car. Despite his disarming smile, I recognized his polite invitation as a gentlemanly directive. We drove no more than a couple of miles and arrived at what appeared to be a sprawling country club.

"Wait here, I'll be right back." There's that smile again. The Sheriff went into the building and returned after a minute or so.

"Stay with me, OK?" I followed him into one of the buildings. It was a large, well-appointed restaurant with a cafeteria-style serving line at one end. There was a separate entrance at the far end, presumably for those who wished to be served at their table rather than making their choices at the cafeteria serving line. There were suits and evening dresses, mostly at the far end, and casual wear and coveralls at our end.

As I followed the Sheriff to the serving line, there was a slight dip in the ambient noise level. Heads turned in our direction, then turned away. Someone was going from table to table, probably explaining that this was the Army pilot in command of the big helicopter that had been keeping their cattle alive and healthy until the roads could be cleared. Even so...

Had I simply arrived there with my crew, I wouldn't have made it to the front door. I may well have been the only black man ever to enter that facility as a customer rather than a worker. The Sheriff may have taken quite a risk bringing me to this place. The guests at one table near the far end pushed their chairs back and left. Two more tables followed. Maybe it meant nothing. Maybe they had finished their meal. Maybe the Sheriff would be dealt with later.

My steak was like none I'd ever tasted. These farmers knew how to keep the best for themselves.

Later that evening, as I settled down for the night, I tried to look at the world through their eyes. They would have grown up in an America that had been won and tamed by gritty heroic white men and their families through hard work and the grace of God. Their ancestors persevered against harsh conditions and attacks by savage Indians, eventually building towns and great cities from coast to coast and border to border. Blacks and people of color were allowed to live and raise their families in their own areas and even get jobs in white areas as long as they obeyed the law and didn't cause trouble. This orderly way of life propelled America to become the greatest nation in the world. But black agitators and their white collaborators began to tear down the systems that had made America great, creating chaos and trying to force hard-working white people to treat black people the same as whites!

These deeply cherished views, artfully woven from half-truths and romanticized fiction, were the stories that these people grew up with. For many of them, this was their truth and the basis of their pride in their country and themselves. This lavish facility was, for them, a sanctuary where they could have the America their ancestors worked so hard to create, where they could be with their own kind and speak their mind without offending some immigrant or coloured person or having to treat them like they're white; cause they're not.

To bring a black man into their space was a desecration.

Of course, these people may not have been like that at all. I realized that my thoughts were, at least in part, a reflection of my own biases. There would certainly have been some diversity of views among the many guests at the facility. Some might be actively working to reduce and eliminate racial discrimination in their communities. My crew and I may have been warmly welcomed had we just shown up and told them who we were. I reminded myself not to make negative assumptions about people I didn't know.

Then again, all those deliberate precautions taken by the Sheriff...

I felt fortunate to be a soldier and an officer. Civilian life in America for a black man seemed chaotic and dangerous. Military life was much more orderly and predictable.

The next day the farmers seemed much more relaxed and approachable. Family members were brought out to see the large twin-rotor helicopter and were given brief impromptu tours of the aircraft. As we prepared to head out, the Sheriff eased the small crowd away from the helicopter. They were treated to a cloud of hay dust as we took off and resumed our bovine search and rescue. We went further afield and found several more strays and, tragically, a few carcasses. By midday, all heads were accounted for. It was time to say our goodbyes and head back to our base at Ft Sill. There were warm handshakes and broad grins as the locals seemed genuinely moved by our efforts to help them recover from the devastating blizzard. Without our help, it would have taken them much longer to get to their animals, and there would have been many more losses. And maybe for just a few of the locals, their image of a black person's role in society may have shifted just a little toward the positive. As we headed towards home, I decided to formally apply to become a career Army Officer by extending my service commitment indefinitely.

A few days later, my crew and I were presented official citations signed by the Governor of Arkansas recognizing our valuable assistance to the State in the aftermath of the terrible blizzard.

I was promoted to Captain and assigned as a staff officer at Battalion Headquarters. This was an important and coveted assignment. I was sure I could handle it. But without the comfort and reassurance of regular flying, my old insecurities threatened to emerge from wherever they had hidden themselves. What was I supposed to be doing? Desk work had always been subordinate to my flying duties. Now the roles would be reversed. A senior staff officer took the role of mentor and guided me through the intricacies of battalion staff work. The battalion commander seemed pleased with my work, and my self-confidence was restored. The army was my world now; it was all I knew, and the future was looking bright. I submitted an application to become a career army officer.

Our first child was born on 8th October 1971, at the Army hospital at Ft Sill. I immediately bonded with my tiny new daughter; each day, the bond grew stronger. I finally had a sense of purpose, a cause to give my all for.

At first, it was whispered furtively among the officers; the big RIF was coming. I was too embarrassed to ask what a big RIF was. I soon learned that a RIF was a Reduction in Forces. Without a war to fight, the army suddenly had far more warfighters than it needed during peacetime. There would be a demobilization. People would be returned to civilian life, involuntarily if necessary. I felt confident I wouldn't be among those being let go.

By late 1971, the US involvement in the war, the savage upheaval that had been, in one way or another, at the center of my life since entering the army, was winding down. Behind the lacey fig leaf of Vietnamization, America was re-clothing its army in the starched tunics and spit-shined boots of peacetime service. The fate of Vietnam would be left in the hands of the Vietnamese. "The only war we've got" was coming to its end. This would be a wrenchingly painful decision for the proud and powerful Army of the United States: to stop fighting, having neither won nor lost, to abandon the cause for which so many fellow soldiers had given their lives. Yet it would also mean sacrificing no more lives for a cause that had been misconstrued from the beginning. Vietnam was never a threat to the United States or its allies. Many years later, I would look back on this decision to stop fighting and go home as heroic in its simplicity: let the Vietnamese people determine their own future; let us mourn our dead in peace.

"The Colonel will see you in his office at 0900 hours tomorrow". Major Droder always looked stressed and unapproachable, as if he were about to be blamed for someone else's screw-up and, out of a deeply ingrained sense of honour, would not consider defending himself.

"Yes, Sir. Do you know what it's about?"

"0900 tomorrow".

Since becoming a Battalion Staff Officer, the feedback from peers and superiors had been all positive. Yet I couldn't help worrying that, in a relaxed or distracted moment, I'd made a serious misstep. I quickly recognized my knee-jerk reflex of protecting myself by expecting the worst and preparing for Licks. Then I remembered my application to become a career officer. Maybe the Colonel wanted to interview me himself before approving the application.

At 0900, a junior officer knocked loudly and then held the door open for me to enter. I stepped in, came to attention, and saluted. He returned my salute and surprised me by inviting me to sit. He surprised me again by complimenting me on a paper

I'd written before being assigned to Battalion Headquarters. We chatted about that for a while, and then he briefly held up a document and returned it to his desk.

"I have your application here. (pause) And I'd be happy to recommend approval. You have an excellent military record; I've been through your file (he slapped a thick folder on his desk). You've been highly decorated; you've shown judgement, leadership, and decisiveness under fire."

He paused again and reclined slightly in his chair.

"We're getting out of Vietnam. We've done all we can for the South Vietnamese. We've been training them to take over the fight for a couple of years now. The Army will be going through a major transition – it's already started, and it's going to be very disruptive. A lot of good people are going to be let go. The qualities you've shown are among the most valued in an officer – during wartime. The ability to get the difficult jobs done with the minimum of casualties, to keep your cool and help others keep theirs when the situation is falling apart fast; that's what gets you promoted – during wartime. The peacetime army is very different; other factors begin to take precedence. Did you graduate from West Point? Did you grow up in a military family? Were your father, your grandfather, field grade officers with combat experience? Bluster, bragging, and organizational politics don't count for much when we're facing a resilient and determined enemy, when our troops are under fire, and someone has to go into the middle of the battle and resupply them or get them out. But politics plays a big role in the peacetime army".

There was a long pause. Maybe he'd said more than he intended to. Maybe the rest couldn't be said. He continued.

"The army is launching a huge RIF program, Reduction In Force. War's over; we've got too many people: peace dividend and all that. Getting the numbers down will take precedence over everything. People will be sent home by the thousands. If you volunteer for the RIF program, the army will pay you the equivalent of several months' salary to help you transition back into the wild jungle of civilian life. Now, I can send your application forward with my strong recommendation, and normally, that would pretty much guarantee approval. But with all that's going on and as fast as things are moving, my expectation is – I don't know this, but my expectation is – it won't be approved. By the time that rejection works its way through the administrative channels, they may no longer be paying people to get out. And even if it is approved, you may find it hard to get promoted because of all the guys with more education and stronger connections to the military than you have. You could even be demoted back to Warrant Officer.

That's the reality, Captain. Think about it and let Major Droder know your decision by noon tomorrow".

I headed to my desk in a mass of conflicting emotions. I'd just had the best compliment I'd received since joining the army and from a senior Lt Colonel, the Commanding Officer of the Aviation Battalion. But despite his cautious choice of words, it was a devastating letdown. One way or the other, my military career was coming to an end, maybe in just a few weeks.

But the army was all I knew. I had a wife and a 5-month-old daughter. We had just bought a new 14ft wide mobile home. Maybe I should risk it and hope to be retained despite the RIF. I replayed the Battalion Commander's monologue in my head. Why would such a senior officer take the time to give me such a careful and detailed explanation of my options and their likely outcomes? Because he knew. He already knew that in the current situation, such applications were not being accepted. It was the only answer that made sense. The order for the RIF had come from the Secretary of the Army, possibly even higher. No approving authority would stick their neck out that far for a young, recently promoted Captain with no significant senior connections. Why me and not the hundreds of others who would be applying to be retained? I began to realize what Lt Colonel Keller was trying to say, the words that couldn't be spoken: A black officer who was also an immigrant would not be given precedence over the many white officers with university degrees and stronger military connections. It was time to get off my butt, formulate a plan, and charge into the battles that waited beyond the world of army life.

Part 3: American Awakening

ERAU

When I was growing up in Trinidad, my dad would bring home old issues of Popular Mechanics magazine from the Ford car company where he worked. Starting around age 14, my friends and I would have fun leafing through them. There were pictures of speedy new sports cars and sleek fighter planes, and sometimes, pretty women in shorts or swimsuits, leaning against the cars or standing near the planes. We got excited arguing about which cars and planes were the fastest and which girls were the prettiest. I began to notice that in each issue, there was a small advertisement for the Embry-Riddle Aeronautical Institute. One of my friends said that's where guys went to become pilots, but you had to be super-bright to go there. Even Trinidad's brightest students weren't bright enough to go there. We argued briefly about that and quickly moved on to the cars and the planes, and the girls. Back then, I knew I wasn't bright enough to ever become a pilot, so it didn't matter. But my older brother might be bright and bold enough to be a pilot. Whenever I got another copy of the magazine, I looked to see if the ERAI advertisement was still there. It always was. I daydreamed about what it might be like to attend an aeronautical institute.

Now I was a seasoned army aviator with 3000 flight hours, including more than a thousand in the Army's most sophisticated helicopter. Embry-Riddle was now an aeronautical university, ERAU. Military pilots could receive credit towards a degree based on an assessment of their military aviation training and experience. I applied for admission to the ERAU Aeronautical Science degree program and dared to hope for the realization of another teenage dream.

After completing our processing and arranging the sale of our mobile home, Tricia, baby Karyn, and I drove past the gate at Ft Sill for the last time and headed for our temporary home at my parents in Queens, New York. I sent job applications to a few helicopter operators and waited. I interviewed with Island Helicopters in New York. While I considered their offer, I received an acceptance letter from Embry-Riddle for the Aeronautical Science Degree program. I was eager to have a good job and a steady income again. But I was hungry for that Aeronautical Science degree. We packed up again and headed for Daytona Beach, Florida.

We found an apartment we liked, but the manager seemed to be concocting a reason not to rent to us. I had little patience for racial nonsense. I said I would give him six months' rent up front, consuming a major chunk of my resettlement funds. This piqued his interest, and we settled on the first and last month plus two months' security deposit.

A few weeks after starting the program, I became concerned that my funds might be depleted before I completed the degree. I had to get a job. Working while pursuing a degree was something I hadn't given much thought to. The army had structured programs for career officers to obtain a degree. But I was no longer in the Army. I would have to coordinate my work and class schedules, neither of which I knew at the time. But I needed a job.

The lady at the employment office never looked at me, as far as I could tell. In a flash, she must have seen all that she needed to see to know what to do next. For a minute or so, she reviewed my documents, which included a summary of my military service, and then told me to go to the waiting area. There was something of a bus station atmosphere at the facility. Someone announced in a loud voice: "You can only apply for unemployment if we haven't found you a job after two weeks." Eventually, someone shouted my name, and I went to her window. She handed me a slip of paper with a name and address on it.

"This is y'ur contact and y'ur location. One PM tomorrow."

She then shouted another name. I turned and took a couple of steps, then turned back to her. "What kind of job is it?" But she had already moved on to the next job seeker.

From the outside, the two-story building looked tired and worn. There was no sign. The white paint had faded to a depressing grey. It seemed too large to be a family residence, although it may once have been. As I approached the entrance, someone stuck their head out the door and pointed towards the side of the building. I found the side entrance, went up three stairs, knocked, and stepped back down the three stairs. A woman opened the door and said my name. I said, "Yes, good afternoon, ma'am." She seemed to be in her fifties, or maybe she just dressed that way, and she was slightly built. She peered down at me with pursed lips, tilting her head this way and that way as if comparing my features to a wanted criminal poster. I was about to ask if there was a problem. She said, "Come on in. I'll show you where everything is."

She led me down a long, dimly lit hallway at the end of which were closed wooden double doors. She tried doors, "Just making sure it's looked".

All the doors along the hallway were closed except for two rooms. She said, "This is the hallway, and there's the two rooms."

The two rooms were the size of large bedrooms. They were empty. She then took me to a closet. "All the cleaning equipment's in here, mops, cleaners, mop buckets. When can you start?"

"Right now, if that's okay?"

"Like that?" she blurted, looking at the way I was dressed. "I'll tell you what, just do the hallway and the one bathroom, and I'll give you credit for today, okay? You might wanna wear your work clothes tomorrow. What did you say your name was?" I told her. She said, "Just making sure. I'm Miss James, Myrtle James, but everyone just calls me Miss James. I'll be in the office near the door if you need anything. You'll need to sign some forms before you leave."

OK, mister big-time super army captain instructor pilot, Welcome to the real America! You want that degree? This dingy old hallway is standing in your way. All you need to do is make it the cleanest, shiniest floor in Daytona Beach. I began at the end of the hallway near the heavy double doors. As I worked my way down the tiled hallway, I did a mental attitude check. "Don't think about it, don't analyse, just do it, back and forth, side to side, back and forth, rinse, squeeze, back and forth. Focus on the floor. If you can master one of the most sophisticated helicopters in the world, you can handle these little white hexagonal dirt-catching monsters. Don't think; just do it!" I coached my way down the hallway.

As I swung the heavy mop back and forth, the supply officer's words at Bearcat took on added significance; "Don't knock the war; it's the only war we've got".

When I got home, I grabbed the daily paper and flipped to the classified job ads at the back. Tricia had circled a few of them. One caught my eye. I'd seen the name on a job board at the agency. Help Wanted - Jake's Pit Barbecue - Flexible hours. I knew where Jake's was, although I'd never eaten there. There were several restaurants along that strip, and they always seemed busy. I called the number.

The manager led me to a room at the back of the kitchen. On one side of the room, a guy was feeding soiled dishes into an industrial-size dishwasher that puffed steam like a mini locomotive, making the room hot and humid. On the other side of the room were three large stainless-steel sinks piled high with greasy pots and pans. "Those have to be washed by hand", he said pointedly. That was the job I was being offered, washing the dirty pots and pans, plus mopping the floor of the room before leaving at 11 pm. I thought, look on the bright side. The hours would be great for scheduling my classes, and there would be barbecue pork at the end of the shift. I started the next day.

Florida sunshine streamed through our dining room window like a cosmic searchlight, highlighting the documents scattered over the kitchen table where I had abandoned them in frustration the night before. I thought; now the heavens are getting on my case, focusing my attention on the vital unfinished task spread out in disarray on the table. I was stuck, totally lost. "That's it, I'm done with this", I blurted out to myself in frustration. I had no idea that applying for my classes at university would be so complicated and involve so many choices. Booklets and flyers, and forms in several shades lay spread out and incomplete under the brilliant sunlight. I was out of time; today was the deadline, and I still couldn't get my class schedules to work out. The financial aid forms were simply impenetrable.

I remember the young lady had said, "It's pretty straightforward, but if you're having a problem, just come on in, and we'll help you through it." I decided to head down to the Embry-Riddle admissions office and plead for help. I stuffed the papers into my briefcase, gulped down the rest of my coffee, and headed for the door. The phone always rings at the worst possible time. Let it ring. No, it might be important, maybe an offer of a better evening job. The steamy room and the smell of pork grease at work were beginning to get to me.

"Yes, this is Captain McIntosh . . ." I sounded much more irritated than I meant to, especially to someone using my former Army rank.

"This is (unintelligible); I understand you flew helicopters in Vietnam with the US Army?"

"Yes; and who's . . . "

"And you're out of the Army now and studying at Embry-Riddle University in Florida?" Sounded like a British accent, but not quite.

"Yes, who is this, please?"

"Brigadier General Serrette, Trinidad and Tobago Defence Force, and you have, let's see here, over two thousand hours of combat flight experience?"

"Yes, er, Yes, Sir, I do."

"And you're what, 26? 27?"

"I'm 25. I'll be 26 in April. Sir, Can I ask . . ."

"And you were, where is it, twice awarded the Distinguished Flying Cross for heroism in combat?"

"Yes, Sir. Can I ask what this is about?"

The General explained that the Trinidad and Tobago Defence Force was getting two new helicopters and needed pilots to fly them. These would be the first helicopters to be operated by the security forces in the twin-island Caribbean nation of 1.2 million people, the small country where I was born and raised to age eighteen. I would be granted a commission as an Officer in the Defence Force. He had me verify that I was born in Trinidad and held a Trinidad passport.

This was January 1973, six months after leaving the US Army at the rank of Captain. I had just completed my airplane commercial pilot's license and flight instructor qualifications at Embry-Riddle and was preparing to start classes towards my Aeronautical Science degree.

"Sir, I'll be starting classes at university in less than three weeks; when would you need me to start?"

"Right away. We'll send tickets for you and your family to fly to Trinidad, and we'll have a moving company ship all your household goods. You'll be given a standard Officers' residence for you and your family and help to get a new car. After two years, we'll pay your tuition and expenses for you to return to complete your studies. Someone will call you with all the details."

"It sounds very appealing, Sir; I'd like some time to think about it."

"The helicopter training courses start in France next week. I'll call you at 0900 hours tomorrow for your decision."

What's to think about? Despite having been a Captain in the US Army, I was still a black man in the American South. The job at Jake's Pit Barbecue was probably as good as I would get in central Florida. Two weeks later, I moved back to Trinidad after being away for more than seven years. I had verified with Embry-Riddle that I could return in two years to complete my degree, during which time I could save enough that I wouldn't need an evening job and could focus on my studies.

The Old Country

Our arrival in Trinidad was an exciting adventure, despite it being frenetic and chaotic. Our furniture and household goods would not arrive for a few days, and our promised house was not yet ready for us, so we stayed at Tricia's large and roomy family house, not far from where I grew up. The helicopters were being built at the Aerospatiale (now Airbus) facility in Marignane, France, and the training courses were due to commence in a few days. Less than a week after returning to Trinidad from Florida, I was given an official government passport and dispatched to France.

The new SA341 helicopters were fast and sleek, and fun to fly. They were a novelty, a new thing buzzing around the sky, patrolling the beaches, helping the police keep an eye on things in the city, and generating high excitement in the outlying villages when government Ministers and other high-level dignitaries swooped in for a rare visit with the village leaders. A leading newspaper did a piece about one of the pilots having flown helicopters in the Vietnam war, which was still raging at the time.

A few weeks after I returned from France, a big Carnival party was being held at the grounds of the University of the West Indies in Trinidad. It was one of the top annual carnival parties drawing many thousands of revellers ready to be worked into a frenzy by three of the most popular local bands. This would be my first carnival in seven years, and I was starting to feel like a teenager again. As I eased my way through the crowd, trying to get closer to the stage, a familiar voice boomed out over the chatter of the crowd and the pulsating jam from a steelpan band; "COPTERMAN!". I swivelled around toward the source of the voice, still unmistakable after seven years. Wide Mouth Harry worked his way towards me, arms in the air and jaws wide open in his trademark grin. Several of my friends were nearby in the throng of party revellers and heard Harry's raucous call. I was thereafter to be Copterman to many of my friends.

My first carnival back in Trinidad left me with mixed feelings and more questions than answers. After seven years, the place you return to is not the place you left. Before emigrating to the US, I was the 18-year-old bass player and music arranger for the Blue Js, a successful and much-loved party band of the day. But the other band members had either emigrated, as had many of my teenage friends or had moved on to more stable careers. I had barely managed to make it through high school in Trinidad. Now I was a combat-experienced former US Army Captain, Senior Aviator, and Flight Instructor, seeing things filtered through my US military training and experience, seeing how much work needed to be done to make the little country a "better" place. Yet people seemed to put more effort and energy into having a good time on a massive scale than into activities like productivity and getting ahead in their careers. On the one hand, it seemed frivolous and irresponsible. On the other hand, it seemed liberating and socially enriching, with an important message for societies that are more divided and prone to conflict based on perceived differences.

I began to ask myself, what's wrong with a country where people work hard but also devote significant time and resources to getting together to have a good time? Maybe the world needs more of that, not less. What happens when a people, a country with several ethnicities, shuts down the centre of their main city for two days and invites everyone to come out and have a good time in whatever way they care to? Two days off from work, just to have fun and enjoy themselves. No reason required. What a great idea! Does it help people to be less afraid of those who are different? Does it help to dissipate some of the tensions that inevitably build up in any society? Does it contribute to a better society overall? I had expected that my first carnival in Trinidad after an absence of seven years would be a few days of nearly nonstop partying. It turned out instead to be an occasion for observation and introspection.

I had seen the casual cruelty of racism that is still tightly woven into the fabric of American society. I had recently spent two years in the middle of a savage killing contest. Now I was seeing thousands of people of all different backgrounds, filling their city with music and dancing and joy. How did the people of this little country of 1.2 million multi-ethnic, multi-racial people become so homogeneous, so comfortable with their differences?

European colonizers brought Christianity to their Caribbean colonies. In Trinidad, it was largely adopted by the descendants of the enslaved Africans and, to a lesser extent, the descendants of the indentured Indians. Easter Sunday is one of the holiest days in the Christian calendar. It is the celebration of the Resurrection of Christ. The forty days leading up to Easter Sunday are a period of penitence and penance, of turning away from earthly pleasures while reflecting on the suffering of Christ, the Passion. It is the season of Lent, and it begins on Ash Wednesday. In countries with significant Christian populations, the Monday and Tuesday before Ash Wednesday are taken by many as an opportunity to pack into two days and nights the 40 days of fun and revelry they were about to forego as a tribute to Christ. Those two days are known in many places as carnival time. In Trinidad, carnival has blossomed into an enormous outlet for talented artists and musicians, both celebrated and previously unknown. For much of the population, it is a great collective relief valve for the accumulated pressures of everyday life.

In the early days of carnival in Trinidad, rebellious young men from communities around the city would form gangs and compete with other gangs for music-making supremacy. They used bamboo and wooden boxes and metal garbage cans to generate infectious rhythms as they moved about the city, impressing the onlookers and alarming the authorities and the Country Club Class. The gangs also got into fights with each other at carnival time. This caused respectable people to dismiss the rhythmic music as an outlet for the poorer classes, not to be indulged in by decent people.

Drumming has been culturally significant to Africans and Indians for thousands of years. Trinidad had the good fortune (or misfortune) to have large deposits of petroleum. A refinery was built, and many of the valuable products derived from the crude oil were stored in – DRUMS! The empty steel drums made a huge booming sound when banged on either end. If one end of the drum was accidentally dented, it would make a different sound or even two different sounds. It did not require a great intellectual leap to then discover that if you hammered out a grove across the top of the drum and offset it an inch or two away from the centre, you could produce two distinct booms from one drum.

The first gangs to use these steel drums at carnival had changed the game entirely and brought about a new era of music in Trinidad. To produce the desired sound, the top of the steel drum first had to be beaten into a bowl shape using the right kind of hammer to stretch the steel without breaking the surface. Playing music on these steel drums is still known in Trinidad as "beating pan". Years of intense experimentation would see the creation of a new class of musical instruments, the Steel Pan.

By the late fifties, the music had evolved to a level of sophistication that lured educated "respectable" musicians to start working with the steel pan bands. But the inter-gang violence was becoming an impediment to further development. To bolster their image as rebels and "Bad-Johns", some of the gangs and their steel bands took their names from popular American movies: The Desperados, The Invaders, Casa Blanca, Renegades, Tripoli, Tokyo, Red Army. A popular calypsonian of the nineteen fifties and sixties (Joseph Carlton, whose stage name was Lord Blakie) had one of his first big hits in the fifties with a song that described inter-band violence on carnival day.

Invaders beating sweet, Ah-Ha
Comin' up Park Street, Ah-Ha

Tokyo,

Comin' down beating very slow.

Well when de two bands clash

Mama-yo! If you see cutlass

Never me again

To jump up in a Steelband in Port of Spain.

In such fights, the toughest gang members would sometimes damage or destroy each other's steel pans using hidden weapons, including cutlasses. There were rare instances of serious injuries requiring medical attention. Someone introduced the idea of encouraging the gangs to compete with their music instead of with dangerous weapons, including knives and machetes. In return, professional musicians would work with the bands on their musical development.

This turned out to be another breakthrough. In addition to learning all the popular calypso hits, each band would spend many weeks learning and perfecting their Bomb, a sophisticated arrangement of an American jazz classic, or a great show tune, or a European classical piece by Mozart or Handel or Chopin. There was one stipulation; the piece had to be done in a carnival steel pan rhythm. In the wee hours of carnival Monday morning, the bands would converge on the city centre and perform their Bomb at a site agreed upon by the band leaders. At first, there was no formal judging and no losers. Every reveller was a judge, and every band was a winner. The revellers would decide who was best, or at least better than who. Over card games, at cookouts and barbecues, and in rum shops around the country, the matter would be argued over until it was time to go again to the pan yards to listen to the bands rehearsing their new Bomb for the next carnival.

Before dawn on *Jour Ouvert*, (pre-dawn Carnival Monday) circa 1973, I made my way to the panyard of the Invaders Steel band, my favourite band from my high school days, along with three friends from my teenage years. From my early childhood, the Invaders had been the flagship band from the western suburbs and, by the 70s, was always a top contender in the finals of the Carnival Panorama, the annual carnival Steel Band competition. Except for police and emergency vehicles, no traffic is allowed in the city during the two days of carnival. We parked and walked several blocks to join the band. We got there at 4 am. The band had between 80 to 100 steelpan players and was already assembled on Tragarete Road, a main artery leading into the city centre. All the pans were mounted on steel frames with castering wheels that allowed them to be pushed through the streets and onto the stage. The music arranger counted out the beat, and the band came alive with a spicy arrangement of a popular calypso.

The live close-up sound of a large, top-quality steel band is like a beautiful shock therapy that takes all my pains and cares away. Diehard Invaders supporters jostled for a position to help push a pan section along. I was already stationed next to my favourite player, Jack, who was a gifted improviser on the double-second steel pan. The Flagman took up his position at the front of the band, and we moved out along Tragarete Road towards downtown Port of Spain.

There was no fee and no entry requirement for joining the band. We started out with at least a thousand revellers, all moving in sync with the music, and steadily grew as we moved toward the city center. Couples held each other close, letting the music carry them forward as a unit of love, peace, and happiness under the bright pre-dawn stars. That initial feeling of being drawn together in our common yet diverse humanity by the steel pan music, exciting yet soothing, now held a special significance for me after living for years in a divided society. The feeling would come back to me many years later when a yoga teacher suggested this mantra to his class: *I Release All Struggle*. I thought; this is what thousands of people do in unison every carnival Monday morning in Trinidad and Tobago.

As we approached Green Corner, where Tragarete Road joins St Vincent and Park Streets, there were other bands ahead of us. Bands from East Port of Spain were on Park Street, and other western bands were on St Vincent Street. Each band would come to a stop to "drop the Bomb" before moving on. Invaders would have to wait their turn. The band continued their music, and everyone partied in place.

After several minutes, I decided to walk ahead to catch the music of the bands ahead of us. The sky was orange and pink as I eased my way through the crowd on Park Street. As I approached the corner of Frederic Street, I could feel an electric excitement in the air. I began to hear the faint rumble of an unusual bass line as I turned onto Frederic Street. But the crowd was so dense I could go no further. I eased back towards Park Street and was able to climb onto a low wall near a street light pole. Now that I was above the crowd, I could see down Frederic Street and hear the music. The crowd was being driven wild by the music. They were jumping in unison with arms and hands flailing above their heads. Someone said it was the Desperadoes dropping their Bomb.

The music sounded familiar, especially the bass line. I was sure I'd heard it before, but I couldn't quite place it. I'd seen a lot of Trinidad carnivals and heard many exciting steel pan arrangements, but I'd never seen a crowd driven to such a frenzy as this. In the days and weeks that followed, I would find myself repeating that bass line in my head and sometimes out loud. I was sure I'd heard it, maybe in a movie or on the radio. But no matter how I tried, I couldn't recall where or put the whole tune together. The resolution of my little quandary eventually came with the approach of Christmas, when we decorated our home and played music that was reserved for the season.

Handel's Messiah was one of our special Christmas treats, without which it wouldn't be a proper Christmas. I put the album on and happily hummed along with the music as I put the lights on the Christmas tree. I sang along with one of my favourites: *"For Unto Us A Child Is Born"*. And then there it was! "That's it!" I blurted out loudly, almost falling off the chair I was standing on to string the lights. "Every Valley Shall Be Exalted". That's what the Desperadoes were playing. That was their carnival Bomb. Tricia looked at me from the kitchen as if I'd said I'd been contacted by aliens. On Frederic Street, as the sun rose on carnival Monday, they had driven a thousand people into a frenzy playing on their steel pans music George Frederic Handel had written more than two hundred years before. He had written the piece in a spirited tempo that turned out to be readily adaptable to a steel pan carnival rhythm. To many Christians, the words of the piece are considered sacred. It seemed clear to me that the music on its own embodied the joyful message of the words. The band's steel pans - tenors, double-seconds, cellos, and basses – had captured the excited spirit that Handel had built into the piece. But the unusual context and the addition of a driving percussion rhythm section prevented me from recognizing that here, in a former British colony, in the wild and wonderful bacchanal of Trinidad and Tobago Carnival, I was hearing one of the great works of one of England's most celebrated and revered classical musicians.

The large steel pan bands with over 100 players no longer traverse the city on carnival Monday and Tuesday. In the 21st century, the music at carnival is provided primarily by celebrity performers on tractor-trailer trucks with powerful sound systems capable of filling a large stadium with the sounds of the bands' popular hits. They can be heard from a mile away, and with dozens of them moving around different parts of the city, the concussive booming sometimes sounded eerily like Vietnam in the late sixties. No steel pan band, no matter how large, can compete with these super-loud systems, with their star performers whipping the revellers into a frenzy with their latest hits the way the steel bands used to on carnival days. It's a safe bet they won't be jumping up to the music of George Frederic Handel. But the spirit and atmosphere of the carnival is still as happy and carefree as ever.

The Steel Bands now regularly perform sophisticated music programs at the top concert halls in Trinidad and Tobago and at music venues all around the world. But the movement was born out of the creative energy of some of the poorest communities in and around the country's cities and towns. Its growth was inspired and nurtured by the explosion of creativity that filled the streets at Carnival time.

But carnival was not the reason I was back in the country where I grew up. The joy of flying the sleek, high-performing helicopters around the lush Caribbean islands was soon offset by the challenges of putting together the country's first helicopter organization. As the weeks turned into months, I began to realize that, as Trinis often say, there was more in the mortar than the pestle. The relationship between the government and military seemed, on the surface, to be harmonious and productive. But beneath the surface, simmering low-key tensions were disrupting the development of the helicopter unit.

In 1970, social unrest in the 8-year-old country had alarmed the government, resulting in the declaration of a state of emergency. More than fifty years later, opinions remain strongly divided as to what the event was about. But as I understand it, there were at least three social movements gathering momentum independently of each other, at least initially. First, labour unions were clamouring for better wages and conditions for their members and for working-class people in general. Secondly, students at the University of the West Indies campus in Trinidad were protesting in sympathy with black students, including Trini students, at a Canadian university who were protesting racism at that university. Thirdly, young army officers, among the first from Trinidad to be trained at Sandhurst in England, were finding it impossible to work under superiors who held high ranks but lacked the commensurate military training and experience needed to earn the respect of the eager young officers.

There was a common thread that began to pull these movements together into the social upheaval that pushed the government to take drastic action. That thread was widespread impatience with the slow pace of dismantling the privileges and deference still shown to the colonialist class, both expatriate and local, after eight years of independence. Many people felt that Independent Trinidad and Tobago still seemed too much like Colonial Trinidad and Tobago. Particularly alarming to the government may have been the young army officers' frustration with their superiors and apparent sympathetic stance towards the other two social movements.

Under the state of emergency, the unrest was quickly quelled, and the "rebellious" army officers were arrested. Two years later, as I worked to build a viable helicopter operation, I began to be aware of subtle rumblings within the small defence force, like aftershocks of the 1970 disturbance. There was still a significant level of tension between the military leadership at the defence force and the civilian leadership at the Ministry of National Security. The defence force consisted of a small army unit and a coast guard unit. The Commanding Officers of these two units reported to the Commander of the Defence Force (CDF) at Defence Force Headquarters.

The senior officers of the Defence Force were unhappy that the Ministry of National Security had made the decision to acquire the helicopters without sufficient consultation with the military and had therefore purchased helicopters that were not suitable for the Defence Force. As a result, their support for the helicopter unit was minimal and sporadic. But the basis for their discontent appeared to be broader and deeper. Among higher-ranking officers, the "civilian clowns" at the National Defence Ministry was often cited as the root cause of their problems and the source of their frustration. The young defence force seemed to have already acquired a bunker mentality. As the months turned into years and the civilians and military continued their tug of war, the helicopters gradually became hangar queens due to a lack of replacement parts. I had to face the reality that my career in aviation was going nowhere.

Trinidad is a small twin-island country less than ten miles from the coast of a much larger country: Venezuela. The body of water between the two countries, the Gulf of Paria, is often as placid as a garden pond and easily traversable by small open boats. It's also an ideal surface for super-fast boats capable of outrunning Coast Guard vessels. It seemed reasonable to expect that border security would be an important national objective and that an effective helicopter unit would be needed to achieve that objective. The Ministry seemed surprised at the cost of establishing and sustaining even a small helicopter unit. A small helicopter unit can make a dent in contraband entering the country by sea. But to be fully effective, close coordination would be required between the Unit, the Coast Guard, and the police. But in the aftermath of the 1970 "Rebellion", distrust between these organizations remained high. The required level of coordination was not achievable.

After four years of no progress and little flying, I reluctantly resigned and returned to Embry-Riddle to complete the Aeronautical Science degree.

Office Politics

Helicopters lift themselves vertically by pushing air downward with a force greater than their own weight. That sounds too much like something you'd hear in a classroom. We need a more down-to-earth description of a rather complicated machine. During our August vacation at the end of 8th grade, me and Denny and Frankie discovered this principle when we went up the hill into the woods behind our house to pick Tonka Beans. The mango tree was too big for us to climb, and we had to be content with those that fell off the tree, despite being bruised and split from hitting the ground. But we knew how to climb up the two Tonka Bean trees to pick the sweet gooey fruit at their perfect ripeness.

Frankie's big brother had warned us that one of the branches we liked to stand on to get to the higher part of the tree was cracked and beginning to rot. Black ants the size of wasps were making a home there, and we could break an arm or leg if the thing gave way with one of us on it. We decided to throw a rope over the cracked branch and pull it down. I went to the house and came back with a long rope. After several tries, Frankie got it over the branch. He stepped back a bit so he would not be hit by the falling branch. He braced himself and began to pull. The branch swayed but showed no sign of breaking. He pulled so hard that instead of bringing the branch *down*, he pulled himself *up* and swung back and forth under the tree. I decided to lend a hand, and soon we were both swinging together under the tree. Denny, the heaviest of the group, scrambled over and gave a great tug. There was a loud crack, and the three of us tumbled a few yards down the hill as the branch finally crashed to the ground. There were a few minor bruises but no broken bones; we had been just a foot or so above the ground, but it struck me as odd that the force we used to pull ourselves up was the same force needed to pull the branch down.

Igor Sikorsky is the name most commonly associated with the invention of the helicopter. His early machines were the first to be practical and reliable enough to be acquired and deployed in significant numbers by the US military. But before Igor, and even before the Wright brothers made their historic first airplane flight, engineers and inventors were discovering that heavier-than-air vertical flight was dauntingly complicated. And hundreds of years before these efforts, an Italian genius produced a drawing that illustrated the concept used by today's helicopters to lift themselves and their occupants into the air vertically. His name was Leonardo DaVinci, and he produced a drawing of his rudimentary helicopter circa 1487!

Sikorsky was born and educated in Russia. In 1909, as a promising young engineer, he took up the challenge of turning Leonardo's concept into a practical machine, only to discover that it was far more complicated than it seemed. He turned to something more achievable and, in 1913, produced some of the earliest 4-engined airplanes. He emigrated to the United States in 1919. In the late 1930s, he returned to the challenge of vertical flight.

Leonardo's design would need a few not-so-minor modifications to achieve the dream of powered vertical flight. The machine would need a light but powerful engine – something that did not exist in Leonardo's day – to turn the rotor. It would also require a more efficient rotor to generate sufficient lift to get the thing into the air. For control in forward flight, it would need a way to adjust each spinning rotor blade individually during flight, with each rotation of the rotor, both independently of each other and together. Why? Forgive the cliché; it's truly complicated. Many books and technical papers provide detailed answers to that question. Helicopters don't just rise vertically. They fly forward at nearly two hundred miles per hour as well as hover backwards and sideways. Achieving this required a lot of creative engineering.

With a powerful new engine and a new articulated rotor system, one final modification was needed to make Leonardo's machine fly. As more power is applied to the rotor and the machine is lifted off the ground, the force turning the rotor will begin to turn the rest of the helicopter in the opposite direction, making the helicopter uncontrollable. Sikorsky solved this problem by adding a tail to the machine and putting a small rotor, also driven by the engine, at its tip. The little rotor not only stops the helicopter from spinning round and round but also allows the pilot to gently turn left or right while hovering by pushing the tail one way or the other using rudder pedals.

In 1939, 30 years after his initial attempt at building a helicopter, Sikorsky and his team built and successfully flew the VS-300. After nearly five hundred years, Leonardo's vision had become a reality.

In 1943, another helicopter pioneer, Frank Piasecki, built and flew the PV 2, a small helicopter using the main rotor and tail rotor approach used by Sikorsky. The military was interested but wanted a helicopter that could carry larger payloads and more troops. Frank decided to take a radically new approach. He would do away with the tail rotor and use two main rotors, one up front and one at the rear and slightly higher than the forward rotor. In 1945, he flew the prototype of what would become known as the flying banana. The helicopter needed a much larger fuselage to accommodate the two main rotors. It was big enough to carry ten troops and could lift over 6,000 pounds of cargo. The rotors turned in opposite directions, cancelling their torque reactions and eliminating the need for a tail rotor. The military was hooked. Piasecki's company was awarded a contract to produce tandem-rotor helicopters for the US military.

In the 1950s, the company delivered H-21 helicopters to the Army and H-46 helicopters to the Navy and Marines. Both were used successfully in the Vietnam war. The company was acquired by Boeing and, in 1960, produced the CH-47 Chinook, considered by many to be the most successful helicopter design. It proved itself in Vietnam and is still one of the Army's frontline helicopters. The Chinook is expected to continue in service for several decades and may well be in continual active service for over a hundred years before it is retired.

By the late nineteen seventies, several countries were seeking to acquire the machine for military use, and a major commercial helicopter operator was clamouring for a commercial version. Boeing began hiring to beef up its commercial helicopter sales and marketing operation.

This turned out to be fortuitous for me because just around that time – August 1978 – I graduated Magna cum Laude from Embry-Riddle and sent my resume to prospective employers.

I got early responses from helicopter operators looking for pilots and had a few offers. I felt my chances of being hired by one of the big helicopter manufacturers – Bell, Sikorsky, or Boeing – were close to zero. I was about to accept an offer from Island Helicopters in New York when Sikorsky invited me in for an interview for a position as a pilot. Shortly after this, Boeing asked me to come in for an interview. I was so excited just to be noticed by Boeing I was sure I would mess up at the interview. I kept telling myself that it was just another interview; I just had to be myself. But this was Boeing! The world's number-one aerospace company!

When we were kids, Pop would sometimes take us on outings to the Piarco airport in Trinidad. We would usually see DC-3s arriving and departing, and if we were lucky, a giant Pan Am Stratocruiser with its four thundering piston engines. The departure lounge was completely accessible back then, and we would find airline brochures highlighting the features of their aircraft. From these, I learned that the Pan Am Stratocruiser was made by a company called Boeing. At home, I browsed magazines and checked our encyclopaedia to learn about other machines produced by this company. Boeing and its huge airplanes held the status of science fiction, something that I fantasized about while knowing that, for me, they were as unattainable and unreal as the rocket ships in comic books.

My excitement at being called for an interview was only slightly dampened upon learning that it was not a flying position. In January 1979, I started as a marketing analyst at what was then Boeing Helicopters. It was not my dream assignment, but it was my dream company. It was an exciting new phase for Tricia and me and gave us renewed hope for building a happy family. Later that year, our second child, Larry C, brought further happiness and optimism to our family.

While the Chinook was a huge success with the US Army, having proven its capabilities in Vietnam, demand among commercial operators remained weak. Following an intense commercial certification program, Boeing produced six BV-234s, the commercial variant of the Chinook, for a major commercial operator. But commercial demand for the aircraft dried up, and the company terminated the program.

About a year after joining the company, a pilot position opened up in the Flight Test department. I threw my hat in the ring and finally got my dream assignment, flying Chinook helicopters. I was introduced to the other test pilots, most of whom were much older than I was. They were all cautiously polite, but a few of the older guys were clearly not pleased to meet me or the large elephant that had apparently followed me into the room. I was privy to a masterclass in the body language of resentful indignation. Once again, I had forgotten that this was America in the 1980s, and I was in a predominantly white organization. Test flying, like combat flying, entails a higher level of risk than normal commercial flying. It is important that the two pilots in the cockpit feel comfortable with each other. This was not the start I was hoping for.

In addition to doing pre-delivery test flights on British RAF Chinooks, we also did developmental test flights pursuant to the commercial certification of the aircraft. This entailed pushing the aircraft well beyond normal and emergency operational limits. We always wore parachutes on these flights. My life insurance premiums increased dramatically.

We also had to establish and demonstrate for the FAA, performance capabilities and emergency procedures that had not been required for military certification. This included simulating failures of the flight control system, among several others. One simulated failure caused the flight controls inputs to go from full nose-down to full nose-up, from several times a second to once every second or two. By the end of that test flight, I knew what it would be like to ride a bull at a rodeo. I also gained increased respect for the men and women who had designed and continued to develop this remarkable aircraft.

The flying program fluctuated in sync with the development and delivery schedules. After a year and a half, the flying slowed, and I was transferred to Project Engineering.

I learned how ideas for improvement and further development of the aircraft are incubated and fledged into complete engineering proposals, which can then be priced and proposed to potential customers. I relished the opportunity to interact daily with engineers in every sub-group of the engineering department, including some of the most brilliant engineers in the aviation industry. It was a priceless education that boosted my self-confidence as an aviation professional.

My next assignment was the Integrated Logistic Support (ILS) department, which encompassed all the disciplines dedicated to supporting the flight operations of a Chinook unit. These included the provisioning of spare parts, the development of flight and maintenance technical manuals, the preparation and delivery of training courses for pilots and maintainers, and delivery of a suite of ground support and test equipment. With each new assignment, I was learning more about not just the technical functions but also the coordination and integration processes necessary to produce and deliver a highly sophisticated aircraft, the "big picture" of what made Boeing Helicopters the success that it was.

When I joined Boeing, I was determined not to be distracted by issues of racial discrimination. This is America, I told myself. In a large, almost all-white engineering department, you're going to take some hits. Don't be distracted. Rise above it.

This is simply part of the invisible background tension that pervades American society, like the cosmic radiation left over from the Big Bang. The decimation of America's indigenous peoples and cultures, the systematic industrial process of capturing people from Africa, dehumanizing them, and forcing them to work without pay or rights to produce the goods that enriched their captors; these historic events comprised America's social Big Bang. In the nineteen eighties and nineties, its irrepressible legacy still resonated ominously in the background of American society and, inevitably, around the offices, departments, and operations of America's corporations, large and small.

Our Technical Data and Publications group received a directive to assemble in the auditorium, along with several other groups, for a presentation to be made by someone from corporate HR. Following the presentation, each group was assigned a written task that had to be completed over three days. The group would then make a presentation to HR, including a corporate HR representative. I was chosen by my group to make the presentation.

About 30 seconds into my ten-minute presentation, Bill Davis came in and sat near the back. Bill was a senior vice president, the number two man at Boeing Helicopters, and was considered by many to be the CEO's hatchet man and the next CEO of the company. He was decisive and ruthless, a tall slim man with a permanent scowl. It was surprising and somewhat unnerving to have him just show up in the middle of the presentation. Why was he here? I held my nerve and finished my presentation. Bill Davis left without a word.

Two days later, I was asked to come to Director Cal Helmsley's office. My boss' boss reported to Cal, who reported to Senior VP Bill Davis. Cal smiled from behind his broad desk and held up a sheet of paper. I took it, and as I read it, he said, "Congratulations Larry, you're a manager!" The document said I was promoted to Integrated Logistic Support Manager on the latest Army Chinook upgrade program. Cal's signature was on the bottom. I knew that this would be a lucrative contract for Boeing if the proposal was accepted by the Army. The ILS portion of the program would be a significant percentage of that. I also knew that Senior VP Bill Davis was considered the "father" of the program; his reputation was at stake.

At a time when I had all but given up hope for any advancement, this was a complete surprise. I was elated but wary. Where was my boss in this? I quickly realized he would never have recommended me. He was a white supremacist who deeply resented having to salute a black senior officer when he was serving in the Air Force. My peers seemed genuinely pleased. But predictably, most of my new peers – the management team I would be working with – made no effort to hide their resentment and even anger. They may well have never seen a black person in this type of management position. I might have been seen as depriving a deserving white person of the position just to have a person of color in management. But top management would not have made this assignment just for the "optics", just to avoid having an all-white management team. This program was too important to the company.

I knew many of the younger engineers who would be doing the detailed work on which the proposal would be based. I also knew that the standard authoritarian top-down management approach would not work for me. These engineers were not used to seeing a black person in a position of authority on a highly technical program. I would have to relate to them as a person, not just a manager. I stopped by every couple of days to chat informally and determine their progress as well as their frustrations. I then worked with their functional managers to eliminate potential roadblocks and keep things moving forward on schedule. The engineers soon realized that I knew my stuff; instead of sitting in an office, I was out on the floor every day listening to their problems and getting them solved. I didn't make any converts among the other program managers, but I achieved a level of respect among the working engineers. I realized I could get the job done despite the resentment of the other managers.

After conducting a few interim reviews of the proposals, the Army evaluators came to Boeing for their final review. They cited several discrepancies that they considered unacceptable because they did not meet the requirements of the contract. They emphasized that the proposal would be rejected if they weren't rectified. However, the Integrated Logistic Support portion of the proposal was positively cited for its overall quality and as a good model for the other departments to follow. This announcement was received by the other managers, like the homily at a funeral service. The Army evaluators had been completely objective in their assessment. They didn't know me, and I didn't know them. But it was clear from the reaction of my peers and superiors in the room that I was now more alienated and isolated than ever.

The program was successful, and Boeing was awarded a major contract. A few months later, Cal Helmsley left the company. Bill Davis became seriously ill and retired. With the two executives who had promoted and supported me now out of the way, any further advancement was extremely unlikely. I was shifted "temporarily" to a supporting role on another program. To move up at a large corporation, you need the support of either your boss or his boss, preferably both. Or you need to catch the eye of a very senior executive. If you have none of these and you're black in a nearly all-white department, *crapaud smoke yuh pipe*! (It's a Trini thing.)

Dan Evans stopped by my cubicle at about 9 am on a Tuesday morning. I'd been away the previous day.

"What happened?!" he said with an expression of concern bordering on alarm.

"Nothing happened. Why? What's up?" I said, wondering if I'd missed out on something.

"No, sorry, you just looked like . . . I just thought maybe . . . Nothing, forget it."

I knew what he wouldn't say - I looked awful. The stress of life for a black engineer in this environment, which I thought was well hidden from my colleagues, was becoming evident from my "normal" facial expression. An hour later, Dan stopped by again. "Hey, has Rob talked to you yet?"

Rob was our new manager, newly hired for the job. Our group was responsible for producing the flight manuals for the various versions of the Chinook helicopter. A single error in a manual could result in a fatal crash. Rob had never flown a Chinook.

"No, talked to me about what?"

Dan looked surprised. "There's a management slot opening up. He's interviewed everyone in the group. Everyone said they told him you're the obvious choice for the job. You've got the most experience, you know the systems inside out, you've got thousands of hours on the aircraft, you're overdue for the job. You even impressed the Army as ILS manager on the Chinook program. You're the one we all come to when we get stuck. You're really like the leader of our group."

He paused and turned away as if the explanation was slowly dawning on him. When he turned back to me, I smiled, quenching the fire inside.

He said, "You oughta go talk to him, man, find out what's going on."

I said, "Dan, I already know what's going on. This isn't the first time it's gone on, or the second, and it won't be the last. Let's see how it plays out".

Over the years, I had developed my own "thought experiment", a mental exercise that I use when blindsided by the reality of the inequities in American society. I do this to keep my perspective balanced, my sanity intact, and my rage under control. I climb into my mental rocket ship and fly far out into space. I then made a long slow turn, like a Boeing 747, until I could see the little Earth. But not just one. There would be thousands of them, going back into history to the Pharaohs and beyond. I could zoom in on any of them with my own special space telescope to see how the people lived, how they cared for each other, how they fought their fights and struggled among themselves for dominance, so they could have all the best things the little earth could offer.

I could see the Romans, their conquests and their great empire, the people of Rome, waiting *"/ with patient expectation/ to see great Pompey pass the streets of Rome:/"*, just as William Shakespeare described in his immortal play, Julius Caesar. I could marvel at all the wars between the peoples of Europe, driven by the lure of empire and conquest. I could see America long before Christopher Columbus was born, teeming with vibrant well-organized societies, building their towns and cities, having their conflicts and wars, and performing their rituals as they pursued their hopes and their dreams, knowing nothing of another world far away, or the terminal disaster that would arrive aboard three ships being built there; the Nina, the Pinta, and the Santa Maria: the end of the world.

I could see from my spaceship wealthy Europeans at seaports on the African coast, haggling over the price of a captured villager who left behind his mother running from their family home, running up the road and into the bush in the middle of the night, holding his little sister with one hand while cradling the baby with the other; "Hurry, Run, Run!", running away from the screams of the women and their children who were now captives of the dreaded people hunters, fleeing into the bush where even in the blackness of a moonless night, they knew every step, every stone, every protruding root, every safe hiding place where the spirits of their ancestors would protect them, where the people hunters would not follow for fear of getting lost in the bush and falling prey to dangerous animals or angry spirits.

I switched my view to the State of South Carolina in the 1830s and zoomed in on a large plantation where hundreds of black men and black women worked long hours every day to produce the crops that had made the plantation owner's family enormously wealthy. So wealthy they established other businesses like factories and banks that provided mortgages that allowed white people to own their homes and pass them on to their children. Yet despite all their hard work that produced much of this wealth, these black men and women owned nothing; not the land they tilled, not the products they harvested, not the clothes they wore, or the huts where they slept at night, not even their children! Not even themselves. Even so, at night, when they were finally left to themselves, they sang and danced and smiled at each other and fell in love. But there was a rumour. Tomorrow twenty-six of them would be taken to the auction in the city for Black people and sold away from their families, their children, and their husbands. No one knew who was on the list. Their tormentors called them slaves, a name intended to erase their humanity. But the buyers and the sellers of Black people were the ones who had discarded their own humanity in their pursuit of wealth and power, and dominance through this gruesome enterprise. How else could they have turned this bizarre and atrocious activity into something generally accepted as normal commerce?

Then I zoomed in on my grandmother's grandfather as he told his young granddaughter in his gravelly voice of the terrible slavery times, the beatings and suffering, the tearing apart of families, the disappearance of some of his children, her relatives. "But that was not the worst of it", he was telling her now through tears, "they never paid us anything! Even just a penny or two each week, I could have saved up, I could have had something to leave for your mother and you."

I could see how she admired the resilience and resourcefulness of the people who never gave in or gave up hope in their quest for freedom and dignity. Dignity. And never succumbed to the lure of hatred and violence towards their persecutors.

Then I surveyed my father's time, the 1930s, 40s, 50s, and beyond. There he is, repairing a US Army Air Force vehicle at Fort Reid in Trinidad as the World War raged on. Then later, leading his band as they provided dance music at the US Navy Officers Club at picturesque Chaguaramas in Trinidad's northeastern peninsula. Here I paused.

Had he been born in America instead of Trinidad, could he have had a job at the great Boeing Company? Could he have been a test pilot or an ILS program manager? Could my space telescope show me that? Maybe he might have been a janitor, mopping up the cafeteria kitchens and taking out the trash? Maybe. He may also have been taken by America's oldest terrorist organization, the Ku Klux Klan, and hung by the neck from a tree in front of a cheering mob for walking down a street just when a black man was needed for a lynching to keep other black people in their place, to maintain and perpetuate the dominance of the white people, so that they could have for themselves all the good things the good earth had to offer.

And now I could see the earth of the very recent past. There I was, feeling angry, upset, and unappreciated because I knew I had done an excellent job. I knew because the Army evaluators said so. But what had I expected? What did I have to be upset about? Through the efforts and sacrifices of those who went before me, I was able to achieve so much more than they could have done. Now it was my turn. Eventually, it would not be unusual, or even remarkable, to see people of color in positions of leadership in all spheres of life. My presence at this great aerospace organization was both a result of the long struggle and a part of it. I checked my telescope for a view of the future. But the future was not accessible.

The future was being created. I smiled. I had so much to be happy about, so much to celebrate. I felt a deep sense of gratitude to all those of every colour and ethnicity who had helped to make it possible for this descendant of people captured in Africa and sold into slavery in the Caribbean to graduate from a highly respected aviation university and work for the company of his dreams. I pointed my little mental rocket towards the earth of the present; it was time to go home, to exit my daydream and return to doing the best job I could without rancour, or recrimination, or blame, just as my father and mother and their parents had done going all the way back to the villages and towns from where they had been rounded up and captured and sent far away from everything they knew.

The anger and the rage had been soothed for the moment, but they were still there. Maybe I no longer knew how to be happy.

A Second Chance

One parent is always ready to make her world a happier place, bringing fun, laughter, and joy to everyone around her; the other parent often broods over ways to make right the ills of the world. Mom is always organized and efficient, with everything in its place; Dad is always ready to challenge the complex scientific theories underpinning the obscure distinctions between tidy and not tidy. One spouse in the living room dancing to rhythmic *Soca* music with her friends while the other spouse in the next room struggled doggedly on his piano to master a Chopin etude – something he was less likely to achieve than getting to the top of Everest in just his shorts and sneakers.

These may not seem like irreconcilable differences, but they reflect deep incompatibilities that were there from the beginning, wearing away at the relationship like a bad bearing deep in the engine of a luxury car. Despite some truly happy times, Tricia and I were gradually making each other more unhappy. As the pressures of daily work in a socially dysfunctional environment steadily took their toll, the stresses of keeping alive an ill-advised marriage became unbearable. Our marriage was teetering towards an end that was likely to be sudden, chaotic, and damaging to our children unless we took control of its ending. After thirteen years and several counselling sessions, Tricia and I agreed we had done our best. Our children needed something we had not been able to give them for some time - happy parents.

The separation and divorce were enormously painful for the four of us. But we know that the trauma would have been worse had we continued our downward trajectory. Even so, the pain of not coming home to my precious children every night was a prolonged torture whose scars will always be with me.

Ballade

When I was a child in Trinidad, it was normal for the girls in aspiring families to be sent to piano lessons. My two older sisters went to Ms Roberts twice a week after school and sometimes on weekends. My oldest sibling, Kay, had an aptitude for the instrument and progressed steadily through the musical grades. Initially, her monotonous practice of scales at home would sometimes be distracting. But as she entered her teenage years, she began to play pieces that formed a pleasant backdrop to the normal activities around the home. Starting around age eleven, I would lay in bed at night, enjoying her playing as I drifted off to sleep. Eventually, certain pieces began to stick in my head so that I could enjoy them as I went to sleep, even when she wasn't playing.

By age fourteen, I was figuring out how to play some of the popular calypsos of the day on our piano. My friend Earl started taking jazz piano lessons, and he showed me some of what he was learning. I soon felt I knew enough to try playing some of my sister's pieces and began pestering her to show me how to play them. With some irritation, she showed me the rudiments of music notation and left me to find my way through one of her music books. Fortunately, I knew what the pieces were meant to sound like. Even so, I spent long hours struggling at first with just a single bar, then two, then three.

Just hearing myself playing those first few bars was like discovering I had wings. I began to believe that I could play these pieces if I just worked hard enough at it.

I soon discovered that the three pieces that I struggled to play were written by the same composer. At first, it was just a passing curiosity; the name was unusual but otherwise meant nothing to me. I didn't give it much thought. On Sunday afternoons, there was a classical music radio program on one of the two radio stations in Trinidad. At the end of a beautiful piano piece, the presenter gave the name of the piece and its composer. My mom had been listening, and she repeated the composer's name but with a French accent. She said it loudly as if she were introducing him at some grand 19th-century event: "Frederic Chopin!" His Father was French, and his mother was Polish. Both countries claimed him as their own.

My fascination with his music grew stronger with each discovery of another of his works. They seemed to speak to me directly, especially at times of great stress or disillusionment, as if he knew exactly what I was going through and what I longed for. His music brought me comfort and strength as nothing else could. Born in 1810, he produced some of the most enduring piano music even though he died at the young age of thirty-nine.

Following the divorce, young Larry was now at his mom's during the week. I had him on weekends. He had started piano lessons after school, and Tricia asked if I could pick him up after his lesson. I met his piano teacher, and we chatted a bit about my interest in music. She brought me a brochure for a concert at the University of Delaware at which she would be playing. Among other items on the program was:

"Ballade No 4 in F Minor" by Frederic Chopin.

I knew nothing of this work and was eager to expand my knowledge of Chopin's music. The last time I had attended a live Chopin recital was probably in my teens in Trinidad. I couldn't think of any of my very few friends who might enjoy this music, so I looked forward excitedly to a pleasant evening out on my own.

There was quite a substantial audience which I expect included many of her university students and their families, as well as her faculty colleagues. She bowed gracefully and took her place at the piano.

With just the first few bars of the piece, that quiet whisper of an opening like no other I know of, I was captivated. As she moved beautifully through the stages of the piece, building in intensity from a gentle, mystical theme to the climactic coda, I was lifted out of myself, suspended, overwhelmed. With the final notes, her hands rose from the keyboard. The audience was exuberant. Everyone was on their feet. I came out of my trance and back to my senses. I stood and applauded. She bowed again and again. She left the stage. The hall lights came up; it was the intermission.

I followed the buzzing, energized audience out to the lobby. I felt a bit unsteady and confused? I took a few deep breaths. My throat felt tight; I needed some air. I walked out to the parking lot. The late fall evening air was crisp and chilly. Maybe I was coming down with a cold. A few couples and families were coming to the hall for the second half of the program. I walked to my car and leaned against the passenger door, breathing deeply amid a swirling mass of incoherent emotions. I was wearing just a light jacket and felt cold from the evening breeze. I went around to the driver's side, unlocked the door, and sat for a moment, trying to calm myself down, to relax my breathing. A loud sob erupted from me as if I had choked on something. It took me by surprise. I tried to compose myself and suppress the impulse that was rising again. I couldn't hold it back; I was crying loudly, the way a small child cries. The more I tried to stop it, the stronger and louder it became. *What is happening to me?!* My shoulders heaved; I was shaking, bawling, and couldn't stop. Two couples emerged from the darkness, heading toward the concert hall. I worried they would notice the car shaking. I tried again to stop, to smother it, but that just made it worse. I gave up and just let it all out, crying like a child in pain, tears pouring out, falling onto my jacket. I no longer cared what anyone thought about the shaking car.

After a while – maybe ten minutes, I really don't know how long – it subsided. I dried my eyes and my face, blew my nose, then sat for a while, hunched over, sniffing inward with each breath. I was no longer cold. I just sat and stared into the night, seeing nothing. The car keys tinkled like little bells when I finally started the car. I drove slowly towards the exit, then out into the street. The night air was so clear; I could see the stars. The lights in the store windows glowed warmly. The streetlights and traffic lights looked bright and sparkly. It would soon be Christmas.

New Year's Day

A few weeks after the Chopin concert, young Larry had a special request: The Christmas holidays were fast approaching, and for New Year's Day 1994, he wanted his Dad to take him to the movies to see Mrs Doubtfire. Among 14-year-olds, this was a must-see item! "Everyone's talking about it, Dad".

He was waiting for me when I pulled up at his mom's. We headed off, and he filled me in on all his amazing Christmas presents. When we got there, Mrs Doubtfire was sold out. I tried to cheer him up. "How about one of the other movies, and we'll try again in a day or two?"

No. He was very disappointed. So was I. We hung around the video game arcade until he was ready to go home. I took him back to his mom's with a promise to take him to the movie before the start of school. We waved goodbye, but there wasn't the usual bright smile. He looked so sad. As I eased my foot off the brake to head back to my tiny studio apartment, Tricia came running toward the car, "Wait, wait!"

I thought, "Ok, what have I forgotten to do this time."

I eased the window down.

She said, "I thought you might like to come in. There's some people I wanted you to meet."

I said, "Come in? I know we're cool, but we don't do 'come in'."

She said, "Just for a few minutes, you can meet everyone, have a drink, and y'know, relax a bit."

I looked at her as if she might be having a hallucination. I couldn't imagine relaxing in her new house with her new husband and their new friends. Why would she suggest such a thing? I shook my head, "Bye, Trish".

As I eased my foot off the brake, she scolded, "It's the holidays; can't you just be sociable for a few minutes? Why are you being such a scrooge?"

Tricia had always been a terrific scolder. I paused. She was right; I was being a Scrooge. I felt like a Scrooge. It seemed to be my default demeanour of late. Maybe I was becoming a full-time Scrooge. I glanced towards her front door. Young Larry was standing there looking so despondent. I couldn't leave him standing there like that. I parked the car and walked toward her door, smiling at my son but full of trepidation at my imminent embarrassment.

The current teenage hysteria over Mrs Doubtfire had brought me to the street in front of Tricia's house twice in less than an hour. This would turn out, in retrospect, to be only the last of a series of improbable coincidences leading to what would happen next. And while I could not rule out Tricia's playfully mischievous hand in what was to follow, it was young Larry who had just saved me from driving away from a blissfully happy future.

I stepped past the foyer into the living room, where five people my age or older were in quiet conversation. A Christmas tree sparkled near the window. I recognized two of Trisha's friends and said Hi. They wished me a happy new year and asked how I'd been. Tricia then introduced me to her new husband, Paul, and the two people I'd never met. We made small talk for a few minutes, and they resumed the conversation I'd interrupted.

In contrast to her ex-husband, Trish was never lost for words and kept the conversation moving along. But before long, I could feel the claws of acute discomfort creeping up my spine. As I mentally rehearsed my "thank you" and "goodbye", Paul must have noticed what I thought was my well-hidden discomfort. He said with a smile, "Larry, whyn't you relax, go to the kitchen, get yourself a drink, and meet the others."

I felt like a new pupil at a strange school, but I was glad for the opportunity to do something other than make an awkward exit.

The house was much longer toward the back than it was wide. The rooms were laid out in tandem. I walked through the dining room and into the kitchen. Two attractive women who looked to be in their 30s were having a riotous laugh as they sat at a small table with their backs to the wall. A few other people were getting drinks or food. The room overflowed with laughter and animated conversation. I was introduced to everyone and took a seat at the table. Someone put a glass of champagne on the table in front of me. I couldn't take my eyes off Sarah. She was warm, spirited, with brown eyes that sparkled and drew me to her. Her laughter was enchanting music. She had well-thought-out views on a wide range of issues and, unlike most Americans I knew, was happily unconcerned about offending tender sensibilities. She radiated an enticing combination of wit, insight, and carefree irreverence towards accepted wisdom. In ten minutes, I was hooked. I had to know everything I could about this amazing person. But I didn't know what to say, how to let her know. We talked and laughed and partied into the night. Tricia put on party music from Trinidad, and her living room became our dance floor. Around midnight, everyone prepared to leave. My heart raced like a nervous 15-year-old. I followed Sarah out the door and into the rain. As she was about to close Vivian's passenger door, I said clumsily, "I have to . . . I'd like to see you again. How can I get in touch with you?", and immediately felt foolish and smiled sheepishly.

"I'm staying at Vivian's. Tricia has her number." Her smile lit up my heart.

"I'll call you in the morning," I shouted as Viv drove her away into the rainy night.

I called her at Vivian's the next morning, and she suggested lunch. Her overnight flight to London was scheduled to depart Philadelphia at 9 pm. I picked her up, and we went to a nearby restaurant.

"Where in England are you from?"

"I grew up in a small village in Cambridge, but I live and work in London."

"Sounds interesting. What kind of work do you do?"

"I work at the Franco-British Council. It's an organization that promotes good relations between the two countries. I lived and worked in France for two years when I was younger. I enjoy it, but it's not my dream job. How about you? What do you do?"

"Boeing has a facility just outside Philadelphia, about 45 minutes from here, where they build Chinook helicopters for the Army. I flew Chinooks in Vietnam and got a job there when I left the Army."

She raised an eyebrow. "You don't seem like an army type. Do you still do army things, go on parade, training exercises, that sort of thing?"

I smiled. "Oh no, I've been out a long time. I'm not in the reserves or anything like that. I don't do 'army things' anymore."

She said, "While you were fighting your war in Vietnam, I was marching in the streets of London with my placard, protesting the war at the top of my voice." She looked at me, waiting for my reaction. I reflected a bit on what she said. I suppose, in some sense, it was my war.

I said to her, "You probably helped to save a lot of lives. The decision to enter and escalate the war may well have been driven by a mixture of hubris and noble intentions, but it turned out to be an incredibly costly neo-colonial overreach. Well, that's a bit pedantic – the war was a mistake. I wasn't trying to impress. It's just that I've thought about this for a long time. That's the way I came to see it anyway. I don't think that's a widely held opinion, at least not in this country."

"What made you choose the army?" she said without looking up from her lunch.

I thought about it for a moment. "Well, it's all because I wouldn't do my homework when I was growing up", I said with a little laugh. "I'm only half-joking. It's a long story."

I told her how much fun it had been growing up in Petit Valley in Trinidad before it became developed and overcrowded. She said, "It sounds lovely. Your little valley should have been called Paradise Valley."

I laughed, "It was a great place to grow up, especially for people of colour. But it was no paradise. It's a tiny country with serious challenges, but race and ethnic differences are not near the top of the list. But I want to know what brought you to Paul and Tricia's house on New Year's Day."

Her irresistible smile warmed the room. She put down her knife and fork and took a sip of her wine. "Strange, wasn't it? I mean, I had a great time last night. I think you did, too, didn't you."

Now I got more clearly, the fleeting sense that had remained out of reach at the table the night before and on my drive home. Deep within this lively, lovely woman was a tender flower that had been trampled upon and was now kept well protected; I needed to be careful. We smiled at each other and began to unravel the mystery of how we met in the most unlikely place imaginable.

She said, "Viv and I go back a long way. We played netball together in our youth. Paul and I worked at the same company in Cambridge around that time. It was my first real job. It's now a major international chemical company. Seems like yesterday. Paul and Vivian got married and had two children. We remained close friends, and over the years, I was like an aunt to their kids. Paul turned out to be a top-notch chemical engineer, and the company offered him a position at their Delaware facility. So, he and Viv and the kids moved to the US. He did quite well here work-wise, but it was tough on Viv and the kids - well, on him too, I suppose - and eventually, the marriage began to fall apart. They agreed to stay together until their daughter's wedding, then get a divorce. Viv's been doing ok. She's a tough lady, but after all those years, it must have been hard on her. So I try to be there for her, she really is a lovely person, a lot of fun. Anyway, Viv's daughter worked at the school where your ex Tricia worked, and she invited Tricia to her wedding. That's where Tricia met Paul."

She paused and looked at me. I said, "That was really special of you - to come all the way from London to ring in the New Year with your friend."

"Oh no, no. I mean, yes and no. I flew out to LA to have Christmas with my brother and his wife and young daughter." She showed me a photo of her hugging her niece of five or six.

She continued, "I called Viv to wish her Happy Christmas, and she told me that Paul's new wife had invited her to lunch at their home on New Year's Day. Viv found it a bit strange and couldn't decide how she should respond. Lunch with her ex and his new wife? She wasn't sure she was up to something like that. We discussed it and decided we'd get all tarted up and bounce in there as if we owned half of Delaware!"

"Tarted up?" I asked curiously.

"You know," she gestured with her hands and arms and a subtle movement of her body, "all dressed up and done up and looking like the main attraction. So, I booked a stop-over in Philadelphia, and that's how I ended up with one of my best friends in her ex's kitchen. So how did you end up in your ex-wife's kitchen? Does seem a bit weird, doesn't it, the more I think of it? Did she invite you too?"

"Oh no, no. Well, I guess it's also yes and no." I told her the story of young Larry and Mrs Doubtfire. We enjoyed a good laugh and agreed it all seemed like a series of improbable coincidences.

She said, "You know if the movie hadn't been sold out, Viv and I would not have been at Paul's when you brought your son back, and we would never have met. Viv, and I only stuck around because you" she paused, "you seemed like an interesting person and a fun guy. But you also seemed, I don't know, different. There must be a special someone around somewhere?"

I smiled nervously, "Not really, I tried dating years ago after the divorce, but after a few trips to popular bars and night spots with colleagues from work – which they referred to as meat markets, a term I still find degrading and offensive – I gave up. I find the rules of socializing in this country bewildering, impenetrable, really. So, I've reluctantly resigned myself to living on my own. How about you? Is someone eagerly awaiting your return home?"

I was expecting a smile, but she became serious and reflective. "I have a good circle of friends, we drop by each other regularly or meet at the pub, and I spend a lot of time with my brother and his wife and two lovely daughters." She paused; I waited. "I was in a relationship with a guy I knew from a sport club. I became very attached to his two young kids. But things got a bit rough, and anyway, it's been long over, and I quite like being free to travel and do things I enjoy. I'm doing a master's program in European Studies, and I'll be graduating this summer."

"Congratulations! Maybe I can take a trip to London this summer, and you can show me around."

She beamed her sparkly smile, "Please, do come. I think you'd really love London. And there's a lot more to England than London."

I couldn't tell if that was real or just English politeness. I said excitedly. "Is it ok if I write to you? I'd like to keep in touch."

We exchanged addresses and phone numbers.

I drove her back to Vivian's. We hugged and looked longingly at each other. I'd met her less than 24 hours ago. Now she was headed back across the Atlantic. I drove home, scolding myself for feeling like a teenager. I was a man in his upper forties with a career, a daughter in university, and a son in a prestigious high school. I had a chance meeting with a person passing through on her way home to London. That was all. But it wasn't all. In that short, strange encounter, she had taken a piece of my heart with her.

I wrote to her, my letters long and rambling in my effort to capture my excitement at meeting her and my near-hysterical desire to see her again. In my clumsy handwriting, I invited her to come back for a visit and stay with Karyn and me and young Larry at our home in Delaware. She called me and revealed that she had been just as excited about meeting me as I was about her. In the summer, I went to see her in London, and a few weeks later, she spent a week with us in Delaware. As the time approached for her to leave again, going back to her other world a million miles across the ocean, it was almost unbearable. We may have felt like giddy teenagers, but we were level-headed forty-somethings. We had to make a go/no-go decision.

Through several more transatlantic visits, we reviewed our options and worked out the challenges associated with each.

We decided that Sarah would obtain a fiancé's visa that allowed her to move to the US but gave us a brief window during which we had to get married, which was just fine with us.

On August 19th, 1995, nineteen months after we'd met at Paul and Tricia's house that New Year's evening, Sarah and I were married in Vivian's garden at her home in Newark, Delaware.

You Can Stop Fighting

I came home from work one evening after the customary sixty-to-ninety-minute traffic-snarled commute from work. Sarah and I greeted each other with a hug and some commentary about the true cost of overcrowded highways. We'd been happily married for three years and reminded ourselves almost daily how lucky we were to have each other. Sarah worked at an international investment bank in Delaware and had a much shorter drive to work than I had. I came back downstairs after changing out of my work clothes.

Sarah said to me, "You're getting out of that place before it kills you."

"What brought that on," I said, somewhat taken aback. I looked at her and smiled. But she wasn't smiling.

"Did I forget to leave my grumpy work face at work again?" I joked, trying to read her mind. I walked over to her, and we hugged gently. As we relaxed our embrace, she said, "I read an article today about the cumulative effect of stress over the course of work life. It cited a study that showed that the average American draws a pension or retirement check for nine months. That's it! Work all your life, and nine months after you retire; you're gone. Maybe even before you retire, well, that's not happening to us."

I said, “Of course, it won’t. We take care of ourselves. We eat right, exercise regularly, and we’re both in pretty good shape.”

She looked at me in mock exasperation, “That’s not what I mean.” I waited.

“You go in early and stay late every day. You go in on weekends to make sure their projects stay ahead of schedule. You’re complimented on the quality of your work by their *customers* but not by the people you work for. We both know they’re never going to promote you because you’ll never fit in with their ‘old boys’ management network, ‘good ole boys’, whatever you call it.”

I looked at her. “You’re serious. You really want me to quit my job.”

She moved a bit closer. “Listen, love. It’s a very toxic environment. You’ve said it yourself. You’re going in there day after day, and it’s taking a toll on you. You may not notice it, but it’s weighing you down, stifling your spirit. And that’s worse for your health than triple cheesy bacon burgers and super-creamy milkshakes or whatever. What about your former boss, who got so angry when you got promoted at that time? What happened to him?”

"Yeah, just after that, we went on Christmas break for a week. He never came back, died of cancer. He was a heavy smoker and proud of it."

"And the VP who got you promoted, what happened to him?"

"Cancer got him too."

"And what about that big shot director who was so incensed at having a black man on his program he slammed his fist on the conference table and stormed out of the meeting? Is he still around?"

"No, I heard he died of cancer too."

I sat at the table. She sat next to me, took my hand, and waited. After a few moments of looking at the table, we looked at each other and smiled.

I said, "You know, when I'm in Trinidad, I'm just a person, and I'm completely comfortable with who I am. I've never felt any better or worse than anyone else, and I've never been made to feel that way. No matter where I go on those islands and who I'm with, I'm never aware of my ethnicity or my race or skin color, or any of that crap. It was only after I was in this country for a while that I realized that from kindergarten on, every class I'd been in at school in Trinidad was like a mini–United Nations, with roots that reached all around the world, not just Africa and India, but to Europe, the Middle East,

China, South America, and who knows where else. For us, diversity was normal and completely unremarkable. People were not meant to be all the same. That was our normal; that was our reality.

"But now, when I'm in the US, I'm constantly aware that I'm not just a person, I'm not just an American; I'm a "something" American – African American or Black American – and that "something" means you are placed in a box with a label that describes the contents, so no one needs to go to the trouble of having to get to know who you are; it's all on the label. But I don't fit into any of their boxes, and that's just fine with me."

She knew I needed to talk and waited for me to go on.

"But it also means that I'm part of this incredible multigenerational struggle to go from slave – an African person deprived of personhood so that their commercial value may be legally stolen - to an American without any prefix. But this process, this huge historical transformation, is something I can't talk about with my friends and colleagues unless they're also African American or persons of colour. And there aren't many of us at work. This tension permeates American society, and Boeing is no exception. So it's not 'Boeing', it's America."

I got up and looked out the window for a few moments, then turned around.

"We all know at work why I won't be promoted again, and it has nothing to do with my ability or performance. But we can't talk about it. So we can't fix it. So, yeah, it does bother me, it infuriates me. But this is America. I'm a black immigrant. Both my children were born in this country. They're African Americans. The struggle for equality and the struggle against racism is a part of living in this country. I can't have it both ways. My responsibility is to suck it up and continue doing a great job. So I *have* to go in early and put in the extra time, not just to stay ahead of my peers, but for my own self-respect. What my employers do is up to them. I could get another job, but it won't be any different, will it? Sorry love, I didn't mean to go off on a rant like that."

I sat at the table again. She said quietly, "You're so different when you're in Trinidad. It's like, a whole hidden side of you comes alive, like, you become your whole self. You'll always be an American. I know how deep your commitment to America goes. You'll always be ready to defend this country if you're called on. But it is what it is; you can't change America overnight, and you're right; you can't have it both ways. That struggle you mentioned is taking its toll. And you've done so much for this country already, haven't you."

We sat quietly for a few more moments. She smiled and said, "I don't know if I told you this, but when I was a child in

England, I hated the way people kept their houses so cold in winter. I still do. My parents used to scold me for sitting on the radiators to warm myself up. When I was about six, we were all gathered in the living room watching England play a cricket test match against the West Indies. My whole family were cricket fanatics. I was cold and sat on the radiator. My mother scolded me and said I would get piles (she had trained as a doctor). I got off the radiator and sulked for a bit, then asked, 'Why are they all wearing summer clothes?' and Dad said, 'They're in Trinidad, in the Caribbean. There's no winter there; it's always warm and sunny all year round. That's why the cricket matches are played there during winter.' So I said, 'When I grow up, I'm going to marry a man from Trinidad and go there to live so I don't have to be cold all the time and be scolded for sitting on radiators!' Then I stormed off in a huff to my room to warm myself up on the radiator."

"You're not serious, are you? You just made that up", I said incredulously.

"Nope, it's the absolute truth. You can ask my brothers; it became a family joke." She retrieved her laptop. "OK, let's think about this. When will you be eligible for early retirement?"

"In two years, maybe a bit less. But I'll only be 52; I won't get much if anything."

“That’s ok. We have a little time. Let me work at this, and we’ll see what I come up with. Supper will be ready in twenty minutes.”

I said, “But I was gonna make dinner tonight.”

She smiled. “Don’t worry. I’m already half done.”

We enjoyed her dinner without much conversation at first. Eventually, I said to her, “For a person of colour, there is this paradox in emigrating from a truly multicultural community to the United States. On the one hand, it can be exhilarating to be part of the struggle to help the great United States realize the full potential of its diverse population and to see people of colour excelling in all spheres right alongside whites. There’s so much going on socially and economically here. The momentum is almost tangible. You can feel it.

On the other hand, the near-constant reminders of the grand crime of American slavery – the exclusion, the resentment, the desperate struggle to maintain white dominance – it all gets so tedious. Sometimes I really miss just being a person and being comfortable with everyone without even thinking about ethnicity or even being aware of it really. Just to go on a good lime with some interesting people; I really miss that, you know? But it feels like a betrayal of my commitment to the struggle for equality here. I don’t know if I’m making any sense.”

She laughed, "A good lime?"

"Oh, yeah, it's a Trini thing. A lime is just an enjoyable and relaxing time or event. It can also be like an informal, loosely structured group of friends and acquaintances who enjoy each other's company. It's very flexible, so people drift in an out of the lime, although there's usually a core group of three or four who've hung out together for years and have become quite close, almost like a family. You can have an impromptu lime at a local cricket or soccer game, or you can join a lime at the beach, or your house can be the venue for the next great lime. You can be part of more than one lime, and you can be a regular or an occasional limer. I'm probably overselling it a bit, but that's only because I miss it so much. It's a great way to meet new people in a relaxed atmosphere or just hang out. Singles of any age can learn a lot about someone before deciding to try dating. The thing is, the group would always include people of different "ethnicities," quote-unquote, but I never noticed that until I lived in this country for a while and realized how rare that is in America. We had something almost like that when I was in Army flight school and was still new to this country. It almost restarted the Civil War, though. I'll tell you about that sometime."

She said, "The pubs in England are a bit like that. You can meet all sorts of people, even if you don't drink. Whole families pop in for dinner, although I wish they wouldn't bring their large dogs." She looked at me. "Pet peeve. I guess Pubs wouldn't really work in this country, would they? You'd need pubs for whites and pubs for Blacks and people of colour – without any signs indicating that, of course. People here just seem to know. That wouldn't really be like a proper English pub, though, would it, although England has its own style of racist division. People at work didn't know I'm married to a black guy. You wouldn't believe the awful things they would sometimes say. They know now, so I don't hear the worst of it anymore, thank God."

I jumped up from the table, pacing and flailing my arms. "It's such a ridiculous way to live. I think you have to grow up in this country to know how to live comfortably with all this division and resentment. I mean, I'm not complaining – maybe I am - I know it's important and necessary to keep up the struggle. If we don't keep things moving forward, we'll just slide backwards into another Jim Crow era."

I was now torqued right up to my red line. "I just get so damn tired of it sometimes. I mean, I get it when some white Americans ask in frustration, 'Why does everything have to be about race?' Not everyone is a historian, and sometimes people just want to live peacefully with their neighbours. The natural reaction to the extreme ugliness of some of America's past is to look away. But America can't keep hiding from the reality of what happened. Simple questions – who lived here before Columbus was born? What happened to them? Where did the black people come from? How did they get here? Why were they brought here? They all worked hard all their lives, so why were they all poor? How were they compensated for all the work they did? Why are all the poor people black? Why are there no white poor people? These are basic questions any 9-year-old might ask about what happened in America. And they contain the answers to the question, 'Why does everything have to be about race?' We have to keep fighting until we achieve equality for all citizens without regard to 'race' and skin colour. And that won't happen until we acknowledge all aspects of our history, not just the good parts. We're talking generations; it won't happen in our lifetime."

Sarah got up and took my hand again. She said, "Earlier this week, on the way home, I heard this guy on the radio. I think he was a psychologist or psychiatrist, I'm not sure. Someone called the program to get advice about a close relative she was having verbal fights with over a family issue. I think the fight was with one of her parents. She described the situation at some length. The fights had been going on for months and were getting more acrimonious. But no matter how hard she tried, she could not make this relative see the value in what she was saying. She was tired of all the fighting.

It was now causing a growing rift between them so that they were seeing less and less of each other. He listened very patiently. She was clearly quite anguished and exasperated and probably in tears. When she finally asked him what she should do, he said slowly, in a very gentle and caring voice: 'I have good news and bad news. First, the bad news: you lost the fight. Now the good news: you can stop fighting.'

On January 3rd, 1999, the day I achieved twenty years of employment at Boeing, I stopped fighting. It was time to pursue the fight in a more constructive and gratifying way. Sarah and I wanted to enrich our lives by making positive connections and contributions to the lives of others without regard to race or ethnicity. The deep racial disconnects in the US in the 1990s made that impossible for us. I resigned from my dream company, the world's foremost aerospace corporation, an organization from which I had learned so much and which I continue to admire despite all the senseless rejection and exclusion I experienced there.

We didn't have very much money, but we were confident of our ability to find a more gratifying life based on our abilities and combined professional experience. Sarah wanted to experience more of Trinidad and Tobago. We spent a week or two driving to the various towns and areas of interest around the islands. A real estate agent suggested to Sarah that we should visit the villages in the northeast corner of Trinidad. I had avoided these areas because they were so remote and still largely undeveloped. After a two-and-a-half-hour drive from West Port of Spain, we stopped at the picturesque village of Toco at the Northeastern tip of the island hoping to find lunch. Something was going on at a small church near where we had stopped. We were invited by some of the villagers to come into the church.

We walked into a lively discussion about a large industrial project being planned for the village and the negative effects it would have on the environment and the lives of the villagers. We sat quietly and listened in growing amazement at the depth and breadth of the villagers' knowledge of climate change, and their love for the natural environment, and commitment to preserving it. They did not want their village to become a bustling industrial complex no matter how many jobs it might create. They decided to schedule a village meeting a few days later to decide on what should be done.

As we drove back to Port of Spain later that day, I realized that Sarah had become enchanted by both the beautiful coastal village and its lively spirited villagers. We attended the village meeting, and Sarah immediately began doing volunteer work with some of the community organizations. A few months later, her work came to the attention of the Caribbean Natural

Resources Institute (CANARI), a small but highly influential NGO based in Trinidad, and doing research and sustainable development with governments and rural communities in several Caribbean countries. She accepted a position at CANARI and eventually became its Executive Director.

CANARI (canari.org) had always struggled to raise funds to be able to do its work independently of government support. Under Sarah's leadership, her team prepared and submitted a funding proposal to the MacArthur Foundation. CANARI was awarded a substantial grant which allowed it to focus a bit less on raising funds and more on its essential work including helping rural and coastal communities prepare for the effects of climate change and rising sea levels.

I accepted a consultancy position with the Ministry of National Security to develop the helicopter division of their Defence Force.

But it wasn't all work. We have dressed in our costumes and "jumped up" in carnival bands all day through the streets of Port of Spain with thousands of happy revellers of all combinations of races and ethnicities (and LOVED it). We've been on many great "limes" in Trinidad, England, France, St Lucia, and elsewhere, deepening our connection to and appreciation for the great diversity of the human family. We also spend much time in the US with our American children and grandchildren. They are all proud African Americans, bursting with optimism about America's future and their place in that future.

For my birthday not long ago, Sarah bought me a stylish shirt from an upscale store at a popular shopping mall in Delaware. It was a perfect fit. She has such an amazing eye for colour and style. I thanked her with a smile and a big hug and kiss. When I took it off, she smiled mischievously and said, "Look at the tag." It said, Made in Vietnam. She embraced me and whispered, "Happy Birthday, Husband." We held each other close for a while longer. It's become my favourite shirt. I wear it all the time.

Postscript

On 30th April 1975, not long after the chaotic and embarrassing exit of the last US personnel from Saigon, North Vietnamese tanks rolled into the capital, and the South Vietnamese government surrendered. The Vietnam War was over. Unification had been achieved.

More than fifty-eight thousand American military service men and women were killed in the failed bid to prevent the unification of Vietnam under a communist system of government. American servicemen and women had fought as honourably and heroically as they had in any other war. Over a million North Vietnamese soldiers and Viet Cong fighters died in the war to achieve the independence and reunification of their country. Some estimates of Vietnamese civilians killed range between one and four million.

About the Author

Larry D McIntosh was born and raised in Trinidad and Tobago. He moved to the US at age 18 and served in the Army for six and a half years. He returned to Trinidad and worked in national security for four years. He then returned to the US, earned a degree in Aeronautical Science from Embry-Riddle Aeronautical University, and worked for Boeing Helicopters for twenty years. He lives in Trinidad and Newark, Delaware.

Get in contact with the author:

larrym621@gmail.com

www.ingramcontent.com/pod-product-compliance
Ingram Content Group UK Ltd.
Pitfield, Milton Keynes, MK11 3LW, UK
UKHW062259290726
14090UKWH00017B/789

9 798869 169617